Designing and Developing ASP.NET Applications Using the Microsoft .NET Framework 3.5

Lab Manual

EXECUTIVE EDITOR	John Kane
EDITORIAL PROGRAM ASSISTANT	Jennifer Lartz
DIRECTOR OF SALES	Mitchell Beaton
DIRECTOR OF MARKETING	Chris Ruel
SENIOR PRODUCTION AND MANUFACTURING MANAGER	Micheline Frederick
SENIOR PRODUCTION EDITOR	Kerry Weinstein

ISBN 978-0-470-57813-1

Printed in the United States of America

10 9 8 7 6 5 4 3 2 1

BRIEF CONTENTS

CONTENTS

LAB 1
DESIGNING WEB APPLICATIONS WITH SUITABLE CONTROLS

This lab contains the following exercises and activities:

Exercise 1.1	Using Common Controls
Lab Review Questions	
Lab Challenge 1.1	Using the Multiview and View Controls
Lab Challenge 1.2	Using Web Parts

BEFORE YOU BEGIN

Lab 1 assumes that the lab setup has been completed as specified in the setup document and that StudentXX-A, StudentXX-B, and StudentXX-C have Microsoft .NET Framework 3.5 and Microsoft Visual Studio 2008 installed on their computers.

> **NOTE** *In this lab, you will see the characters XX. When you see these characters, substitute the two-digit number assigned to your computer.*

SCENARIO

You are developing a web application that asks the user to subscribe to the Web site by providing user details such as name, e-mail ID, date of birth, and zip code. The Web site uses various .NET controls and validation strategies.

In Lab Challenge 1.1, you will use Multiview and View controls to display data in different formats. In addition, in Lab Challenge 1.2, you will use Web Parts to create user customizable web pages.

After completing this lab, you will be able to:

- Use standard controls
- Use rich controls
- Use validation controls
- Use Web Parts

Estimated lab time: 125 minutes

Exercise 1.1	Using Common Controls
Overview	You are developing a web application using various server controls in ASP.NET. You are planning to implement server-side validation methods. In this lab exercise, you will understand the usage of standard controls, rich controls, and validation methods. You will use Microsoft Visual Studio 2008 to create a Web site. This task is complete when you create a Web site that demonstrates the use of various controls and server-side validation methods. To complete this lab exercise, all the student computers such as StudentXX-A and StudentXX-B must be started and must have network access.
Completion time	60 minutes

1. From the Start menu, select Microsoft Visual Studio 2008, and then select Microsoft Visual Studio 2008.

2. Select File → New Project → ASP.NET Web Site, and enter the name, **UsageOfControls**. This creates a new Web site with the Default.aspx page in it. Rename Default.aspx to **Subscribe.aspx**.

3. Add two new folders to the Web site—**XML** and **Images**.

4. Add the controls in Table 1-1 to the Subscribe.aspx page.

Table 1-1
Controls in the Web Page

<table>
<tr><th>Control</th><th>ID</th><th>Properties</th></tr>
<tr><td>Label</td><td>lblDate</td><td>Text = “ ”</td></tr>
<tr><td>TextBox</td><td>txtName</td><td></td></tr>
<tr><td>TextBox</td><td>txtEmailId</td><td></td></tr>
<tr><td>TextBox</td><td>txtZipCode</td><td></td></tr>
<tr><td>TextBox</td><td>txtDOB</td><td></td></tr>
<tr><td>RadioButtonList</td><td>rdbCountry</td><td>RepeatDirection = Horizontal</td></tr>
<tr><td>Label</td><td>lblSuccess</td><td></td></tr>
<tr><td>Button</td><td>btnAdd</td><td>Text = “Subscribe”</td></tr>
<tr><td>Button</td><td>btnView</td><td>Text = “View my Details”</td></tr>
<tr><td>GridView</td><td>gvDetails</td><td></td></tr>
<tr><td>Ad Rotator</td><td>AdRotator1</td><td>AdvertisementFile = “Advertisements.xml”</td></tr>
<tr><td>RequiredFieldValidator</td><td>rqdValName</td><td>ControlToValidate = txtName ErrorMessage = Please enter name</td></tr>
<tr><td>RequiredFieldValidator</td><td>rqdValEmail</td><td>ControlToValidate = txtEmail ErrorMessage = Please enter Email Id</td></tr>
<tr><td>RequiredFieldValidator</td><td>rqdValZip</td><td>ControlToValidate = txtZipCode ErrorMessage = Please enter ZipCode</td></tr>
<tr><td>RegularExpressionValidator</td><td>regValDOB</td><td>ControlToValidate = txtDOB ErrorMessage = Please enter date in mm-dd-yyyy format
ValidateExpression = (0[1-9]|1[012])[- /.](0[1-9]|[12][0-9]|3[01])[- /.](19|20)\d\d</td></tr>
<tr><td>RegularExpressionValidator</td><td>regValEmail</td><td>ControlToValidate = txtEmailId
ErrorMessage = Email Id Format is incorrect
ValidateExpression=\w+([-+.']\w+)*@\w+([-.]\w+)*\.\w+([-.]\w+)*</td></tr>
</table>

Question 1	*What would you do to validate the number of characters in the name field?*

5. Add two list items to the rdbCountry RadioButtonList control namely—**USA** and **Others**.

6. Write the following code for the `OnPageLoad` method:

```
private void OnPageLoad()
{
  // Check whether the page is requested for the first time using
IsPostBack property
    if (!IsPostBack)
    {
      // If yes, set the rdbCountry to select the USA option
      rdbCountry.SelectedIndex = 0;
      // Disable the control that accepts zip code
      txtZipCode.Enabled = false;
      // Change the background color of the zip code control to light gray
      txtZipCode.BackColor = System.Drawing.Color.LightGray;
      // Set the lblDate label control to the current date time value
      lblDate.Text = DateTime.Now.ToString();
    }

    if (txtZipCode.Enabled == true)
    // Enable the RequiredField Validator for the txtZipcode control to
true, if txtZipCode is enabled
      rqdValZip.Enabled = true;
    else
      // Otherwise, disable the validator
      rqdValZip.Enabled = false;

    if (Session["Details"] == null)
    // If the Session variable Details has no data, disable the btnView
button control
      btnView.Enabled = false;
    else
      // Otherwise, enable the btnView button control
      btnView.Enabled = true;
```

```
        // Set the visibility of gvDetails grid view control to false
        gvDetails.Visible = false;
        // Clear the lblSuccess label control
        lblSuccess.Text = "";
    }
```

7. Call the `OnPageLoad` method in the `Page_Load` method:

```
    protected void Page_Load(object sender, EventArgs e)
    {
        OnPageLoad();
    }
```

8. Write the following code for the `btnAdd_Click` method:

```
    protected void btnAdd_Click(object sender, EventArgs e)
    {
        // Call the SaveDataToSession method to save the user supplied data
in a session variable
        SaveDataToSession();
    }
```

9. Write the following code for the `SaveDataToSession` method:

```
    private void SaveDataToSession()
    {
        // Clear the Session variable
        if (Session["Details"] != null)
          Session["Details"] = null;
        // Create a data table
        DataTable  dtDetails = new DataTable();
        // Call the CreateDataTable method to create columns for the data
table corresponding to the input fields
        CreateDataTable(dtDetails);
        // Create an empty row in the data table
        DataRow dr = dtDetails.NewRow();
        // Set the value of each column in the row with the values entered in
the respective text box control
        dr["Name"] = txtName.Text;
        dr["EmailId"] = txtEmail.Text;
        dr["DOB"] = txtDOB.Text;
        if (txtZipCode.Enabled)
```

```
          dr["Country-Code"] = rdbCountry.SelectedValue + "-" +
txtZipCode.Text;
        else
          dr["Country-Code"] = rdbCountry.SelectedValue;
        // Add the row to the data table
        dtDetails.Rows.Add(dr);
        // Store the data table in the session variable Details
        Session["Details"] = dtDetails;
        lblSuccess.Text = "Click View my details...to verify your details!";
        // Enable the btnView button control to let the user click the
control to see the values stored in the session variable in a grid view
control
        btnView.Enabled = true;
    }
```

10. Write the following code to the `CreateDataTable` method:

```
    private void CreateDataTable(DataTable dtDetails)
     {
      // Add columns to the data table
      dtDetails.Columns.Add(new DataColumn("Name"))
      dtDetails.Columns.Add(new DataColumn("EmailId"))
      dtDetails.Columns.Add(new DataColumn("DOB"))
      dtDetails.Columns.Add(new DataColumn("Country-Code"))
     }
```

11. Write the following code for the `btnView_Click` method:

```
    protected void btnView_Click(object sender, EventArgs e)
     {
       Call the DisplayDetailsInGrid method to display the values stored in
the Session variable "Details" in the GridView control
       DisplayDetailsInGrid();
     }
```

12. Write the following code for the `DisplayDetailsInGrid` method:

```
    private void DisplayDetailsInGrid()
     {
       // Set the data source property of the gvDetails GridView control to
the Session variable "Details"
       gvDetails.DataSource = (DataTable)Session["Details"];
       try
```

```
        {
          gvDetails.DataBind();
        }
        catch(Exception ex)
        {
           lblSuccess.Text = ex.Message;
        }
        // Set the GridView control to be visible
        gvDetails.Visible = true;
    }
```

13. Define the `RowDataBound` event for the GridView as given here. This displays a status message to the user indicating that he or she did not enter a value for the data of birth field, when the respective field value is empty:

```
    protected void gvDetails_RowDataBound(object sender,
GridViewRowEventArgs e)
    {
      // Check if the value in the third column (DOB field) of the grid
view row is empty
      if (e.Row.Cells[2].Text == " ")
        // If yes, display a status message to the user accordingly
        e.Row.Cells[2].Text = "Sorry, you didn't specify one!";
    }
```

14. Write the following code to `SelectedIndexChanged` event of the RadioButtonList:

```
    protected void rdbCountry_SelectedIndexChanged(object sender, EventArgs
e)
    {
      // Call the EnableDisableZipCode method to enable or disable the
txtZipCode Textbox control depending on the selection of item in the
RadioButtonList control
      EnableDisableZipCode();
    }
```

Question 2	*You have defined and implemented the SelectedIndexChanged event for the RadioButtonList. However, you observe that it is not triggered. What may be the reason?*

15. Write the following code for the `EnableDisableZipCode` method:

```
private void EnableDisableZipCode()
{
  if (rdbCountry.SelectedValue.ToLower() == "others")
  {
    // Enable the txtZipCode control if the user has selected the option for the country as "Others"
    txtZipCode.Enabled = true;
    txtZipCode.BackColor = System.Drawing.Color.Empty;
    rqdValZip.Enabled = true;
  }
  else
  {
    // Disable the txtZipCode and the corresponding RequiredField Validator control if the user has selected the option for the country as "USA"
    txtZipCode.Enabled = false;
    txtZipCode.BackColor = System.Drawing.Color.LightGray;
    rqdValZip.Enabled = false;
    txtZipCode.Text = "";
    btnView.Enabled = false;
  }
}
```

Question 3	*When you use validation controls, you observe that on postback all the desired validators display their messages. However, you need to display validation messages in a sequence. How can you achieve this?*

16. Build the application by clicking on the Build menu and choosing Build Solution (ctrl+shift+B).

17. Run the aplication by clicking on the Debug menu and choosing Debug Application(F5).

18. Click the Subscribe button without entering any details. The required field validators should show up with the corresponding error messages.

19. Enter the date in a wrong format. The regular expression validator prompts an error.

20. Enter an incorrect form of e-mail ID. The regular expression validator prompts an error.

21. Select Others from the options and do not enter the zip code. Enter all other details and click Subscribe. The required field validator prompts an error.

22. Enter all the details correctly and click Subscribe.

23. The View My Details button is enabled and a message appears to view the details.

24. Click View My Details to see your details in a grid view.

25. Note that DOB is not a required field and if you do not enter a value in the DOB field in the grid view, it shows the message: "Sorry, you didn't specify one!"

LAB REVIEW QUESTIONS

Completion time	**15 minutes**

1. The scenario in Lab Exercise 1.1 requires you to display details entered by the users in a grid view control. Also, consider a scenario that requires you to click the username in the grid view and display the user details (more details than in grid view). Which ASP.NET control would be the most ideal for this scenario?

2. In the given lab, how will you check that the date of birth entered by the user falls earlier than the current year?

3. Consider that you want to edit and update the details in the grid view discussed in review question 1. You have the `Edit` and `Update` buttons in the grid view rows to achieve this. Which event of the GridView control will you use to code for this?

4. What is the significance of the `Impressions` property in the Ad Rotator advertisements file?

LAB CHALLENGE 1.1: USING THE MULTIVIEW AND VIEW CONTROLS

Completion time	**30 minutes**

Now that you have created the Subscribe functionality, you need to modify the Subscribe.aspx page so that it has four sections or four tabs: Subscribe, Login, About us, and Contact us. Modify the Subscribe.aspx page to include the tabs.

LAB CHALLENGE 1.2: USING WEB PARTS

Completion time	**20 minutes**

ASP.NET Web Parts enable users to create web pages that present modular content and also allows users to change the appearance and content to suit their preferences. In the Subscribe.aspx page described previously, you can achieve this functionality using Web Parts. Create a user control named Subscribe.ascx and embed the code of Subscribe.aspx (except the date label) in a user control.

LAB 2
DESIGNING WEB SITES

This lab contains the following exercises and activities:

Exercise 2.1	Using Master Pages, Themes, and Skins
Lab Review Questions	
Lab Challenge 2.1	Using Nested Master Pages
Lab Challenge 2.2	Setting the MasterPageFile Property from Code

BEFORE YOU BEGIN

Lab 2 assumes that the lab setup has been completed as specified in the setup document and that StudentXX-A, StudentXX-B, and StudentXX-C computers have Microsoft .NET Framework 3.5 and Microsoft Visual Studio 2008 installed.

> NOTE
> *In this lab, you will see the characters XX. When you see these characters, substitute the two-digit number assigned to your computer.*

SCENARIO

You are creating a Web site that requires maintaining a consistent layout and look and feel. You use master pages to achieve a consistent layout. You use skins and style sheets to achieve a consistent look and feel throughout the Web site.

In the Lab Challenges, you will use nested master pages. In addition, you will dynamically change the master page reference.

After completing this lab, you will be able to:

- Use master pages
- Use themes
- Use skins
- Use nested master pages
- Modify the master page reference through code

Estimated lab time: 90 minutes

Exercise 2.1	Using Master Pages, Themes, and Skins
Overview	You are creating a Web site using master pages; you use skins and themes to design the user interface. In this lab exercise, you will use master pages and access the master page from content page and vice versa. In addition, you will apply skins and themes. You will use Microsoft Visual Studio 2008 to create the Web site. This task is complete when you create a Web site that demonstrates the use of master pages, skins, and themes. To complete this lab exercise, all the student computers such as StudentXX-A and StudentXX-B must be started and must have network access.
Completion time	40 minutes

1. From the Start menu, select Microsoft Visual Studio 2008, and then select Microsoft Visual Studio 2008.

2. Select File → New Web Site → ASP.NET Web Site, and enter the name **MasterPagesAndThemes**. This creates a new Web site with the Default.aspx page in it. Delete Default.aspx.

3. Add three new folders to the Web site—**XML**, **Images**, and **Master Pages**.

4. Add a master page to the Master Pages folder by selecting Master Pages folder → Add New Item → Master Page and name the page **SiteMasterPage.master**.

> **NOTE**
> *Visual Studio creates a Default.aspx page when creating a new ASP.NET application. This Default.aspx page isn't bound to a master page. To bind the Default.aspx page to a master page, delete the Default.aspx page and re-add it by checking the "Select Master Page" check box.*

5. Re-add the Default.aspx page. To perform this:

   a. Right click on the project name in the Solution Explorer and choose Add New Item → Web Form.

   b. In the Add New Item dialog box that appears, name the web form as Default.aspx and select the Select Master Page check box. The Select Master Page dialog box appears. Select the Master page from the corresponding folder.

6. Add ASP.NET folder App_Themes to the Web site and rename the Theme1 folder **Blue**. Add another theme folder to App_Themes and name it **Pink**.

7. Add a style sheet and a skin file to each of the two theme folders by selecting Theme Folder → Add New Item → Stylesheet/Skin File. Name the style sheet in the Blue folder **BlueCSS.css** and name the skin file **BlueSkin.skin**. Name the style sheet in the Pink folder **PinkCSS.css** and name the skin file **PinkSkin.skin**.

8. Add the following code to BlueCSS.css. The given css sets the background color of the body element to blue and sets the top, right, left, and bottom padding of a table element:

```
body
{
  background-color: #99ccff;
}

table
{
  padding-right: 5px;
  padding-left: 5px;
  padding-top: 5px;
  padding-bottom: 5px;
}
```

9. Add the following code to PinkCSS.css. The given css sets the background color of the body element to pink and sets the top, right, left, and bottom padding of a table element:

```
body
{
  background-color: #ffccff;
}

table
{
  padding-right: 5px;
  padding-left: 5px;
  padding-top: 5px;
  padding-bottom: 5px;
}
```

10. Add the following code to BlueSkin.skin. This control skin sets the specified font properties for Label, Button, and TextBox controls placed on the Default.aspx page. Note that the setting also has control skins named “Success” and “button”:

```
    <asp:Label runat="server" Font-Family="verdana" Font-Size="10px" Font-Weight="bold"/>

    <asp:Label runat="server" Font-Family="verdana" Font-Size="12px" Font-Weight="bold" ForeColor="red" SkinId="Success"/>

    <asp:TextBox runat="server" Font-Family="verdana" ForeColor="blue" Font-Size="10px" Font-Weight="bold"/>

    <asp:Button runat="server" Font-Family="verdana" Font-Size="10px" Font-Weight="bold"/>

    <asp:Button runat="server" Font-Family="verdana" Font-Size="12px" ForeColor="red" Font-Weight="bold" SkinId="button"/>
```

11. Add the following code to PinkSkin.skin. This control skin sets the specified font properties of Label, Button, and TextBox controls placed on the Default.aspx page. Note that the setting also has control skins named “Success” and “Button”:

```
    <asp:Label runat="server" Font-Family="calibri" Font-Size="10px" Font-Weight="bold"/>

    <asp:Label runat="server" Font-Family="calibri" Font-Size="12px" Font-Weight="bold" ForeColor="red" SkinId="Success"/>

    <asp:TextBox runat="server" ForeColor="Blue" Font-Family="calibri" Font-Size="10px" Font-Weight="bold"/>

    <asp:Button runat="server" Font-Family="calibri" Font-Size="10px" Font-Weight="bold"/>
```

```
<asp:Button runat="server" Font-Family="calibri" Font-Size="12px"
ForeColor="maroon" Font-Weight="bold" SkinId="button"/>
```

12. Add a style sheet named StyleSheet.CSS to the App_Themes folder and register it in the Master Page using the link element. The link element adds the StyleSheet.CSS to the document:

```
<link rel="Stylesheet" href="~/App_Themes/StyleSheet.css" id="css1" />
```

13. Add the following code to StyleSheet.css. Note that the given setting uses class selectors .header and .SaveButton to be applied to the table column and SaveButton controls, respectively, placed on the Master Page in Step 16:

```
body
{
}

.header
{
  background-color:Maroon;
  font-weight:bold;
  font-family:Book Antiqua;
  font-size:24pt;
  color:White;

}
td
{
  font-family:Book Antiqua;
  font-size:medium;
}
.SaveButton
{
  font-family:Book Antiqua;
  font-weight:bold;
  background-color:silver;
}
```

NOTE	*You can use the class selector to specify style settings for a group of elements. Using a class selector, you can set a particular style for any HTML element that references the class.*

14. Add the same controls and code to Default.aspx and Default.aspx.cs as in Lab 1. Set the skin id property of lblSuccess to Success and the skin id property of btnView to button. This is to ensure that the property settings in the named skins Success and Button are applied to these controls, respectively.

15. Add a RadioButtonList control to Default.aspx and add two list items, **Pink Theme** and **Blue Theme**, and set the value propeties to pink and blue.

16. Add a button named **btnSave** to the Master Page. Provide the text for the button as **Save Records** and set its CssClass property to **SaveButton**. The following is the HTML design of the master page. Note that the class selector header is applied to the column in the first row of the table:

```
<body>
  <form id="form1" runat="server">
    <table style="width:100%;height:100%;">
     <tr>
       <td colspan="2" align="center" class="header">
         MASTER PAGE SAMPLE
       </td>
     </tr>
     <tr>
         <td colspan="2" align="right">
           <asp:Button ID="btnSave" runat="server" Text="Save Records"
CssClass="SaveButton" OnClick="btnSave_Click"></asp:Button>
         </td>
     </tr>
     <tr>
        <td style="width:80%;">
          <asp:contentplaceholder id="ContentPlaceHolder1"
runat="server">
          </asp:contentplaceholder>
        </td>

     </tr>
    </table>
  </form>
</body>
```

17. Add a class named SaveRecords to the App_Code folder and write the following code in this class:

```
public class SaveRecords
{
  // Declare a public method named SaveRecordsToCSV with two arguments
namely csvPath that contains the physical file path and a datatable. The
SaveRecordsToCSV method saves the data in the datatable in the specified file.
  public static void SaveRecordsToCSV(string csvPath,DataTable dt)
  {
    // Use a StreamWriter object to write a file with the contents in
the data table
    StreamWriter sw = new StreamWriter(csvPath);
    string strVals = string.Empty;
    // Iterate the rows and columns in the datatable to write the data
stored in it to the specified file
    for (int i = 0; i < dt.Rows.Count; i++)
    {
      for (int j = 0; j < dt.Columns.Count;j++ )
      {
        strVals = dt.Rows[i][j].ToString();
        sw.Write(strVals);
```

```
            sw.Write(',');
          }
        }
        sw.Close();
      }
    }
```

18. To switch between pink and blue themes by clicking the radio buttons, add the following code to the PreInit event of the Default.aspx page:

```
protected void Page_PreInit(object sender, EventArgs e)
{
  // Add an event handler named Master_SaveClicked to the SaveClicked
event of the master page. The SaveClicked event has been declared in step 19a.
  Master.SaveClicked += new EventHandler(Master_SaveClicked);
  // Check whether an item has been checked in the RadioButtonList
rdbLstTheme using the Request.Form property. The Request.Form property gets a
collection of form variables.
  if (Request.Form["ctl00$ContentPlaceHolder1$rdbLstTheme"] != null)
    // If yes, then set the Page.Theme property to the selected value in
the RadioButtonList
    this.Theme =
ConfigurationManager.AppSettings[Request.Form["ctl00$ContentPlaceHolder1$rdbLs
tTheme"]].ToString();
}
```

Question 1	*What would happen if you add a label to your content page and try to assign a value to it in the PreInit event?*

19. To save records to the CSV file by clicking the Save Records button in the Master Page, you need to do the following:

    a. Declare an event in the master page:

```
public event EventHandler SaveClicked;
```

    b. In the Save button click event, write the following code:

```
if (SaveClicked != null)
  // Raise the SaveClicked event of the master page. The
EventArgs.Empty field in the code represents that the SaveClicked event has no
event data
  SaveClicked(this, EventArgs.Empty);
```

    c. In the MasterSaveClicked event handler, write the following code:

```
private void Master_SaveClicked(object sender, EventArgs e)
{
  // Call the SaveRecordsToCSV method of the SaveRecords class by
passing the file path and the Datatable that holds the personnel details. Note
```

```
that the code uses the Server.MapPath method to get the physical file path of
the specified virual path
            SaveRecords.SaveRecordsToCSV(Server.MapPath("CSV.csv"),
(DataTable)Session["Details"]);
        }
```

Question 2	*What class does the Master Page derive from?*

20. Build the application by clicking on the Build menu and choosing Build Solution (ctrl+shift+B).

21. Run the application by clicking on the Debug menu and choosing Debug Application (F5).

22. Select each radio button and observe that the theme and skins applied to the controls also change.

23. Click Save Records and observe that the records are saved to the CSV file.

LAB REVIEW QUESTIONS

Completion time	**15 minutes**

1. Which event of the aspx page life cycle would you use to load themes dynamically?

2. Compare themes and cascading style sheets.

3. When used within a master page, the controls have different IDs when rendered. These IDs are different from the actual ones assigned to them. Explain.

LAB CHALLENGE 2.1: USING NESTED MASTER PAGES

Completion time	**20 minutes**

The given lab uses a single master page. However, you may need to use nested master pages. For example, consider that you want the Web site to use different layouts depending on the country chosen. Create a parent master page, a child master page, and a child file that uses the nested master pages.

LAB CHALLENGE 2.2: SETTING THE MASTERPAGEFILE PROPERTY FROM CODE

Completion time	**15 minutes**

Setting the MasterPageFile attribute in the @Page directive assigns the page's MasterPageFile property during the Initialization stage, which is the first stage of the page's life cycle. Alternatively, you can set this property programmatically. Set the page's MasterPageFile property through code.

LAB 3
CREATING WEB APPLICATIONS AND WEB SITES

This lab contains the following exercises and activities:

BEFORE YOU BEGIN

Lab 3 assumes that the lab setup has been completed as specified in the setup document and that StudentXX-A, StudentXX-B, and StudentXX-C computers have Microsoft .NET Framework 3.5 and Microsoft Visual Studio 2008 installed.

> **NOTE**
> *In this lab, you will see the characters XX. When you see these characters, substitute the two-digit number assigned to your computer.*

SCENARIO

You are designing a huge Web site that is going to be developed using .NET Framework 3.5. It is necessary to handle the site navigation effectively. Additionally, you also need to manage the requests and the responses to and from the site globally.

In the Lab Challenges, you will implement an HTTP module. In addition, you will secure the navigation to restrict select users.

After completing this lab, you will be able to:

- Work with navigation controls
- Work with HTTP modules
- Work with HTTP handlers

Estimated lab time: 95 minutes

Exercise 3.1	Designing Navigation Mechanisms
Overview	You are designing a Web site, and you need to provide a consistent way for the users to navigate through your site. You need to store links of all the pages in your site in a central location and render those links in lists or navigation menus. You need to achieve bread crumb navigation also. You will use Microsoft Visual Studio 2008 to create the Web site. This task is complete when you design a Web site and provide a consistent way for the users to navigate through your site, store links of all the pages in your site in a central location, render those links in lists or navigation menus, and achieve bread crumb navigation. To complete this lab exercise, all the student computers such as StudentXX-A and StudentXX-B must be started and must have network access.
Completion time	15 minutes

1. From the Start menu, select Microsoft Visual Studio 2008, and then select Microsoft Visual Studio 2008.

2. Select File → New Web site → ASP.NET Web Site, and then select File System mode of creating the Web site. Enter the name **SiteNavigation**. This creates a new Web site.

> **NOTE**
> *Site navigation is a Web site-wide feature, and it needs to be present in all Web site pages. To accomplish this, we need to implement site navigation in the master page.*

3. Create a master page, and add the header "SITE NAVIGATION DEMO."

4. Create a Web site structure as mentioned in the following steps:

   a. Create a folder named Books. In the folder, create four pages: Default.aspx, Fiction.aspx, History.aspx, and Business.aspx. Bind each of these pages to the master page by adding the attribute: `MasterPageFile="~/MasterPage.master"` to the `<%@ Page ...... %>` directive and then add some contents to the pages.

   b. Create a folder named Apparel. In the folder, create a page named Default.axpx. Bind the page to the master page by adding the attribute: `MasterPageFile="~/MasterPage.master"` to the `<%@ Page ...... %>` directive and then add some contents to the page.

   c. Create a folder named Electronics. In the folder, create a page named Default.aspx. Bind the page to the master page by adding the attribute: `MasterPageFile="~/MasterPage.master"` to the `<%@ Page ...... %>` directive and then add some contents to the page.

   d. Create a folder named Computers. In the folder, create a page named Default.aspx. Bind the page to the master page by adding the attribute: `MasterPageFile="~/MasterPage.master"` to the `<%@ Page ...... %>` directive and then add some contents to the page.

5. Add a Web.SiteMap file to the project by right clicking on the project in Solution Explorer → Add New Item—"Site Map." Modify the default content in the SiteMap file, as given here, to reflect the Web site structure created in Step 4:

> **NOTE**
> *The Web.SiteMap file is an XML file.*

```
<?xml version="1.0" encoding="utf-8" ?>
<siteMap>
  <siteMapNode url="~/Default.aspx" title="Home">
    <siteMapNode url="~/Books/Default.aspx" title="Books">
      <siteMapNode url="~/Books/History.aspx" title="History" />
      <siteMapNode url="~/Books/Fiction.aspx" title="Fiction" />
      <siteMapNode url="~/Books/Business.aspx" title="Business" />
    </siteMapNode>
    <siteMapNode url="~/Apparel/Default.aspx" title="Apparel" />
    <siteMapNode url="~/Electronics/Default.aspx" title="Electronics" />
    <siteMapNode url="~/Computers/Default.aspx" title="Computers"/>
  </siteMapNode>
</siteMap>
```

Question 1	*How can you secure custom sitemaps that are stored in files without the sitemap extension?*

6. Add a SiteMapPath control to the master page. The SiteMapPath automatically picks the site navigation links from the Web.SiteMap file.

7. Add a SiteMapDataSource control and a TreeView control to the master page. Set the `DataSourceId` of the Treeview control to SiteMapDataSource1. The SiteMapDataSource control binds to the SiteMap data.

8. Add three hyperlinks to the page, namely **Previous**,**Up**, and **Next** with the IDs **lnkPrev, lnkUp,** and **lnkNext**, respectively.

9. In the `Page_Load` method of the master page, write the following code:

```
// Check whether a previous SiteMapNode object is available on the    same
level as the current one          if( SiteMap.CurrentNode.PreviousSibling
!= null)
 {
     // If yes, set the lnkPrev hyperlink control to the URL of the page
represented by the previous SiteMapNode object


     lnkPrev.NavigateUrl = SiteMap.CurrentNode.PreviousSibling.Url;
     lnkPrev.Text = "< Prev (" + SiteMap.CurrentNode.PreviousSibling.
Title +")>";
 }
```

```
else
{
    // If no, set the NavigateUrl property of the lnkPrev hyperlink
control to empty

    lnkPrev.NavigateUrl = String.Empty;
    lnkPrev.Text = "<Prev";
}

// Check whether the current SiteMapNode object has a parent SiteMapNode

if(SiteMap.CurrentNode.ParentNode != null)
{
    // If yes, set the lnkUp hyperlink control to the URL of the page
represented by the parent site map node
    lnkUp.NavigateUrl = SiteMap.CurrentNode.ParentNode.Url;
    lnkUp.Text = "<Up (" + SiteMap.CurrentNode.ParentNode.Title + ")>";
}
else
{
    // If no, set the NavigateUrl property of the lnkUp hyperlink control
to empty
    lnkUp.NavigateUrl = String.Empty;
    lnkUp.Text = "Up";
}

// Check whether a next SiteMapNode object is available on the same level
as the current one
if(SiteMap.CurrentNode.NextSibling != null)
{
    // If yes, set the lnkNext hyperlink control to the URL of the page
represented by the next site map node
    lnkNext.NavigateUrl = SiteMap.CurrentNode.NextSibling.Url;
   lnkNext.Text = "<(" + SiteMap.CurrentNode.NextSibling.Title + ") Next >";
}
else
{
    // If no, set the NavigateUrl property of the lnkNext hyperlink
control to empty
    lnkNext.NavigateUrl = String.Empty;
```

```
        lnkNext.Text = "Next>";
    }
```

10. Open the web application's default web form default.aspx and bind it to the master page by adding the attribute: `MasterPageFile="~/MasterPage.master"` to the `<%@Page ...... %>` directive as shown here and set the page as the start page:

```
<%@ Page Language="C#" MasterPageFile="~/MasterPage.master"
   AutoEventWireup="true" CodeFile="Default.aspx.cs" Inherits="_Default"
   Title="Untitled Page" %>
```

11. Build the application by clicking on the Build menu and choosing Build Solution (ctrl+shift+B).

12. Run the application by clicking on the Debug menu and choosing Debug Application (F5).

13. Observe the bread crumb navigation and TreeView navigation as shown in Figure 3-1.

14. Observe the functioning of the hyperlinks. The links display the previous or next links as per the hierarchy. Figure 3-1 shows the Apparel page as the current page. Note that the Prev link points to the Books page and the Next link points to the Electronics page as per the hierarchy.

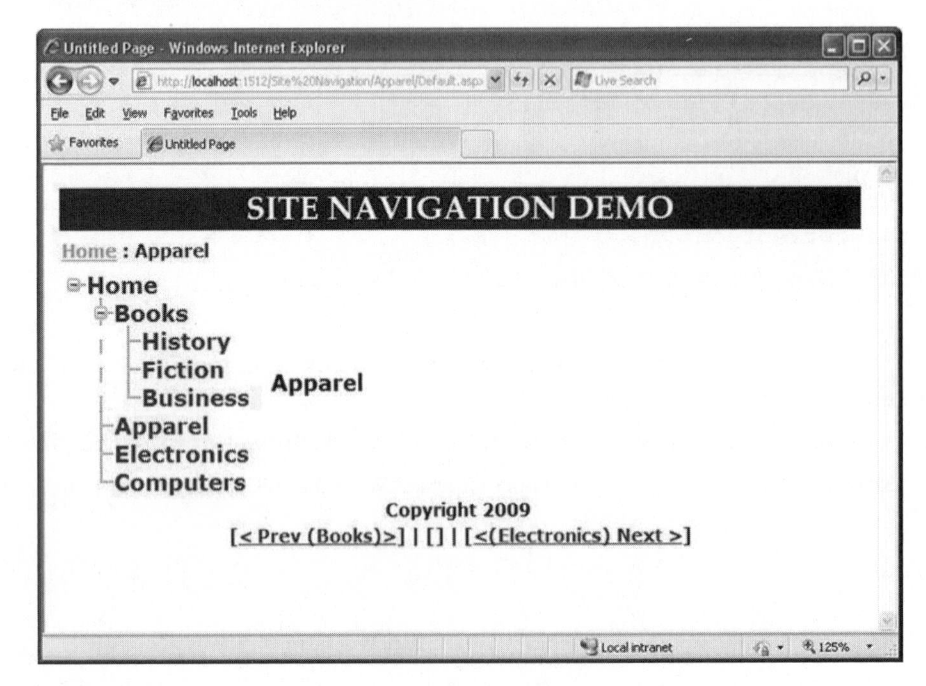

Figure 3-1
Site Navigation Demo

Exercise 3.2 Using HTTP Modules

Overview	You are creating a Web site that needs to assign roles to the current user by using HTTP modules. You will use Microsoft Visual Studio 2008 to create the Web site. This task is complete when you create a Web site that achieves this functionality on every request. To complete this lab exercise, all the student computers such as StudentXX-A and StudentXX-B must be started and must have network access.
Completion time	15 minutes

1. From the Start menu, select Microsoft Visual Studio 2008, and then select Microsoft Visual Studio 2008.
2. Select File → New Website → ASP.NET Web Site → File System and enter the name **HTTPModulesandHandlers**.
3. Add a class to the App_Code folder and name it **SampleModule.cs**.

NOTE	*You can create an HTTP module in the App_Code folder of your Web site. However, if you have a web application project, the preferred way to use an HTTP module would be to create it as a separate class library project and add a reference to the HTTP module's dll to the web application.*

4. Implement the IHttpModule interface in the SampleModule class as follows:

```
public class SampleModule:IHttpModule
```

5. Define the Init method as follows:

```
// Implement the Init method of the IHttpModule interface to register event
   handling methods with the specified events
public void Init(HttpApplication application)
    {
        // Add event handler for the application.BeginRequest event
        application.BeginRequest                    +=                    (new
   EventHandler(this.Application_BeginRequest));
        // Add event handler for the application.EndRequest event
        application.EndRequest                      +=                    (new
   EventHandler(this.Application_EndRequest));
```

```
        // Add event handler for the application.AuthenticateRequest event
        application.AuthenticateRequest                    +=                 new
    EventHandler(Application_AuthenticateRequest);
    }
```

6. Implement the Application_BeginRequest handler to write a message to the requested ASP.NET web page at the beginning of an HTTP request as shown:

```
private void Application_BeginRequest(object sender, EventArgs e)
    {
        // Get the current HttpApplication object
        HttpApplication application = (HttpApplication)sender;
        // Get the current HttpContext object
        HttpContext context = application.Context;
        // Write the required message to the requested ASP.NET page
        context.Response.Write("<h1><font   color=red>Sample   Http   Module:
    Beginning of Request</font></h1>");
    }
```

NOTE	*Application_BeginRequest is raised when any web page in your application is requested. This event allows you to initialize resources that will be used for each request.*

7. Implement the Applicaton_EndRequest handler to write a message to the requested ASP.NET web page at the end of processing the request as shown:

```
private void Application_EndRequest(object sender, EventArgs e)
    {
        // Get the current HttpApplication object
               HttpApplication application = (HttpApplication)sender;
        // Get the current HttpContext object
        HttpContext context = application.Context;
        // Write the required message to the requested ASP.NET page
        context.Response.Write("<hr><h1><font color=red>Sample Http Module:
    End of Request</font></h1>");
      }
```

NOTE	*Application_EndRequest is the only event that is guaranteed to be raised in every request because a request can be short-circuited. For example, if two modules handle the Application_BeginRequest event and the first one throws an exception, the Application_BeginRequest event will not be called for the second module. However, the Application_EndRequest method is always called to allow the application to clean up resources.*

8. Implement the Application_AuthenticateRequest handler to assign roles to the current user as shown:

NOTE	*Application_AuthenticateRequest fires when a security module establishes the identity of the user.*

```
private void Application_AuthenticateRequest(object sender, EventArgs e)
    {
        // Check whether the current request is not null
        if (!(HttpContext.Current.User == null))
        {
            // Check whether the authentication type of the current user is
forms
            if    (HttpContext.Current.User.Identity.AuthenticationType    ==
"Forms")
            {
                // If yes, get the identity of the current user
                System.Web.Security.FormsIdentity id;
                id                                                          =
(System.Web.Security.FormsIdentity)HttpContext.Current.User.Identity;
                // Create roles and assign the roles to the user
                String[] myRoles = new String[2];
                myRoles[0] = "Manager";
                myRoles[1] = "Admin";
                HttpContext.Current.User             =                   new
System.Security.Principal.GenericPrincipal(id, myRoles);
            }
        }
    }
```

Question 2	*When are the Init and Dispose methods of the HttpModule called?*

9. In the Page_Load event of Default.aspx, write the following code to determine the role of the current user:

```
protected void Page_Load(object sender, EventArgs e)
    {
        if (User.IsInRole("Admin"))
        {
            Response.Write("You are an Administrator");
        }
        else
        {
            Response.Write("You do not have any role assigned");
        }

    }
```

10. Add the following setting in the web.config file to register the custom HttpModule SampleModule:

```
<configuration>
  <system.web>
   <httpModules>
    <!-- Added a Custom HTTP Module-->
    <add name="SampleModule" type="SampleModule"/>
   </httpModules>
  <system.web>
</configuration>
```

11. Build the application by clicking on the Build menu and choosing Build Solution (ctrl+shift+B).

12. Run the application by clicking on the Debug menu and choosing Debug Application (F5).

13. Observe the sequence of events in the HttpModule while debugging.

14. Observe the output. When the ASP.NET receives the page request, it first passes through HttpModule. The module events occur first before the page loads in the following sequence:

    a. Application_BeginRequest

    b. Application_AuthenticateRequest

c. Page_Load

d. Application_EndRequest

The output is:

```
Sample Http Module: Beginning of Request
You are an Administrator/ You do not have any role assigned
Sample Http Module: End of Request
```

Exercise 3.3	Using HTTP Handlers
Overview	You are creating an HTTP handler to process the requests from the resources in your .NET application that have a .sample extension. You will use Microsoft Visual Studio 2008 to create the application. This task is complete when you create an HTTP handler that processes the requests for the resources with a .sample extension in your .NET application. To complete this lab exercise, all the student computers such as StudentXX-A and StudentXX-B must be started and must have network access.
Completion time	15 minutes

1. Open the solution HttpModulesAndHandlers that was created in the previous exercise.

2. Add a class file to the App_Code folder and name it **SampleHttpHandler.cs**.

3. Implement the IHttpHandler interface to the SampleHttpHandler class:

```
public class SampleHttpHandler:IHttpHandler
   {
   }
```

4. Implement the ProcessRequest method and the IsReusable property:

```
public void ProcessRequest(HttpContext context)
    {
        HttpResponse Response = context.Response;
        // This handler is called whenever a file ending
```

```
        // in .sample is requested. A file with that extension
        // does not need to exist.
        Response.Write("<html>");
        Response.Write("<body>");
        Response.Write("<h1>Message   from   a   synchronous   custom   HTTP
handler.</h1>");
        Response.Write("</body>");
        Response.Write("</html>");
    }
    public bool IsReusable
    {
        // To enable pooling, return true here.
        // This keeps the handler in memory.
        get { return false; }
    }
```

Question 3	*What are asynchronous HTTP handlers?*

The `IsReusable` property returns false indicating that no other request can use the IHttpHandler instance.

5. Register the HttpHandler in the web.config file:

```
<httpHandlers>
  <!-- Added a Custom HTTP Handler -->
  <add verb="*" path="*.sample" type="SampleHttpHandler"/>
 </httpHandlers>
```

6. Build the application by clicking on the Build menu and choosing Build Solution (ctrl+shift+B).

7. Create a virtual directory in the IIS for this application by performing the following steps:

   a. Go to Administrative Tools and select Internet Information Services, or use Start → Run → inetmgr.

b. Expand "Web Sites" and select "Default Web Site," right click, and select New → "Virtual Directory." A wizard page appears as shown in Figure 3-2. Click Next.

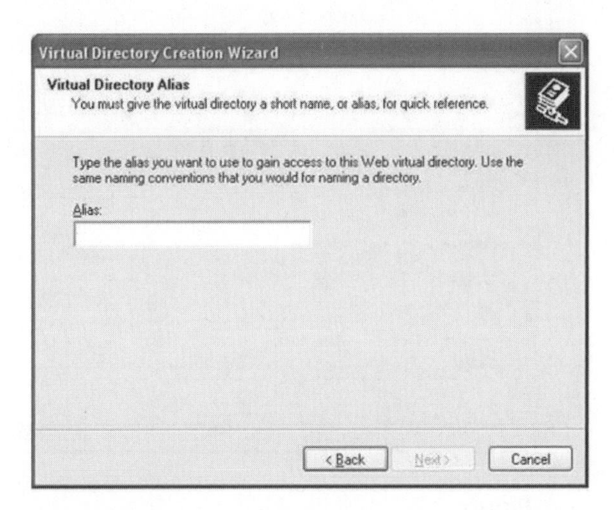

Figure 3-2
Virtual Directory Creation Wizard

c. In the wizard, enter the name you want to assign to your directory.

d. Now browse to the location of your folder in which your Web site files exist. Click Next, and then finish the wizard. Find the virtual directory that has been created.

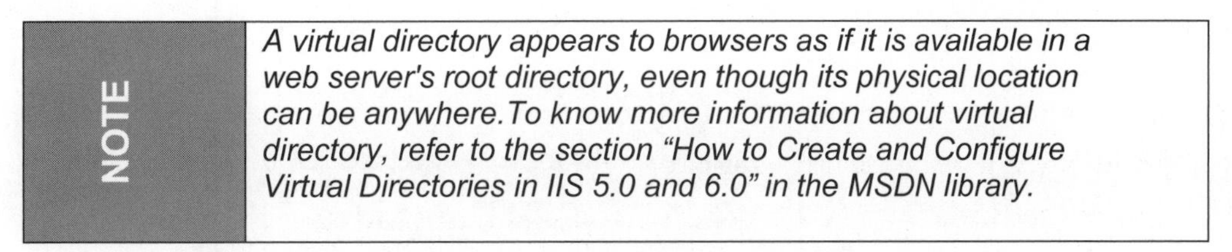
NOTE

A virtual directory appears to browsers as if it is available in a web server's root directory, even though its physical location can be anywhere. To know more information about virtual directory, refer to the section "How to Create and Configure Virtual Directories in IIS 5.0 and 6.0" in the MSDN library.

8. View the properties of the Web site in the IIS using the httpWebSiteProperties dialog box. Click the Configuration button on the Virtual Directory tab of this dialog box. Figure 3-3 shows the httpWebSite Properties dialog box.

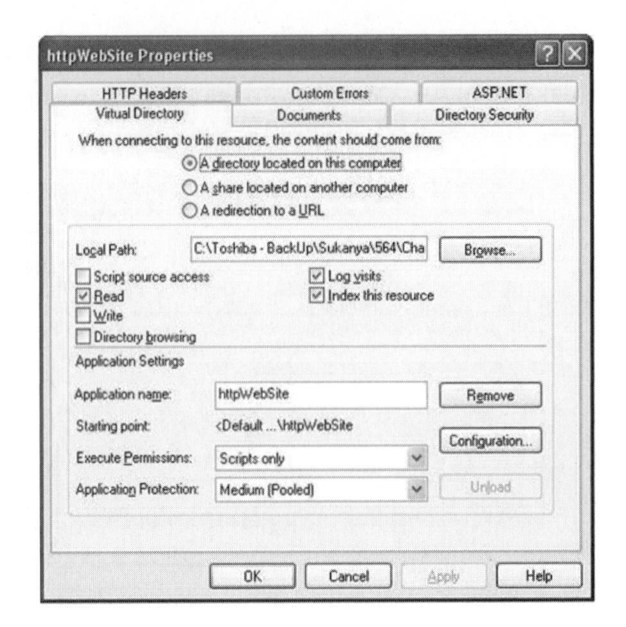

Figure 3-3
Web Site Properties

9. Click the Add button on Application Configuration dialog box. Browse to the aspnet_isapi.dll to get the executable as shown in Figure 3-4. Enter .sample in the Extension textbox and uncheck the "Check that file exists" check box in the Add/Edit Application Extension Mapping dialog box as shown in Figure 3-5.

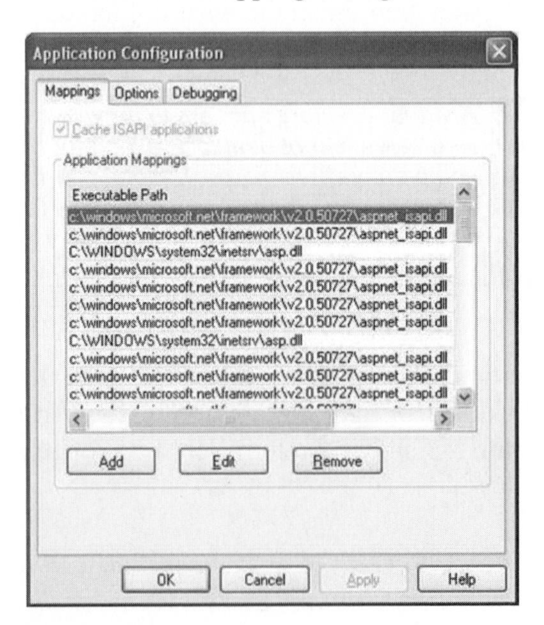

Figure 3-4
Application Configuration Dialog Box

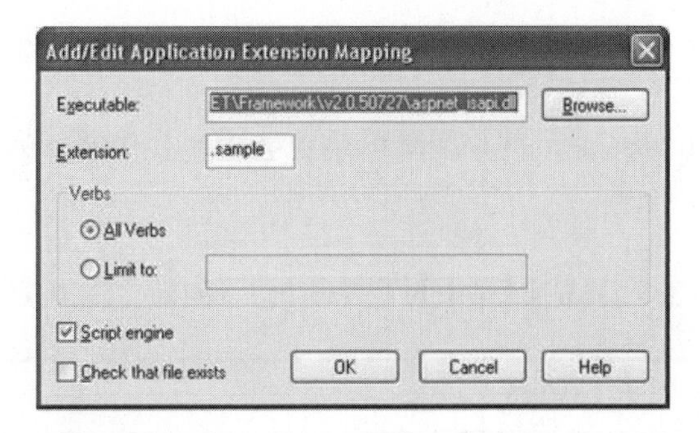

Figure 3-5
Add/Edit Application Extension Mapping Dialog Box

10. Request a page (may not exist) called Test.sample from the application. Observe the text, "Message from a synchronous custom HTTP handler," as shown in Figure 3-6, displayed on the page.

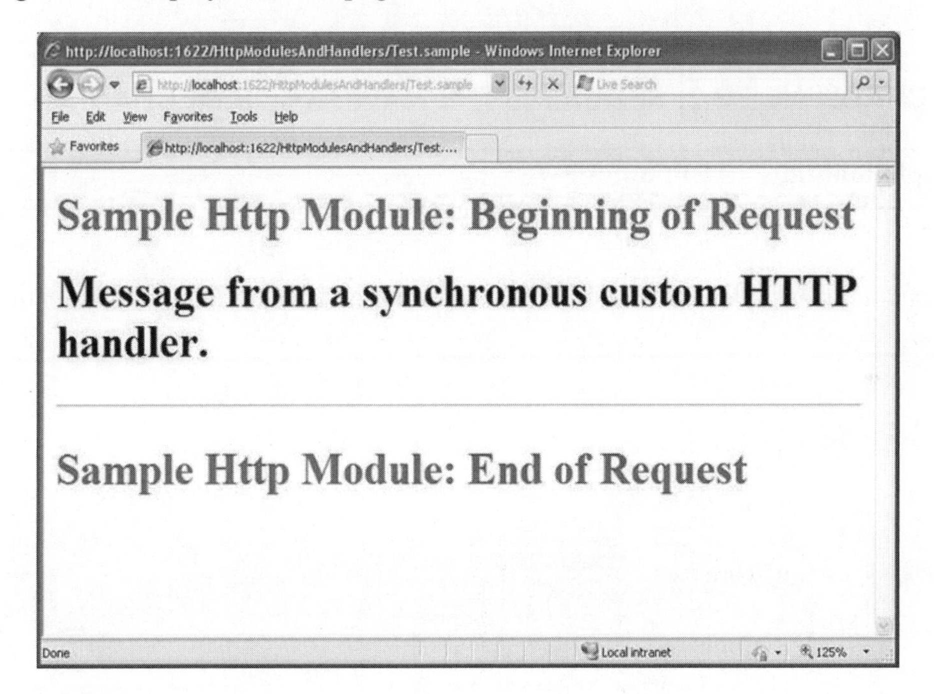

Figure 3-6
Page Showing the Message from the Custom HTTP Handler

LAB REVIEW QUESTIONS

Completion time	**15 minutes**

1. How can an asynchronous HTTP handler improve the performance of an application?

2. How can you maintain session state in HTTP handlers?

3. How can you access a custom site map provider from a parent site map file?

LAB CHALLENGE 3.1: IMPLEMENTING HTTP MODULES

Completion time	**20 minutes**

You are a technical architect in your company and are responsible for designing a big Web site. You are implementing HttpModule in the site to intercept the incoming requests and perform some actions on it. You need to serve the request for the page content from the cache after request authorization. How will you achieve this?

LAB CHALLENGE 3.2: SECURING THE NAVIGATION MECHANISM

Completion time	**15 minutes**

You are creating an ASP.NET Web site that has the following navigational hierarchy:

Home

- Products
    - Hardware
    - Software
    - Discounts
- Services
    - Training
    - Consulting
    - Support

The Support.aspx page should not be visible to clients who are not in Customer role. How can you achieve this?

LAB 4
DESIGNING STATE MANAGEMENT FOR WEB APPLICATIONS

This lab contains the following exercises and activities:

BEFORE YOU BEGIN

Lab 4 assumes that the lab setup has been completed as specified in the setup document and that StudentXX-A, StudentXX-B, and StudentXX-C computers have Microsoft .NET Framework 3.5 and Microsoft Visual Studio 2008 installed.

NOTE	*In this lab, you will see the characters XX. When you see these characters, substitute the two-digit number assigned to your computer.*

SCENARIO

You are designing a huge Web site that is going to be developed using .NET Framework 3.5. You need to design an appropriate state management strategy and effectively utilize the page-lifecycle events.

In the Lab Challenges, you will use a custom control and you will access the profile information.

After completing this lab, you will be able to:

- Manage states

Estimated lab time: 65 minutes

Exercise 4.1	Managing State for Web Applications
Overview	You are designing a Web site and you need to manage the state throughout the Web site using different strategies depending on the scenario. You will use Microsoft Visual Studio 2008 to create the Web site. This task is complete when you design a Web site and manage the state throughout the Web site using different strategies on the basis of the scenario. To complete this lab exercise, all the student computers such as StudentXX-A and StudentXX-B must be started and must have network access.
Completion time	15 minutes

1. From the Start menu, select Microsoft Visual Studio 2008, and then select Microsoft Visual Studio 2008.

2. Select File → New Web site → ASP.NET Web Site, and then select File System mode of creating the Web site. Enter the name **StateManagementAndPageLifeCycle**. This creates a new Web site.

NOTE	*Site navigation is a Web site-wide feature, and it needs to be present in all Web site pages. To accomplish this, you need to implement site navigation in the master page.*

3. Add an XML file to the site and name it **UserData.xml**. This file stores the user data such as username, password, role, and name. For example:

```
<Employees>
  <Employee1>
    <UserName>newUser</UserName>
    <Password>NEWUSER1</Password>
    <UserRole>User</UserRole>
    <FirstName>Jo</FirstName>
    <LastName>Dawson</LastName>
    <OrgRole>Manager</OrgRole>
    <City>Seattle</City>
    <ZipCode>98000</ZipCode>
  </Employee1>
</Employees>
```

> **NOTE** *In this code sample, the root element is <Employees>. You can add more employee elements such as Employee2, Employee3, and so on.*

4. Add two web forms to the site: **Default.aspx** and **Home.aspx**.

5. In Default.aspx, add a login section with two textboxes for username and password and a Login button. Additionally, declare the following variables:

```
string city = string.Empty;
string firstName = string.Empty;
DataTable dtCredentials = new DataTable();
```

6. Create a method named CreateDataTable to store the given XML file data in the data table dtCredentials as shown:

```
private void CreateDataTable(ref DataTable dt, XmlNodeList nodeList)
{
  // Create columns in the data table to map the nodes of the
<Employee1> element of the given XML file
  dt.Columns.Add(new DataColumn("uname"));
  dt.Columns.Add(new DataColumn("pwd"));
  dt.Columns.Add(new DataColumn("role"));
```

```
        dt.Columns.Add(new DataColumn("city"));
        dt.Columns.Add(new DataColumn("fname"));

       // Populate the data table column's with the node values
        foreach (XmlNode node in nodeList)
        {
            XmlDocument doc = new XmlDocument();
            doc.LoadXml(node.OuterXml);
            // Create a DataRow object
            DataRow dr = dt.NewRow();
            dr["uname"]                                              =
   doc.GetElementsByTagName("UserName").Item(0).InnerXml;
            dr["pwd"] = doc.GetElementsByTagName("Password").Item(0).InnerXml;
            dr["role"]                                               =
   doc.GetElementsByTagName("UserRole").Item(0).InnerXml;
            dr["city"] = doc.GetElementsByTagName("City").Item(0).InnerXml;
            dr["fname"]                                              =
   doc.GetElementsByTagName("FirstName").Item(0).InnerXml;
            // Add the created row to the data table
            dt.Rows.Add(dr);
        }
    }
```

7. In the click event of the login button, the XML file is read so that the user credentials can be compared with those in the XML file. This is done by the `GetUserRole()` method to verify that the user is valid user. If the user is a valid user, then the username, password, and user role are added to the session so that they can be accessed across the Web site. If not, then the user is reported as invalid. The city and user's first name are acquired from the datatable dtCredentials and are stored in the variables city and firstName, in order to be passed as QueryString to the Home.aspx page:

```
private bool GetUserRole()
    {
        bool foundUser = false;
        // Create an XmlReaderSettings object to specify a set of features to
   support the XmlReader object.
        XmlReaderSettings settings = new XmlReaderSettings();
        settings.IgnoreWhitespace = true;
```

```
    settings.IgnoreComments = true;
    settings.IgnoreProcessingInstructions = true;
    // Create an XmlReader object to read the contents from the given XML
file
    XmlReader reader = XmlReader.Create(Server.MapPath("UserData.xml"),
settings);
    // Read the contents from the given XML file
    reader.Read();
    while (!reader.EOF)
    {
        if (reader.NodeType==XmlNodeType.Element && reader.Name ==
"Employees")
        {
            // Create an XmlDocument object to create an in-memory tree
representation of the given XML document
            XmlDocument xmlDoc = new XmlDocument();
            // Read an XmlNode (the <Employee1> node in this case) from
the XmlReader object and store it in an XmlNode object
            XmlNode empNode = xmlDoc.ReadNode(reader);
            // Retrieve all the child nodes of the <Employee1> node
            XmlNodeList childNodeList=empNode.ChildNodes;
            // Call the CreateDataTable method to load the child node into
the dtCredentials data table
            CreateDataTable(ref dtCredentials, childNodeList);
            // If the username entered already exist in the data table,
store it in the Session state
            foreach (DataRow dr in dtCredentials.Rows)
            {
                if ((dr["uname"].ToString() == txtUsername.Text) &&
(dr["pwd"].ToString() == txtPassword.Text))
                {
                    Session["UName"] = txtUsername.Text;
                    Session["Pwd"] = txtPassword.Text;
                    Session["Role"] = dr["role"].ToString();
                    city = dr["city"].ToString();
                    firstName = dr["fname"].ToString();
                    foundUser = true;
                    break;
                }
```

```
                }

            }
            else
            {
                reader.Read();
            }
        }
        return foundUser;
    }
```

8. The click event of the login button calls the `GetUserRole()`. If the user is valid, then he/she is directed to the Home page of his/her city:

```
protected void btnLogin_Click(object sender, EventArgs e)
    {
      // Call the GetUserRole method to check if the user is valid.
      if(GetUserRole())
        // Pass the user's city and first name in the query string
        Response.Redirect("Home.aspx?city="+  city+  "&fnm="  +  firstName,
  true);
   else
     Response.Write("You are in invalid user");
}
```

NOTE	*Confidential details, such as user credentials are stored in session; whereas, general details like city and user's first name can be passed as a query string as shown. This is because query strings can be easily tampered with, so you should not store confidential details in them.*

Question 1	*What are the advantages of query strings?*

9. Add two label controls, namely **lblForecast** and **lblDesc**, and two button controls, namely **btnForecast** and **btnSignDesc**, to Home.aspx. Also add a Enter date of birth textbox. When the user clicks view forecast, he can view his forecast depending on his sun sign retrieved from his date of birth. Only then does the btnSifnDesc button become visible.

10. Declare the following variable in the Home.aspx page:

```
string[] arrSigns = null;
```

11. In the **load** event of the Home page, extract the first name and the city of the user from the query string to display a message in the browser window. Extract the user role from session. If the sessions are null, display a message saying “Your session has expired.” Also you need to display the user’s daily forecast depending on the sun sign. Store the twelve zodiac signs as an array and store the array in Viewstate. The load event of the Home page would appear as:

```
 protected void Page_Load(object sender, EventArgs e)
 {
     if (!IsPostBack)
     {
         arrSigns = new string[] {"Aries", "Taurus", "Gemini", "Cancer",
"Leo", "Virgo", "Libra", "Scorpio", "Sagittarius", "Capricorn", "Aquarius",
"Pisces"};
         // Store the string array containing the sun signs in the view
state
         ViewState["Signs"] = arrSigns;
     }


     btnSignDesc.Visible = false;
     lblDesc.Visible = false;
     lblForecast.Visible = false;

     if (Session["UName"] != null && Session["Role"]!=null)
     {
         // Display a greeting message on the page by retrieving the user's
first name from the query string
         Response.Write("<h5>Hello                    "                +
Request.QueryString["fnm"].ToString() + "</h5>");
         // Display an informational message on the page by retrieving the
user's role from the Session state
         Response.Write("<h5>You    are    logged    in    as    :    "+
Session["Role"].ToString() +"</h5>");
         / /Display a greeting message on the page by retrieving the city
name from the query string
         Response.Write("<h2>Welcome to "+ Request.QueryString["city"] + "
city's home page</h2>");
```

```
        }
        else
        {
            Response.Write("<h2>Your session expired. Please login again</h2>");
        }
}
```

12. The click event of forecast button shows the forecast depending on the user's sun sign which is determined by the date of birth entered by the user. This is achieved by calling the ShowSignAsperDate method:

```
protected void btnForecast_Click(object sender, EventArgs e)
{
    lblForecast.Visible = true;
    // Retrieve the sun signs from the view state
    arrSigns = (string[])ViewState["Signs"];
    // Retrieve the month from the user's birth date
    int month = int.Parse(txtDate.Text.Substring(0, 2));
    // Call the ShowSignAsPerDate method to evaluate the sun sign of the user
    string sunSign = ShowSignAsPerDate(month,arrSigns);
    // Store the retrieved sun sign in a View state
    ViewState["UserSunSign"] = sunSign;
    lblForecast.Text = "You could be " + sunSign + " : You shall be always smiling :)";
    btnSignDesc.Text = sunSign + " Traits ";
    btnSignDesc.Visible = true;
}
```

Question 2	*What are the disadvantages of an application state?*

13. The user sun sign is added to the ViewState so that it can be accessed between postbacks on the same page. It can be accessed when the btnSignDesc button is clicked.

14. The ShowSignAsPerDate method is defined as:

```
private string ShowSignAsPerDate(int month,string[] signs)
{
```

```
string sunSign = string.Empty;
// Calculate the sun sign approximately
switch (month)
{
    case 1:
        sunSign = signs[10] + "or" + signs[11];
        break;
    case 2:
        sunSign = signs[11] + "or" + signs[12];
        break;
    case 3:
        sunSign = signs[12] + "or" + signs[1];
        break;
    case 4:
        sunSign = signs[1] + "or" + signs[2];
        break;
    case 5:
        sunSign = signs[2] + "or" + signs[3];
        break;
    case 6:
        sunSign = signs[3] + "or" + signs[4];
        break;
    case 7:
        sunSign = signs[4] + "or" + signs[5];
        break;
    case 8:
        sunSign = signs[5] + "or" + signs[6];
        break;
    case 9:
        sunSign = signs[6] + "or" + signs[7];            break;
    case 10:
        sunSign = signs[7] + "or" + signs[8];
        break;
    case 11:
        sunSign = signs[8] + "or" + signs[9];
        break;
    case 12:
        sunSign = signs[9] + "or" + signs[10];
```

```
                break;
        }
        return sunSign;
    }
```

15. Write the following code in the click event of the **btnSignDesc** button:

```
protected void btnSignDesc_Click(object sender, EventArgs e)
    {
        btnSignDesc.Visible = true;
        lblForecast.Visible = true;
        lblDesc.Visible = true;
        lblDesc.Text = (string)ViewState["UserSunSign"] + " traits : Not
available now";
    }
```

16. Build the application by clicking on the Build menu and choosing Build Solution (ctrl+shift+B).

17. Right click on the Default.aspx page, select Set As Start Page.

18. Run the application by clicking Debug → Start Debugging (F5).

19. In the web page with UserName and Password dialog that appears, enter the username as **newUser** and password as **NEWUSER1**. Click on the Login button.

20. Once the Default page is opened, you can enter the appropriate UserName and Password, and it will take you to another page where you will see the city name per the user.

21. In the Enter your date of birth textbox, enter your birth date in the mmddyyyy format. For example, if your birth date is 17 Feb 1981, then enter in the American date format as 02171981 and click on the Show my forecast button. The program displays your sun sign and a forecast. Do not use the Internet Explorer back button. This may give undesirable results in this application.

LAB REVIEW QUESTIONS

Completion time	**15 minutes**

1. What is the difference between Session State and Application State?
2. Where is View State stored on the form?
3. What are persistent cookies?

LAB CHALLENGE 4.1: USING A CUSTOM CONTROL

Completion time	**20 minutes**

You have written a custom control that has different tabs showing different information. In order for that control to work as expected, it needs to know which tab is selected between round trips. The ViewState property can be used for this purpose, but view state can be turned off at a page level by developers, effectively breaking your control. How will you prevent this?

LAB CHALLENGE 4.2: ACCESSING THE PROFILE INFORMATION

Completion time	**15 minutes**

You want to store and use the user's postal code. When a user visits your site, you need to present the user with region-specific information, such as weather reports. How would you achieve this?

LAB 5
DESIGNING REUSABLE CONTROLS

This lab contains the following exercises and activities:

Exercise 5.1	Working on User Controls
Exercise 5.2	Working on Custom Controls
Exercise 5.3	Working on Derived Controls
Lab Review Questions	
Lab Challenge 5.1	Creating a Sample User Control

BEFORE YOU BEGIN

Lab 5 assumes that the lab setup has been completed as specified in the setup document and that StudentXX-A, StudentXX-B, and StudentXX-C computers have Microsoft .NET Framework 3.5 and Microsoft Visual Studio 2008 installed.

> **NOTE** *In this lab, you will see the characters XX. When you see these characters, substitute the two-digit number assigned to your computer.*

SCENARIO

You are developing an online survey web application. This application requires you to build your own user interface components.

In this lab, you will learn to create user controls, custom controls, and to extend the behavior of an existing server control.

In the Lab Challenge, you will create a user control that will display the current system date and time on a web form.

After completing this lab, you will be able to:

- Create user controls
- Create custom controls from scratch
- Create custom controls by extending the behavior of an existing server control

Estimated lab time: 90 minutes

Exercise 5.1	Working on User Controls
Overview	You are developing a Web site for which you are required to develop a user control. The user control should display a link to a help file. In this lab exercise, you will use Microsoft Visual Studio 2008. This task is complete when you are able to successfully create the user control and use it in the required pages. To complete this lab exercise, all the student computers such as StudentXX-A and StudentXX-B must be started and must have network access.
Completion time	15 minutes

1. From the Start menu, select Microsoft Visual Studio 2008, and then select Microsoft Visual Studio 2008.

2. Select File → New Project → ASP.NET Web Application, and enter the name **WorkingOnUserControl**.

3. Add a new web page in the project and name it **Help.aspx**.

4. Add the following HTML in the Help.aspx:

```
    <form id="form1" runat="server">
  <div>
    Hi, you have successfully created your user control.
    <br />HOW CAN I HELP YOU?
  </div>
</form>
```

5. Add a folder named **UserControls**.

6. Right click on the UserControls folder and select Add → New Item → Web User Control.

7. Name the Web User Control **Help.ascx**.

8. In the Help.ascx user control, add the hyperlink control as shown:

```
      <asp:HyperLink ID="hlnkHelp" runat="server" ToolTip="Click to
navigate to help file"
Target="_blank" NavigateUrl="~/Help.aspx">Help</asp:HyperLink>
```

9. Add a master page by right clicking on the project. Select Add New Item and then select Master Page from the provided templates. Enter the name as **MasterPage.Master**.

10. Add the user control to the master page by registering it. You can register the user control as shown:

```
      <%@ Register TagPrefix="uctrl" TagName="HelpCtrl"
Src="~/UserContols/Help.ascx" %>
```

11. Now add the given HTML in the master page:

```
   <head runat="server">
    <title>Untitled Page</title>
    <asp:ContentPlaceHolder ID="head" runat="server">
    </asp:ContentPlaceHolder>
  </head>
  <body>
   <form id="form1" runat="server">
     <div>
       <asp:ContentPlaceHolder ID="ContentPlaceHolder1" runat="server">
```

```
         </asp:ContentPlaceHolder>
      </div>
      <hr/>
      <div style="text-align:center">
         <uctrl:HelpCtrl ID="hlpCtrl" runat="server" />
      </div>
      </form>
   </body>
   <html>
```

12. Add a new web page by right clicking on the project and by selecting Add New Item. Then select Web Form. Name the form **default.aspx**.

Question 1	*Why do we use Web Content Form instead of Web Form?*

13. You will be prompted to select the master page. Select the added master page.
14. Build the application by clicking on the Build menu and choosing Build Solution (ctrl+shift+B).
15. Select the Default.aspx page, right click, and then choose View in Browser. Observe that the Help hyperlink is displayed on the bottom of the page. On clicking the hyperlink, the Help.aspx page is displayed. The Help.ascx user control is created and placed on the master page in order to be used in all the content pages. If the help file changes, you just need to update the user control so that the changes will be automatically reflected in all pages.

Exercise 5.2 Working on Custom Controls

Overview	You are creating an application to develop customizable pages. You want to allow users to change the font style of text on every button click. In this lab exercise, you will use Microsoft Visual Studio 2008. This task is complete when you are able to create and implement a custom control that allows for changing the text font on every click of the button.

	To complete this lab exercise, all the student computers such as StudentXX-A and StudentXX-B must be started and must have network access.
Completion time	15 minutes

1. From the Start menu, select Microsoft Visual Studio 2008, and then select Microsoft Visual Studio 2008.

2. Select File → New Project → ASP.NET Server Control and name it **WorkingOnCustomControls**.

3. On creation of the project, the Visual Studio creates a custom control named `ServerControl1`.

4. Add a reference to the `System.Drawing` namepsace as shown:

```
using System.Drawing;
```

5. Declare a private string variable named **_text**:

```
private string _text;
```

6. You will find a default property named `Text` being set. Modify the `get` and `set` property procedures as shown:

```
[Bindable(true)]
[Category("Appearance")]
[DefaultValue("")]
[Localizable(true)]
public string Text
{
  get
      {
        return _text;
      }
   set
      {
        _text = value;
      }
  }
```

7. Add the following code in the ServerControl1.cs file. This adds a new property named `Size` to the custom control that stores the index value of the `FontFamily.Families` property array used in Step 9:

```
public int Size
{
    // Retrieves the value of the Size property from view state
    get { return Convert.ToInt32(ViewState["Size"].ToString());}
    // Saves the value of the Size property in view state
    set { ViewState["Size"] = value.ToString();}
}
```

8. Add the following constructor to the custom control. The constructor initializes the value of the `Size` property stored in the view state:

```
public ServerControl1()
{
  // Initialize the value of the Size property in the view state to 1
   ViewState["Size"] = 1;
}
```

9. Override the `RenderContents` method of the base class in the ServerControl1.cs as shown:

```
protected override void RenderContents(HtmlTextWriter output)
{
    // Set the font style of the text to the name of the FontFamily object at
the specified index position of the Families property array
     output.AddStyleAttribute("font-family",
 FontFamily.Families.ElementAt(Size).Name);
     // Set the color of the text
     output.AddStyleAttribute("color",
ColorTranslator.ToHtml(Color.ForestGreen));
     // Set the text to be written in heading 2
output.RenderBeginTag("h2");
     // Write the text on the page
     output.Write(Text);
     output.RenderEndTag();
}
```

NOTE	*The `FontFamily.Families` property used in the given code returns an array of all `FontFamily` objects of the current graphics context.*

NOTE	*The core method of custom controls is the `RenderContents` method. This method is declared in the base `WebControl` class and can be overridden in the derived classes to take control of the rendering of the custom control. Note that the given code uses the parameter `HtmlTextWriter` object of the `RenderContents` method to write the string held in the `Text` property.*

10. Build the WorkingOnCustomControls project.

11. Create a new ASP.NET Web Application project that implements the created custom control. Name the project **UsingCustomControls**.

12. Add a reference to the WorkingOnCustomControls.dll in the web application. To perform this, right click on Add Reference. A dialog box appears. Select the Browse tab and navigate to WorkingOnCustomControl\Bin\Debug and select WorkingOnCustomControls.dll.

13. On the default.aspx page, you need to register the custom control as shown:

```
    <%@ Register Assembly="WorkingOnCustomControls"
Namespace="WorkingOnCustomControls" TagPrefix="cc1" %>
```

Question 2	*What will happen if the TagPrefix is not added in the @register directive while registering the control on the page?*

14. Add the following code in the default.aspx page:

```
<form id="form1" runat="server">
<div>
  <cc1:ServerControl1 ID="ServerControl1" runat="server"
Text="My first custom control" />
  <asp:Button ID="btnChangeFontStyle" runat="server"  Text="Click Me"
onclick="btnChangeFontStyle_Click" />
</div>
</form>
```

15. Add the following event handler for the click event of the `btnIncreaseSize` button control. The handler increases the value of the `Size` property of the custom server control. This in turn changes the text font:

```
protected void btnChangeFontStyle_Click(object sender, EventArgs e)
{
 ServerControl1.Size += 1;
}
```

16. Build the application by clicking on the Build menu and choosing Build Solution (ctrl+shift+B).

17. Run the aplication by clicking on the Debug menu and choosing Debug Application (F5).

18. Verify that on every button click the font style of the text changes.

Exercise 5.3	Working on Derived Controls
Overview	You are creating an online customer survey for a product. You want to maintain a count of the customers who use the product by tracking the number of times a button is clicked. For this purpose, you are required to create a custom control that extends the behavior of the button control. The custom control should maintain the count of the number of times it was clicked. In this lab exercise, you will use Microsoft Visual Studio 2008 to create the custom control. This task is complete when you are able to create the custom control with the specified functionality and implement it in a web application. To complete this lab exercise, all the student computers such as StudentXX-A and StudentXX-B must be started and must have network access.
Completion time	30 minutes

1. From the Start menu, select Microsoft Visual Studio 2008, and then select Microsoft Visual Studio 2008.

2. Select File → New Project → ASP.NET Server Control, and enter the name **DerivedControls**.

3. On creation of the project, the Visual Studio creates a custom control named `ServerControl1`. Rename the ServerControl1 to **DerivedButton**.

4. Add the following code to the DerivedButton.cs file. Note that the custom control inherits from the `Button` class:

```
[DefaultProperty("Text")]
[ToolboxData("<{0}:ServerControl1 runat=server></{0}:ServerControl1>")]
public class DerivedButton : Button
{
  // Constructor initializes the value in ViewState
  public DerivedButton()
  {
      this.Text = "Hit Me";
      ViewState["TotalCount"] = 0;
  }
  public int TotalCount
  {
      get
      {
          return Convert.ToInt32(ViewState["TotalCount"].ToString());
      }
      set
      {
          ViewState["TotalCount"] = value;
      }
  }
  // Override the OnClick to increment the count,
  // Update the button text and then invoke the base method
  protected override void OnClick(EventArgs e)
  {
    ViewState["TotalCount"] =
  Convert.ToInt32(ViewState["TotalCount"].ToString()) + 1;
    this.Text = ViewState["TotalCount"] + " clicks";
  }
}
```

5. Build the DerivedControls project.

6. Create a new web application that implements the created custom control. Name the application **UsingDerivedControls**.

7. Add reference to the DerivedControls.dll in the web application.

8. On the default.aspx page, include an `@register` directive to register the custom control as shown:

```
<%@ Register Assembly="DerivedControls" Namespace="DerivedControls"
TagPrefix="cc1" %>
```

9. Add the following script to the default.aspx page:

```
<form id="form1" runat="server">
  <div>
    <cc1:DerivedButton ID="drvBtn" runat="server" />
  </div>
</form>
```

10. Build the application by clicking on the Build menu and choosing Build Solution (ctrl+shift+B).

11. Run the aplication by clicking on the Debug menu and selecting Debug Application (F5).

12. Click the button a couple of times. Note that the text displayed on the button changes on every click and shows the count of the button click.

LAB REVIEW QUESTIONS

Completion time	**15 minutes**

1. Which directive is used to add a user control to a web form?

2. Explain the differences between user controls and custom controls.

LAB CHALLENGE 5.1: CREATING A SAMPLE USER CONTROL

Completion time	**15 minutes**

Consider that you have to create a user control that will display the current system date and time for your web application. Write code to create the user control.

LAB 6
LEVERAGING SCRIPTING WITH ASP.NET AJAX

This lab contains the following exercises and activities:

Exercise 6.1	Implementing Server-Side Scripting with ASP.NET AJAX
Exercise 6.2	Understanding ASP.NET AJAX Control Toolkit
Exercise 6.3	Implementing Client-Side Scripting with ASP.NET AJAX
Lab Review Questions	
Lab Challenge 6.1	Using Web Services in ASP.NET AJAX
Lab Challenge 6.2	Using Timer Control

BEFORE YOU BEGIN

Lab 6 assumes that the lab setup has been completed as specified in the setup document and that StudentXX-A, StudentXX-B, and StudentXX-C computers have Microsoft .NET Framework 3.5 and Microsoft Visual Studio 2008 installed.

> **NOTE** *In this lab, you will see the characters XX. When you see these characters, substitute the two-digit number assigned to your computer.*

SCENARIO

You are a developer in a company and are required to build applications that provide better performance and faster user interaction. You decide to use ASP.NET AJAX for this purpose. ASP.NET AJAX features enable partial page updates and enhance user experience.

After completing this lab, you will be able to:

- Implement AJAX and its related controls on the server side
- Use AJAX Control Toolkit
- Implement AJAX and its related controls on the client side

Estimated lab time: 110 minutes

Exercise 6.1	Implementing Server-Side Scripting with ASP.NET AJAX
Overview	You are developing an application for a financial institution. Certain pages of your application involve lots of mathematical calculations during postbacks. Therefore, to improve the performance and user interaction of these web pages, you want only specific contents of the pages to be updated during postbacks. You will achieve this by implementing AJAX in your application. In this lab exercise, you will use Microsoft Visual Studio 2008. This task is complete when you are able to successfully implement AJAX functionality in your application. To complete this lab exercise, all the student computers such as StudentXX-A and StudentXX-B must be started and must have network access.
Completion time	20 minutes

1. From the Start menu, select Microsoft Visual Studio 2008, and then select Microsoft Visual Studio 2008.

2. Select File → New Project → ASP.NET Web Application, and enter the name **ajaxImplement**.

3. Drag the controls listed in Table 6-1 from the toolbox to the Default.aspx page.

Table 6-1

Controls in Default.aspx Page of ajaxImplement Application

Control	***ID***	***Properties***
ScriptManager	`ScriptManager1`	None
UpdatePanel	`UpdatePanel1`	None
ContentTemplate	`ContentTemplate1`	None
TextBox	`TextBox1`	None
TextBox	`TextBox2`	None
Button	`Button1`	Text = "Calculate Sum"
Button	`Button2`	Text = "Reset"
Label	`lbl`	None

The following is the Default.aspx page:

```
<html xmlns="http://www.w3.org/1999/xhtml" >
<head runat="server">
  <title>Untitled Page</title>
</head>
<body>
  <form id="form1" runat="server">
   <div>
    <!--ScriptManager control to support partial page rendering -->
    <asp:ScriptManager ID="ScriptManager1" runat="server">
    </asp:ScriptManager>
    <!--UpdatePanel control to enable partial page rendering -->
    <asp:UpdatePanel ID="UpdatePanel1" runat="server">
      <ContentTemplate>
        Enter Number 1::<br />
        <asp:TextBox ID="TextBox1" runat="server"></asp:TextBox><br />
        Enter Number 2::<br />
        <asp:TextBox ID="TextBox2" runat="server"></asp:TextBox><br />
```

```
            <asp:Button ID="Button1" runat="server" Text="Calculate Sum"
onclick="Button1_Click"
                Width="100px" />
            <asp:Button     ID="Button2"     runat="server"     Text="Reset"
Width="50px"
                onclick="Button2_Click" /><br /><br />
            <asp:Label ID="lbl" runat="server"></asp:Label>
          </ContentTemplate>
        </asp:UpdatePanel>
    </div>
  </form>
</body>
</html>
```

4. Add a click event handler for the `Button1` button control as shown here:

```
protected void Button1_Click(object sender, EventArgs e)
{
    int x = 0;
    // Check whether the respective text box controls have values
    if (TextBox1.Text != "" && TextBox2.Text != "")
    {
        // Calculate the sum of the entered values
        x = int.Parse(TextBox1.Text) + int.Parse(TextBox2.Text);
        // Display the resultant sum in a label control
        lbl.Text = x.ToString();
    }
}
```

Question 1	*What does AJAX stand for?*

5. Add a click event handler for the `Button2` button control as shown here:

```
protected void Button2_Click(object sender, EventArgs e)
{
    //Clear all the controls
    TextBox1.Text = "";
    TextBox2.Text = "";
```

```
        lbl.Text = "";
    }
```

> **NOTE**
> *You must use `ScriptManager` control in ASP.NET AJAX applications, because it is responsible for managing the required AJAX features of ASP.NET on the respective pages. Some of the important AJAX features include partial page rendering and JavaScript proxy classes. The proxy classes allows you to call web service methods asynchronously from the client.*

6. Build the application by clicking on the Build menu and choosing Build Solution (ctrl+shift+B).

7. Run the application by pressing Ctrl+F5. You will see a web page with two TextBox controls and two Button controls. Note that this application will produce the sum of two numbers without a postback because you are using AJAX. Enter the required numbers in the TextBox controls. Click the Calculate Sum button. Notice that there is no postback in the page. The small progress bar that you see when you refresh a page or when you click a button in a web page appears at the bottom of the page in the status bar.

8. Now, comment out the script manager control on the page, as shown:

```
<! --  <asp:ScriptManager ID="ScriptManager1" runat="server">
</asp:ScriptManager> -->
```

   Build the application again and then rerun the application. Reenter the numbers in the text boxes and click the Calculate Sum button. Find the occurrence of the postback as the progress bar appears at the botton of the page.

Exercise 6.2 Understanding ASP.NET AJAX Control Toolkit

Overview	You are creating a web application for a movie theatre. You want to provide a TextBox control in your application that shows a pop-up calendar for easy entry of dates. You will use the CalendarExtender control from the AJAX Control Toolkit. In this lab exercise, you will use Microsoft Visual Studio 2008 and AJAX Control Toolkit. This task is complete when you are able to implement the CalendarExtender control on the required page of your application. To complete this lab exercise, all the student computers such as StudentXX-A and StudentXX-B must be started and must have network access.

Completion time	20 minutes

1. From the Start menu, select Microsoft Visual Studio 2008, and then select Microsoft Visual Studio 2008.

2. Select File → New Project → ASP.NET Web Application, and enter the name **AjaxToolKit**.

NOTE	*Before you start working with AJAX ToolKit, you need to download it from http://www.codeplex.com/AjaxControlToolkit/Release/ProjectReleases.aspx.*

3. Add a new tab on the Toolbox. To perform, select View → Toolbox. Right click theToolbox window. From the context menu, select the Add Tab option. Enter the name **Ajax-Toolkit**. This will be an empty tool set under Toolbox.

4. Add the AJAX controls under the newly added tab:

   a. Right click the tab.

   b. Select Add Items from the context menu.

   c. In the Choose Toolbox Items dialog box, browse to the location where you have downloaded the Ajax Control Toolkit and choose "AjaxControlToolkit.dll." Click Open and find the various control names listed under the tab ".NET Framework Components." Click OK.

5. Add the controls given in Table 6-2 to the Default.aspx page.

Table 6-2
Controls in Default.aspx Page of AjaxToolKit Application

Control	*ID*	*Properties*
ScriptManager	`ScriptManager1`	None
TextBox	`TextBox1`	None
CalendarExtender	`CalendarExtender1`	TargetControlID = "TextBox1"

Question 2	*What property of the `CalendarExtender` control will you use if you want the calendar to pop up on a button click?*

The following is the Default.aspx page:

```
<html xmlns="http://www.w3.org/1999/xhtml" >
    <head runat="server">
      <title>Untitled Page</title>
    </head>
   <body>
  <form id="form1" runat="server">
    <h1>Ajax Toolkit Demo</h1>
   <div>
      <!--ScriptManager control to manage the AJAX control placed on the
page -->
      <asp:ScriptManager ID="ScriptManager1" runat="server">
      </asp:ScriptManager>
      Click to Select Date::<br />
      <asp:TextBox ID="TextBox1" runat="server"></asp:TextBox><br />


      <!--CalendarExtender control from the AJAX Toolkit-->
      <cc1:CalendarExtender ID="CalendarExtender1" runat="server"
TargetControlID="TextBox1">
    </cc1:CalendarExtender>
    </div>
  </form>
 </body>
</html>
```

NOTE	*You must configure the `TargetControlID` property of the `CalendarExtender` control.This enables it to attach to the respective control. When the user selects a date, it is displayed in the linked control, which in this case is the `TextBox1` text box control.*

6. Build the application using F5. You will see a text box control on the screen. Click the text box and a calendar control pops up. Select a date from the calendar control. Find the selected date appearing in the text box control.

Exercise 6.3	Implementing Client-Side Scripting with ASP.NET AJAX
Overview	You are developing a web application by using ASP.NET AJAX. The application uses a web service that calculates the square of a number. The web service is called by a client-side script. In this lab exercise, you will use Microsoft Visual Studio 2008. This task is complete when you are able to implement client-side scripting using ASP.NET AJAX. To complete this lab exercise, all the student computers such as StudentXX-A and StudentXX-B must be started and must have network access.
Completion time	20 minutes

1. From the Start menu, select Microsoft Visual Studio 2008, and then select Microsoft Visual Studio 2008.

2. Select File → New Project → ASP.NET Web Application, and enter the name **AjaxClientSide**.

3. Add the controls given in Table 6-3 to the Default.aspx page.

Table 6-3
Controls in Default.aspx Page of AjaxClientSide Application

Control	*ID*	*Properties*
TextBox	`_symbolTextBox`	None
Button (HTML)	`_lookupButton`	Text = "Square"
Label	`_resultLabel`	None
ScriptManager	`ScriptManager1`	EnablePageMethods = "true"

4. Add the following script pertaining to the web service in the Default.aspx as shown:

```
<head runat="server">
  <script runat="server">
   // Expose the public method GetSquare as part of the XML Web service
using the WebMethod attribute
    [System.Web.Services.WebMethod]

     public static int GetSquare(int x)
     {
         // Calculate the square of the given number
         return x*x;
     }
   </script>
   <script type="text/javascript">
     function OnLookup()
     {
        /*Get the id of the text box control in which the user entered the
number*/
        var stb = document.getElementById("_symbolTextBox");
        /*Invoke the Web method GetSquare. Note that the second parameter
OnLookupComplete is the name of the JavaScript function that processes the
received result from the Web method*/
        AjaxClientSide.GetSquare(stb.value, OnLookupComplete);
     }
    /* OnLookupComplete method that processes the result returned from the
Web method*/
    function OnLookupComplete(result)
    {
      // Get the id of the label control
      var res = document.getElementById("_resultLabel");
      // Display the result returned from the GetSquare Web method in the
label control
      res.innerHTML = "<b>" + result + "</b>";
```

```
    }
  </script>
</head>
```

NOTE	*You must mention the following attributes preceding a web service:* `[System.Web.Services.WebMethod]` *This attribute is needed to declare the* `GetSquare()` *method as a web service method.*

5. Invoke the OnLookUp JavaScript function on the click of the input button as shown:

```
<input onclick="OnLookup();" id="_lookupButton"
         type="button" value="Lookup" />
```

6. Build the application using F5. You will see a text box control on the screen. Enter a number in the text box control. Click the Square button. This will asynchronously call the GetSquare function without a postback, and you will see the output of the function displayed in the label control.

LAB REVIEW QUESTIONS

Completion time	**15 minutes**

1. Explain the role of the `UpdatePanel` control in ASP.NET AJAX.
2. Explain the role of the `ScriptManagerProxy` control in ASP.NET AJAX.
3. Can multiple `ScriptManager` controls be added to a page?

LAB CHALLENGE 6.1: USING WEB SERVICES IN ASP.NET AJAX

Completion time	**20 minutes**

Consider that you are required to create a web service. The web service should display a welcome text along with the current date and time. How will you call this web service from the client-side script in an AJAX-enabled ASP.NET client application?

LAB CHALLENGE 6.2: USING TIMER CONTROL

Completion time	**15 minutes**

Consider that you want your ASP.NET AJAX Web application to perform a certain operation at a regular interval of time through the use of a timer control. How will you achieve this?

LAB 7
TROUBLESHOOTING WEB APPLICATIONS

This lab contains the following exercises and activities:

Exercise 7.1	Error Handling with Tracing Techniques
Exercise 7.2	Event Logging and Exception Handling
Exercise 7.3	Debugging with a Custom Error Page
Exercise 7.4	Working with Asynchronous Pages
Exercise 7.5	Debugging with Visual Studio 2008
Lab Review Questions	
Lab Challenge 7.1	Using Trace Listeners
Lab Challenge 7.2	Implementing Asynchronous Processing

BEFORE YOU BEGIN

Lab 7 assumes that the lab setup has been completed as specified in the setup document and that StudentXX-A, StudentXX-B, and StudentXX-C computers have Microsoft .NET Framework 3.5 and Microsoft Visual Studio 2008 installed.

> **NOTE**
>
> *In this lab, you will see the characters XX. When you see these characters, substitute the two-digit number assigned to your computer.*

SCENARIO

You are building an application to perform mathematical calculations such as calculating the result of square roots and divisions. This application requires you to handle errors with different techniques.

In this lab, you will learn to use various error handling techniques such as debugging using the Debugger, exception handling, event logging in log files, and customized error handling. In addition, you will learn to implement asynchronous page processing.

In the Lab Challenge, you will use trace listener objects to log error details. In addition, you will implement asynchronous processing when calling web services.

After completing this lab, you will be able to:

- Use tracing techniques to handle errors
- Use event logging and exception handling
- Debug using a custom error page
- Implement asynchronous page processing
- Use Visual Studio Debugger

Estimated lab time: 140 minutes

Exercise 7.1	Error Handling with Tracing Techniques
Overview	You are creating an application to calculate square roots. You want to add trace messages to your application at various stages. In this lab exercise, you will use Microsoft Visual Studio 2008. This task is complete when you are able to display the trace messages through your application. To complete this lab exercise, all the student computers such as StudentXX-A and StudentXX-B must be started and must have network access.
Completion time	15 minutes

1. From the Start menu, select Microsoft Visual Studio 2008, and then select Microsoft Visual Studio 2008.

2. Select File → New Project → ASP.NET Web Site, and enter the name **TraceLab**. Visual Studio creates a new Web site that contains the Default.aspx page.

3. Add the controls given in Table 7-1 to the Default.aspx page.

Table 7-1
Controls in Default.aspx Page of TraceLab Application

Control	*ID*	*Properties*
Label	`Label1`	Text = "Enter the number"
TextBox	`txtVal`	
Button	`btnSqr`	Text = "Square Root"
Button	`Button1`	Text = "Custom error"

4. Add a reference to the Diagnostics namespace in the code behind page, default.aspx.cs as shown:

```
using System.Diagnostics;
```

5. In the `Page_Load` method, add the following code:

```
// Write the value supplied in the text box in red to trace log
Trace.Warn("TraceLab", txtVal.Text.ToString());
// Write the Page.IsPostBack value in red to trace log
Trace.Warn("TraceLab", "Postback=" + Page.IsPostBack);
```

Question 1	*What is the difference between `Trace.Warn` and `Trace.Write` methods?*

6. In the `btnSqr_Click` method, which is the click event handler of the `btnSqr` button control, add the following code:

```
// Calculate the square root of the given number using Math.Sqrt method
txtVal.Text = Math.Sqrt(Convert.ToDouble (txtVal.Text)).ToString();
```

```
// Write the result returned in red to trace log
Trace.Warn("TraceLab", txtVal.Text.ToString());
// Write the value of the Page.IsPostbBack value in red to trace log
Trace.Warn("TraceLab", "Postback=" + Page.IsPostBack);
```

7. You must set the `Trace` attribute of the `@Page` directive to `true` in the default.aspx page to enable tracing at page level.

> **NOTE**
>
> *You can also enable tracing at the application level by modifying the trace tag in the web.config file as in Step 10.*

8. Build the application by clicking on the Build menu and choosing Build Solution (ctrl+shift+B).

9. Run the application and view the trace messages appearing on the default.aspx page. Figure 7-1 shows the default.aspx page with the trace information displayed at the bottom of the page.

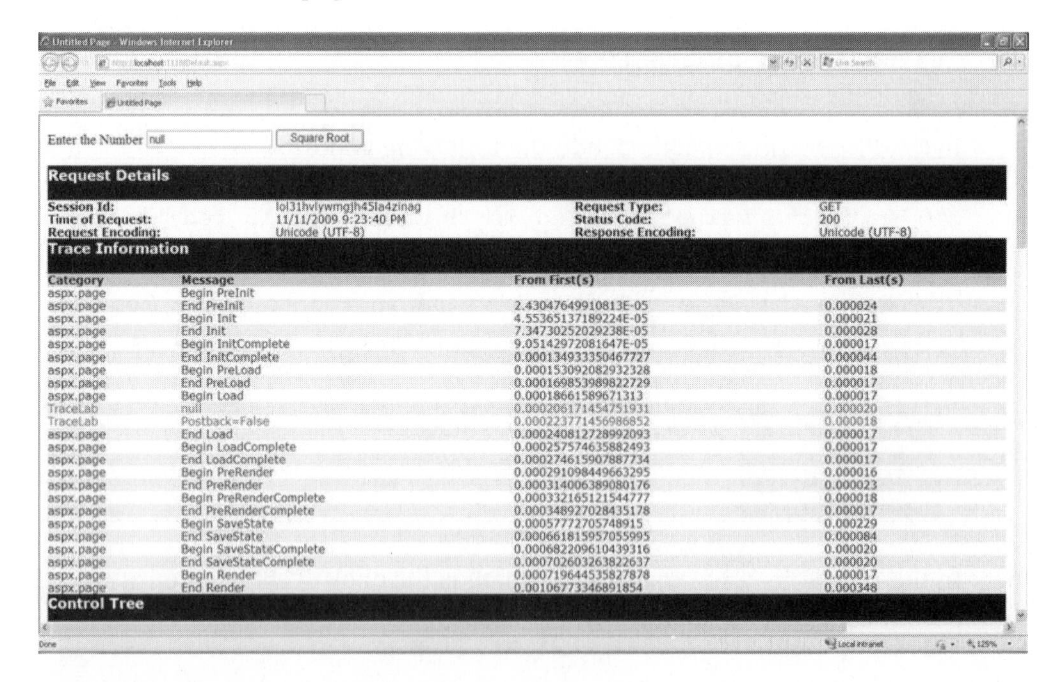

Figure 7-1
Default.aspx Page with the Trace Information

10. To enable tracing at the application level, modify the trace tag in the web.config file by setting the `pageOutput` to true as shown:

```
<trace enabled="true" requestLimit="10" pageOutput="true"
localOnly="true" />
```

11. Build the application by clicking on the Build menu and choosing Build Solution (ctrl+shift+B).

12. Run the application and view the trace messages appearing on the page.

Exercise 7.2	Event Logging and Exception Handling
Overview	You are creating a web application to perform division. This application must use exceptions to catch the division by zero error and log this event into an error log. In this lab exercise, you will use Microsoft Visual Studio 2008 to handle exceptions in a web application. This task is complete when you are able to handle the division by zero error and log the event into a log file successfully. To complete this lab exercise, all the student computers such as StudentXX-A and StudentXX-B must be started and must have network access.
Completion time	15 minutes

1. From the Start menu, select Microsoft Visual Studio 2008, and then select Microsoft Visual Studio 2008.

2. Select File → New Project → ASP.NET Web Site, and enter the name **ErrorLog**. Visual Studio creates a new Web site that contains the Default.aspx page.

3. Add the controls given in Table 7-2 to the Default.aspx page, as shown in Figure 7-2.

Table 7-2
Controls in Default.aspx Page of ErrorLog Application

Control	***ID***	***Properties***
Label	`Label1`	Text = “Enter Value1”
Label	`Label2`	Text = “Enter Value2”
Label	`Label3`	Text = “Result”

TextBox	`TextBox1`	
TextBox	`TextBox2`	
Button	`btnDivision`	Text = "Division"

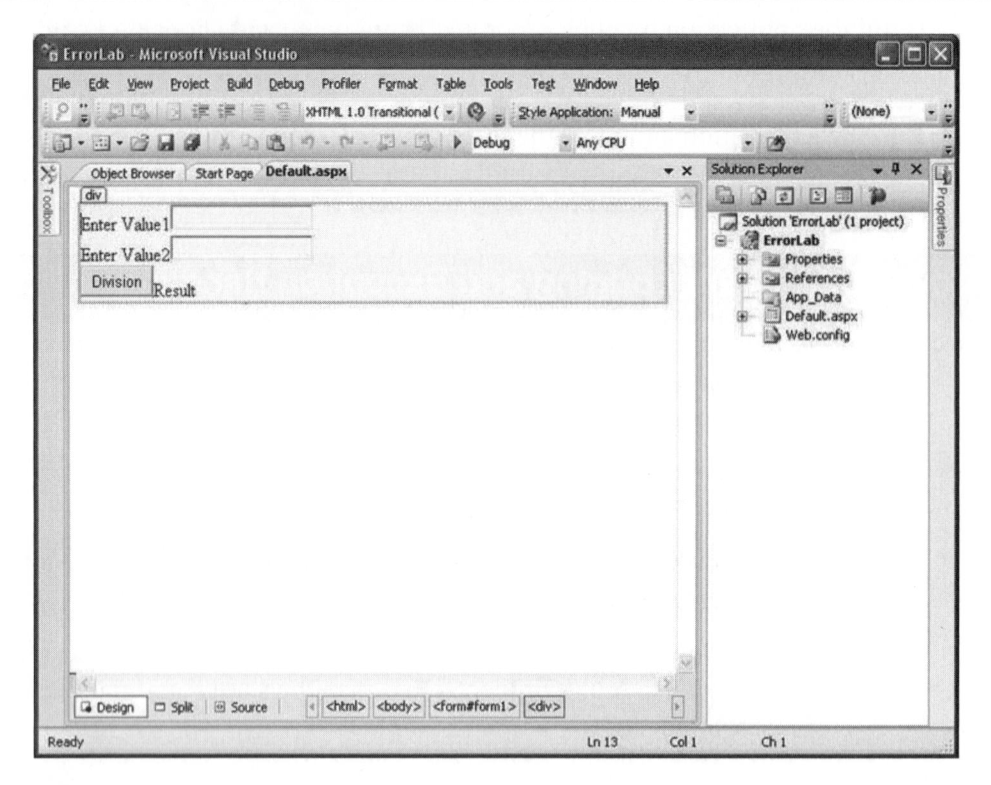

Figure 7-2
Design View of Default.aspx Page

4. Add reference to the Diagnostics namespace in the code behind page, default.aspx.cs as shown below:

```
using System.Diagnostics;
```

5. Declare two global string variables to save the error log message and error log name:

```
string sSource,sLog;
```

NOTE	*The variables declared in Step 4 are used in various methods in the code behind file, therefore they are declared as global variables.*

6. In the `Page_Load` method, use two static methods of the `EventLog` class to check whether your log source exists. If the log name that you specify does not exist, then a log is created automatically when you write your first entry to the log. By default, if you do not supply a log name to the `CreateEventSource` method, the log file is named "EventLogDemo":

```
protected void Page_Load(object sender, EventArgs e)
{
    sSource = "Error Log App";
    sLog = "EventLogDemo";
    // Check if the source already exists using the
EventLog.SourceExists method
    if (!EventLog.SourceExists(sSource))
        // If source is not registered already, create the source
        EventLog.CreateEventSource(sSource, sLog);
}
```

NOTE	*The `EventLog.SourceExists` method used in the given code accesses the registry to determine whether an event source is registered on the local computer. Therefore, you must have the appropriate registry permissions on the local computer; otherwise, a SecurityException will be thrown.* *Additionally, if you are using Windows Vista, Windows XP Professional, or Windows Server 2003, you must have administrative privileges to search for an event source. Otherwise, the `SourceExists` method will throw a SecurityException.*

Question 2	*Can you implement event logging through the web.config file?*

7. In the `btnDivision_Click` method, add the division functionality with the try/catch block. Add code to trap any error that occurs and write to the event Log as follows:

```
protected void btnDivision_Click(object sender, EventArgs e)
{
    try
    {
        // Convert the value entered in the textbox to integer
datatype before performing division
        int x = Convert.ToInt32(TextBox1.Text);
        int y = Convert.ToInt32(TextBox2.Text);
```

```
                // Divide the numbers
                int res = (x / y);
                // Display the result in the label control
                Label3.Text = res.ToString();
            }
            catch (Exception ex)
            {
                // Display the message that describes the exception in a label
control
                Label3.Text = ex.Message.ToString();
                // Write the string representation of the frame in the stack
trace to the event log
                EventLog.WriteEntry(sSource, ex.StackTrace.ToString());
                // Write the message that describes the exception as warning
in the event log
                EventLog.WriteEntry(sSource, ex.Message.ToString(),
EventLogEntryType.Warning, 234);
            }
            finally
            {
                // Release the resources
                sSource = null;
                sLog = null;
            }
        }
```

8. Build the application by clicking on the Build menu and choosing Build Solution (ctrl+shift+B).

9. Enter values in the two text boxes and check the output.

10. Enter 0 for the second text box and check the output.

11. Open the System Event Viewer by using Start → Run → Eventvwr.msc. Notice that there is a custom event log `EventLogDemo` created as shown in Figure 7-3. Examine the error.

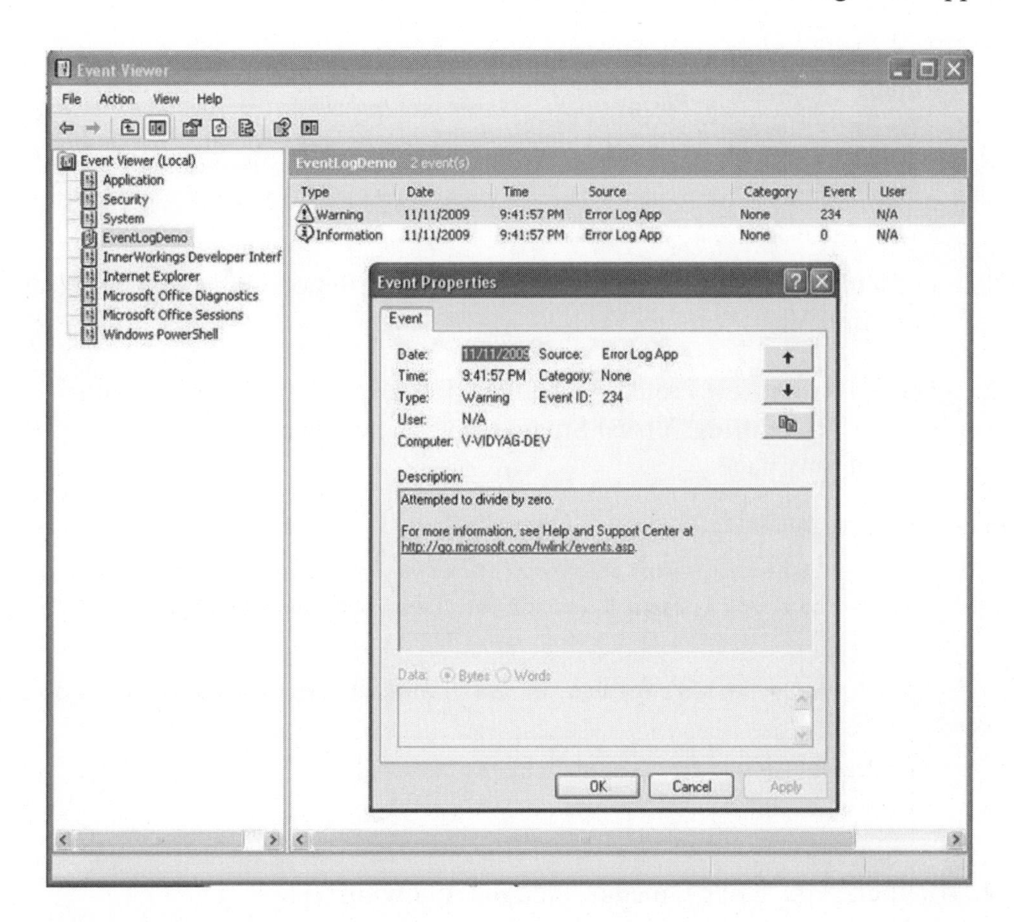

Figure 7-3
Event Viewer Displaying the Custom Event Log EventLogDemo

Exercise 7.3	**Debugging with a Custom Error Page**
Overview	You are creating a web application in which you want to handle errors at both page and application levels. You also want to redirect users to a page containing a friendly error message in case users encounter an error in the application. In this lab exercise, you will use Microsoft Visual Studio 2008. This task is complete when you are able to create a web application and redirect users to a custom error page when they encounter errors. To complete this lab exercise, all the student computers such as StudentXX-A and StudentXX-B must be started and must have network access.
Completion time	30 minutes

> **NOTE**
> *In this exercise, you will first handle errors in your application at page level using the `Page_Error` method.*

1. From the Start menu, select Microsoft Visual Studio 2008, and then select Microsoft Visual Studio 2008.

2. Select File → New Project → ASP.NET Web Site, and enter the name **EventErrHandling**. Visual Studio creates a new Web site that contains the Default.aspx page.

3. In the `Page_Load` method, add the following code:

```
    protected void Page_Load(object sender, EventArgs e)
    {
      // Throw an exception to be handled at the page and application
level
      throw (new ArgumentNullException());
    }
```

4. In the `Page_Error` method, add the following code:

```
  // Handle the thrown exception at the page level using the Page_Error
method
    private void Page_Error(object sender, EventArgs e)
    {
        // Write the title of the page in red to the trace log
        Trace.Warn("Page Information", Page.Header.Title.ToString());
        // Write the status code of the output returned to the client in
red to the trace log

        Trace.Warn("Status Code", Response.StatusCode.ToString());
        // Write the description of the error that occurred in red to the
trace log
        Trace.Warn("ERROR: ", Server.GetLastError().Message);
    }
```

5. Build the application by clicking on the Build menu and choosing Build Solution (ctrl+shift+B).

6. Right click the page, and then click View in Browser to run the page. Notice that the `ArgumentNullException` is thrown and reported according to the code specifications.

> **NOTE**
> *In the following steps, you will handle the thrown exception at the application level, using the `Application_Error` event handler.*

7. In the Solution Explorer, right click on the project, select Add New Item, and choose the Global Application Class template from the dialog box. This adds a new Global.asax file to the project.

8. Add the following code to the `Application_Error` event handler in the `Global.asax.cs` file:

```
    // Handle the thrown exception at the application level using the
Application_Error event handler
    protected void Application_Error(object sender, EventArgs e)
    {
        // Get the base exception that is the root cause of one or more
exceptions
        Exception objErr = Server.GetLastError().GetBaseException();
        // Retrieve the required information from the objErr Exception
object in a string
        string err = "Error Caught in Application_Error event\n" +
                "Error in: " + Request.Url.ToString() +
                "\nError Message:" + objErr.Message.ToString() +
                "\nStack Trace:" + objErr.StackTrace.ToString();
        // Log the exception in the event log
        System.Diagnostics.EventLog.WriteEntry("Event_Error_Handling",
err, System.Diagnostics.EventLogEntryType.Error);
        // Clear the error to prevent it from bubbling to the higher level
        Server.ClearError();
    }
```

> **NOTE**
> *You may notice that the code issues a call to Server.ClearError. This prevents the error from continuing to the application configuration file.*

9. Build the application by clicking on the Build menu and choosing Build Solution (ctrl+shift+B).

10. Right click the page, and then click View in Browser. In this case, the page will be blank. However, notice that a new entry has been added in the event log. This code example makes an entry in the Application log, which is accessible from the Event Viewer. You can access Event Viewer either from Administrative Tools or by executing Eventvwr.msc from the Run menu. In the Event Viewer under the Application node, you can see an entry of your application at the time you ran it with an error under Source. Double click on the entry to view further details. To redirect the user to a user-friendly error page after logging the error in the application log, perform the steps listed.

Question 3	*After logging the error, you might want to redirect the user to another more user-friendly error page, or perform some additional actions if needed. How can we achieve such handling through web.config?*

11. In the Solution Explorer, right click on the Project, select Add New Item, and choose Web Form from the dialog box. Name the form **CustomErr.aspx**.

12. Add a button control to this page, and set its id to `btnCustomErr`. Add the following code to the click handler of this control:

```
protected void btnCustomErr_Click(object sender, EventArgs e)
{
    Response.Redirect("abc.aspx");
}
```

13. Open the web.config file and modify the customErrors element as shown:

```
<customErrors mode="On" defaultRedirect="GenericErrorPage.htm">
    <error statusCode="403" redirect="NoAccess.htm" />
    <error statusCode="404" redirect="error.htm" />
</customErrors>
```

14. Add an html file and name it **error.htm**. Add some text to this html page.

15. Comment on the `Server.ClearError` method called in the Application_Error event handler in the global.asax.cs file. This allows the error to bubble up to the application configuration file and can be handled based on the setting in the customErrors section of this file.

16. Build the application by clicking on the Build menu and choosing Build Solution (ctrl+shift+B).

17. Select the CustomErr.aspx page, right click, and choose View in Browser. You can see that a page with a button is loaded. Click on the button to log the error entered in Step 13 to the Event Viewer.

18. Under the Application node, you can see an entry of your application at the time you ran it with an error under Source. Double click on the entry to view further details. Notice that the error makes more sense and is easy to read. Additionally, notice that you have been redirected to the error.htm page.

Exercise 7.4	**Working with Asynchronous Pages**
Overview	You are creating an application to allow asynchronous page requests. In this lab exercise, you will use Microsoft Visual Studio 2008 to implement asynchronous page processing into a web application. This task is complete when you successfully implement asynchronous page processing into your web application. To complete this lab exercise, all the student computers such as StudentXX-A and StudentXX-B must be started and must have network access.
Completion time	15 minutes

1. From the Start menu, select Microsoft Visual Studio 2008, and then select Microsoft Visual Studio 2008.

2. Select File → New Project → ASP.NET Web Site, and enter the name **AsyncLab**. Visual Studio creates a new Web site that contains the Default.aspx page in it.

3. Set the `Async` attribute of the `@Page` directive to `true`, as shown:

```
    <%@Page Language="C#" AutoEventWireup="true"
CodeBehind="Default.aspx.cs" Async="true" %>
```

4. Add the controls given in Table 7-3 to the Default.aspx page.

Table 7-3
Controls in Default.aspx Page of AsyncLab Application

Control	*ID*	*Properties*
Label	`Label1`	Text = ""
Label	`Label2`	Text = ""
Label	`Label3`	Text = ""
TextBox	`result`	Multiline = true

5. Add a reference to the `System.Net` namespace in the code behind page, default.aspx.cs, as shown:

```
using System.Net;
```

6. Declare a global variable of type WebRequest as shown:

```
WebRequest myRequest;
```

Question 4	*What will you do to perform several asynchronous I/O operations in an asynchronous page that does not involve remote web service/database calls?*

7. In the `Page_Load` method, add the following code:

```
protected void Page_Load(object sender, EventArgs e)
{
        // Get the currently running thread and display its hash code in a
label control
        Label1.Text = "Page_Load: thread #" +
System.Threading.Thread.CurrentThread.GetHashCode();
        // Register the handler that will handle the asynchronous
operation
        BeginEventHandler beventhandle = new
BeginEventHandler(this.BeginGetAsyncData);
        //Register the handler that will handle the callback of the
asynchronous operation
        EndEventHandler eeventhandle = new
EndEventHandler(this.EndGetAsyncData);
```

```
        // Add the registered handlers to the asynchronous page by calling
the AddOnPreRenderCompleteAsync method
        AddOnPreRenderCompleteAsync(beventhandle, eeventhandle);

        // Initialize the WebRequest.
        string address = @"http://www.wikipedia.org";
        // Initialize the myRequest instance of WebRequest to the
specified URL
        myRequest = System.Net.WebRequest.Create(address);
    }
```

> **NOTE**
>
> *You are actually calling the* `AddOnPreRenderCompleteAsync` *method to register the begin and end methods. The* `BeginAsyncOperation` *can launch an asynchronous operation such as a database call, or web service call, and return immediately. When this operation is completed, another thread continues from the* `EndAsyncOperation` *method to complete the request and send the response back to the client.*
>
> *You can decide if the task will run in parallel or sequentially by the fifth parameter of the* `PageAsyncTask` *constructor.*

8. Define the `BeginGetAsyncData` method with return type `IAsyncResult` to begin the async processing as follows:

```
    IAsyncResult BeginGetAsyncData(Object src, EventArgs args,
AsyncCallback cb, Object state)
    {
        // Display the hash code of the current thread in a label control
        Label2.Text = "BeginGetAsyncData: thread #" +
System.Threading.Thread.CurrentThread.GetHashCode();
        // Asynchronously start the request for the target resource
        return myRequest.BeginGetResponse(cb, state);
    }
```

9. Define the `EndGetAsyncData` method of page response into the control as follows:

```
    void EndGetAsyncData(IAsyncResult ar)
    {
       // Display the hash code of the current thread in a label control
```

```
          Label3.Text = "EndGetAsyncData: thread #" +
System.Threading.Thread.CurrentThread.GetHashCode();
          // Retrieve the target resource by calling the EndGetResponse
method
          System.Net.WebResponse myResponse = myRequest.EndGetResponse(ar);
          // Display the data stream from the target resource in the textbox
control by calling the GetResponseStream
          result.Text = new
System.IO.StreamReader(myResponse.GetResponseStream()).ReadToEnd();
          myResponse.Close();
      }
```

10. Build the application by clicking on the Build menu and choosing Build Solution (ctrl+shift+B).

NOTE	*The HttpRequest can take a long time to return.*

Exercise 7.5	**Debugging with Visual Studio 2008**
Overview	You want to use Visual Studio Debugger to debug your web application. In this lab exercise, you will use Microsoft Visual Studio 2008 to debug your web application. This task is complete when you are able to use the debugger to debug your application. To complete this lab exercise, all the student computers such as StudentXX-A and StudentXX-B must be started and must have network access.
Completion time	15 minutes

1. From the Start menu, select Microsoft Visual Studio 2008, and then select Microsoft Visual Studio 2008.

2. Select File → Open Project and enter the name **ErrorLog project**.

3. Go to the `btnDivision_Click(object sender, EventArgs e)` method and set a breakpoint there by clicking in the left-hand margin or by pressing F9.

4. Run the web application in debug mode by clicking Start on the Debug menu.

5. Enter values into both the text boxes and click on the button.

6. VS.NET enters the debugger at the breakpoint; notice the information as shown in Figure 7-4:

    - The CallStack window displays the name of the function.

    - The Autos window displays the name and value of variables in the current statement.

    - The Locals window displays the name and value of all the local variables in the current scope.

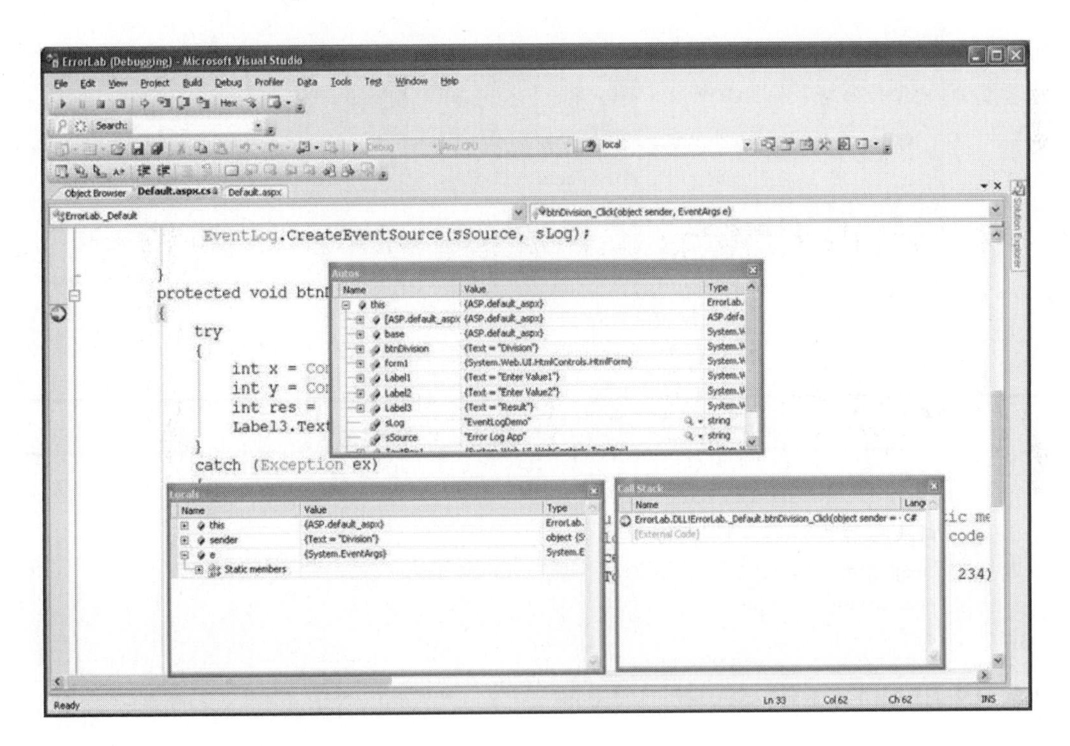

Figure 7-4
Breakpoint with Debug Windows

7. Pause the mouse on the variable x and view its current value.

8. Click Step Over (F10) again and again. Notice that the CallStack and Local window variables change. You can use Step Into (F11) to any method definition as shown in Figure 7-5, if required. Once you have stepped into all of the statements, the browser window becomes active again. Finally, you will see the normal ouput.

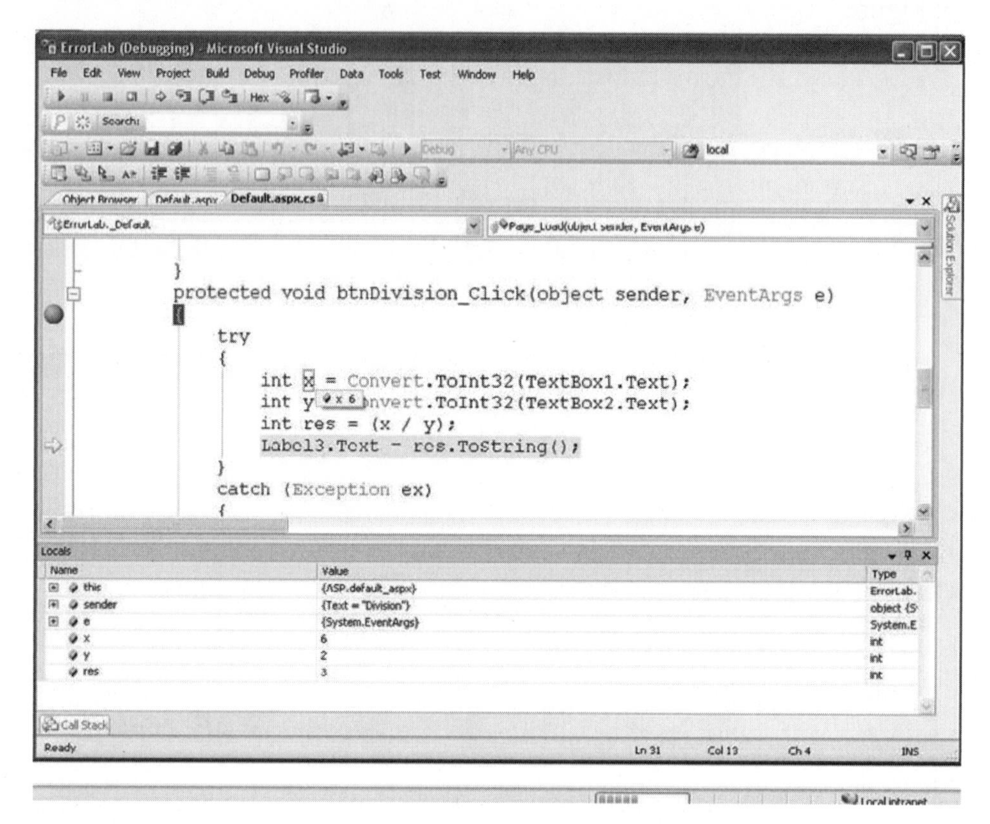

Figure 7-5
Step Into with Locals Window

LAB REVIEW QUESTIONS

Completion time	**15 minutes**

1. What is the difference between the `Trace` object and the `Debug` object?

2. Consider the code snippet given here and explain why the string values are set to null in the finally block:

```
    protected void btnDivision_Click(object sender, EventArgs e)
    {
        try
        {
            int x = Convert.ToInt32(TextBox1.Text);
            int y = Convert.ToInt32(TextBox2.Text);
            int res = (x / y);
            Label3.Text = res.ToString();
        }
        catch (Exception ex)
        {
            Label3.Text = ex.Message.ToString();
            EventLog.WriteEntry(sSource, ex.StackTrace.ToString());
            EventLog.WriteEntry(sSource, ex.Message.ToString(),
EventLogEntryType.Warning, 234);
        }
        finally
        {
            sSource = null;
            sLog = null;
        }
    }
```

3. What levels of errors can the Global.asax file handle?

LAB CHALLENGE 7.1: USING TRACE LISTENERS

Completion time	**15 minutes**

Consider that you want to write error details into a `TraceListener` object rather than an error log. Write code to achieve this.

LAB CHALLENGE 7.2: IMPLEMENTING ASYNCHRONOUS PROCESSING

Completion time	**20 minutes**

Create a web service and implement asynchronous processing when calling a web service.

LAB 8
ACCESSING AND DISPLAYING DATA

This lab contains the following exercises and activities:

Exercise 8.1	General Data Saving and Data Retrieval with Bound Controls
Exercise 8.2	Pagination in Data-Bound Controls
Lab Review Questions	
Lab Challenge 8.1	Binding a Data-Bound Control to a Stored Procedure
Lab Challenge 8.2	Implementing Pagination Using a Stored Procedure

BEFORE YOU BEGIN

Lab 8 assumes that the lab setup has been completed as specified in the setup document and that StudentXX-A, StudentXX-B, and StudentXX-C computers have Microsoft .NET Framework 3.5 and Microsoft Visual Studio 2008 installed.

> **NOTE** *In this lab, you will see the characters XX. When you see these characters, substitute the two-digit number assigned to your computer.*

> **NOTE**
> *For this lab, open the SQL server and copy the pubs database script or .mdf/.ldf files. Run the query or attach the database into SQL Server Management Studio.This step is detailed in the Lab Setup document.*

SCENARIO

You are working as a senior web developer in an organization. You should provide database functionality to your organization's Web site. Additionally, you should implement record pagination in the Web site.

In this lab, you will learn to retrieve and store data in a database through data-bound controls. Additionally, you will also learn to implement pagination through data-bound controls.

After completing this lab, you will be able to:

- Perform database interactions in an ASP.NET application
- Implement pagination in data-bound controls

Estimated lab time: 115 minutes

Exercise 8.1	General Data Saving and Data Retrieval with Bound Controls
Overview	You are creating a web application that stores personal details of users in a SQL Server database. The application also retrieves and displays the stored information according to the user's selection. In this lab exercise, you will use Microsoft Visual Studio 2008 and SQL Server pubs database. This task is complete when you are able to successfully store and retrieve data from the pubs database using ADO.NET classes. To complete this lab exercise, all the student computers such as StudentXX-A and StudentXX-B must be started and must have network access.
Completion time	45 minutes

NOTE

This lab assumes that the SQL Server is located on the local machine. The connection string setting in Step 5 uses the value "(local)" for the attribute Data Source to indicate this. In addition, this lab assumes that you have a pubs database available in your SQL Server Management Studio. In SQL Server Management Studio click on New Query and then create a table named tblPersonalDetail in the pubs database using the following SQL statement:

```
Use pubs
go
create table tblPersonalDetail
(
name varchar(20),
age int,
address varchar(30)
)
go
```

1. From the Start menu, select Microsoft Visual Studio 2008, and then select Microsoft Visual Studio 2008.

2. Select File → New Project → ASP.NET Web Site, and enter the name **DataGetSet**. Visual Studio creates a new Web site that contains the Default.aspx page.

3. Add the controls given in Table 8-1 to the Default.aspx page.

Table 8-1
Controls in Default.aspx Page of DataGetSet Application

Control	*ID*	*Properties*
Panel	`Panel1`	
Panel	`Panel2`	
Label	`Label1`	Text = "Enter the name"
Label	`Label2`	Text = "Enter the age"
Label	`Label3`	Text = "Enter the address"
Label	`record`	Text = ""

Label	select	Text = "Select Name"
Label	Name	Text = "Name"
Label	Age	Text = "Age"
Label	Address	Text = "Address"
TextBox	txtName	
TextBox	txtAge	
TextBox	txtAddress	
TextBox	getName	
TextBox	getAge	
TextBox	getAddress	
Button	btnSave	Text = "Save"
Button	btnReset	Text = "Reset"
Button	btnRetrieve	Text = "Retrieve"
DropDownList	ddlName	

NOTE	*Place the controls with the following ID in Panel1:* *1. Label1* *2. Label2* *3. Label3* *4. record* *5. txtName* *6. txtAge* *7. txtAddress* *8. btnSave* *9. btnReset* *Place the controls with the following ID in Panel2:* *1. select* *2. ddlName* *3. Name* *4. Age* *5. Address* *6. getName* *7. getAge* *8. getAddress* *9. btnRetrieve*

4. Add the following statement in the Default.aspx.cs file:

```
using System.Data;
```

5. Define a method named **GetConnectionString** to establish connection to the pubs database:

```
private string GetConnectionString()
{
        return "Data Source=(local);Initial Catalog=pubs;"
        + "Integrated Security=SSPI;";
}
```

6. Define a method named **ClearData** to reset the value of the server controls:

```
private void ClearData()
 {
    txtName.Text = "";
    txtAge.Text = "";
    txtAddress.Text = "";
}
```

7. Call the ClearData method in the `btnReset_Click` event:

```
protected void btnReset_Click(object sender, EventArgs e)
{
  ClearData();
}
```

8. Define a method called PopulateList. The method retrieves all the values of the name field from the tblPersonalDetail table and lists them in the `ddlName` DropDownList control:

```
private void PopulateList()
{
  // Retrieve connection string
  string connectionString = GetConnectionString();
  using(SqlConnection connection = new SqlConnection(connectionString))
  {
    // Create a SQL query to retrieve all the names from the table
tblPersonalDetail.
    string str = "Select name from tblPersonalDetail";
    // Define SqlCommand object and pass the query and connection
object
    SqlCommand cmd = new SqlCommand(str, connection);
    // Open the connection
    connection.Open();
    // Define a SqlDataReader object that is read only,forward only
cursor to iterate through the records and execute the specified command
    SqlDataReader sdr = cmd.ExecuteReader();
    // Add all the retrieved names into drop-down control DataReader's
Read() method execution

    while (sdr.Read())
    {
      for (int i = 0; i < sdr.FieldCount; i++)
      {
        ddlName.Items.Add(sdr.GetValue(i).ToString());
      }
    }
    sdr.Close();
  }
}
```

Question 1	*Is it mandatory to close `SqlDataReader` object after data retrieval?*

9. Add a click event handler for the `btnSave` button as shown:

```
protected void btnSave_Click(object sender, EventArgs e)
{
    string connectionString = GetConnectionString();
    using (SqlConnection connection = new
SqlConnection(connectionString))
    {
        //Create a query to insert the record into the table
tblPersonalDetail.
        string qry = "insert into
tblPersonalDetail(name,age,address)"+
"values('"+txtName.Text+"','"+txtAge.Text+"','"+txtAddress.Text+"')";
        SqlCommand cmd = new SqlCommand(qry,connection);
        // Open the connection to the database.
        connection.Open();
        // Call the ExecuteNonQuery method to save the record in the
table
        int rowsAffected = cmd.ExecuteNonQuery();
        // Call the PopulateList method to refresh the drop-down list
        PopulateList();
        record.Text = string.Format("<b>Record successfully save<b>");
        // Clear the controls.
        ClearData();
    }
}
```

Question 2	*What is the significance of the `using` statement in the given code?*

10. Add a click event handler for the `btnRetrieve` button as shown here. The handler retrieves values from the database in the respective TextBox controls:

```
protected void btnRetrieve_Click(object sender, EventArgs e)
```

```
{
  // Retrieve the selected name from the drop down
  string name = ddlName.SelectedItem.Text;
  string connectionString = GetConnectionString();
  using (SqlConnection connection = new
SqlConnection(connectionString))
  {
    // Select the respective record for the selected name
    string str = "Select name,age,address from tblPersonalDetail where
name='" + name + "'";
    SqlCommand cmd = new SqlCommand(str, connection);
    connection.Open();
    SqlDataReader sdr = cmd.ExecuteReader();
    // Display the field values in the respective TextBox controls
    while (sdr.Read())
    {
      getName.Text = sdr.GetValue(0).ToString();
      getAge.Text = sdr.GetValue(1).ToString();
      getAdd.Text = sdr.GetValue(2).ToString();
    }
    sdr.Close();
  }
}
```

11. Call the PopulateList method in the `Page_Load` method of the Default.aspx page as shown:

```
protected void Page_Load(object sender, EventArgs e)
{
   if(!IsPostBack)
   {
       PopulateList();
       record.Text = "";
   }
}
```

12. Debug the application by pressing F5. Perform the following actions:

a. Enter values in the txtName, txtAge, and txtAddress text box controls. Click the Save button. Note that the DropDownList control is populated with the entered values.

b. Select a name listed in the DropDownList control. Click the Retrieve button. Find the corresponding record displayed in the respective text box controls.

Exercise 8.2	**Pagination in Data-Bound Controls**
Overview	You are creating a web application that performs database interaction. You want to display the retrieved information from the database into a GridView control. To make the displayed data more presentable, you use the pagination feature. In this lab exercise, you will use Microsoft Visual Studio 2008 and the SQL Server pubs database. This task is complete when you are able to implement pagination in the specified data-bound control. To complete this lab exercise, all the student computers such as StudentXX-A and StudentXX-B must be started and must have network access.
Completion time	20 minutes

1. From the Start menu, select Microsoft Visual Studio 2008, and then select Microsoft Visual Studio 2008.

2. Select File → New Project → ASP.NET Web Site, and enter the name **Pagination**. Visual Studio creates a new Web site that contains the Default.aspx page.

3. Add the controls given in Table 8-2 to the Default.aspx page.

Table 8-2
Controls in Default.aspx Page of Pagination Application

Control	***ID***	***Properties***
GridView	`GridView1`	None

4. Add the following statements in the Default.aspx.cs file:

```
using System.Data;
using System.Data.SqlClient;
```

5. Configure the desired format for the GridView control using AutoFormat. You can find the AutoFormat option on the Smart Tag when you right click on the GridView control as shown in Figure 8-1.

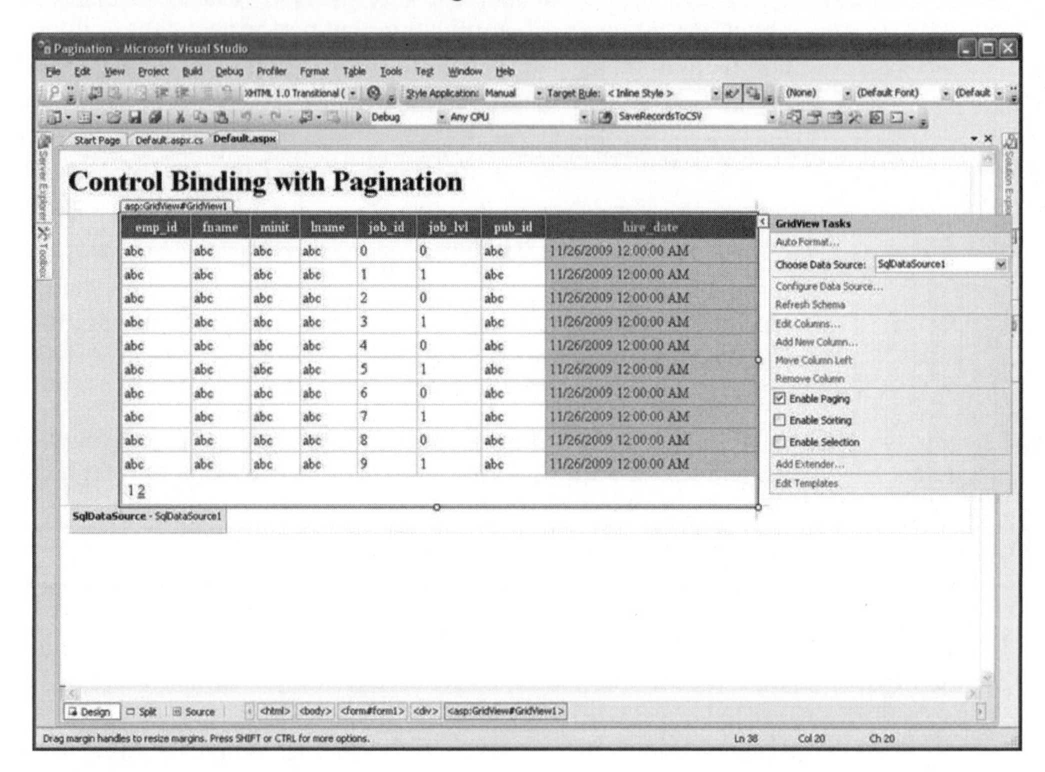

Figure 8-1
Auto Format Option in GridView Smart Tag

6. Select Smart Tag again and in the "Choose Data Source" drop-down option, choose <New data source…> as in Figure 8-2.

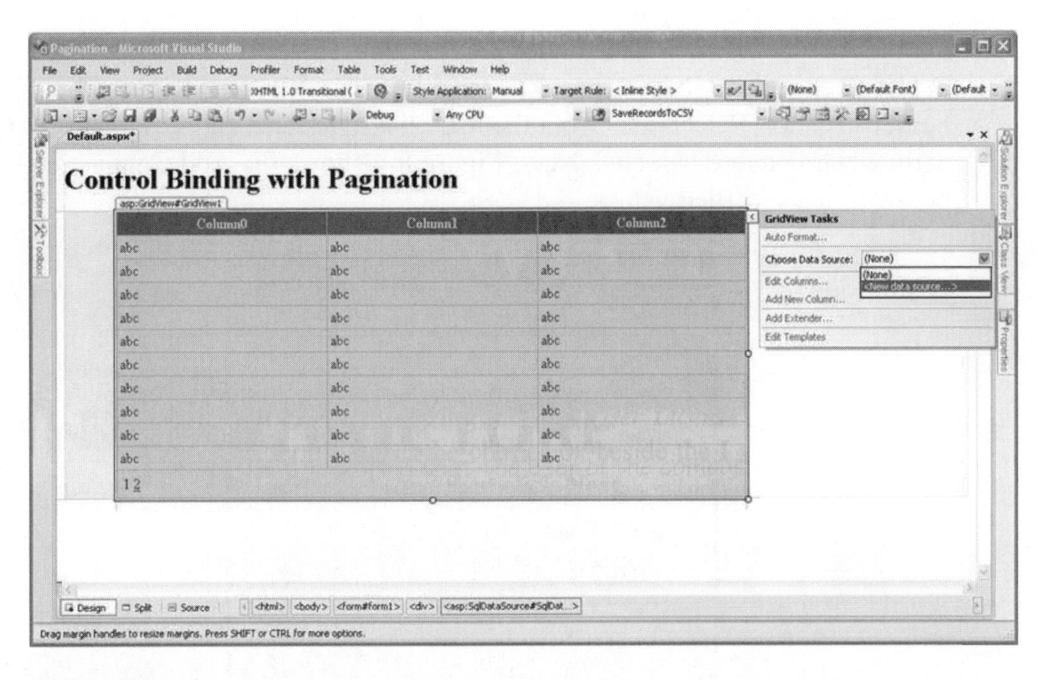

Figure 8-2
New Data Source Option in GridView Smart Tag

7. Select the Database option in the Data Source Configuration Wizard dialog box and enter the ID for the data source as SqlDataSource1 as shown in Figure 8-3. Click OK.

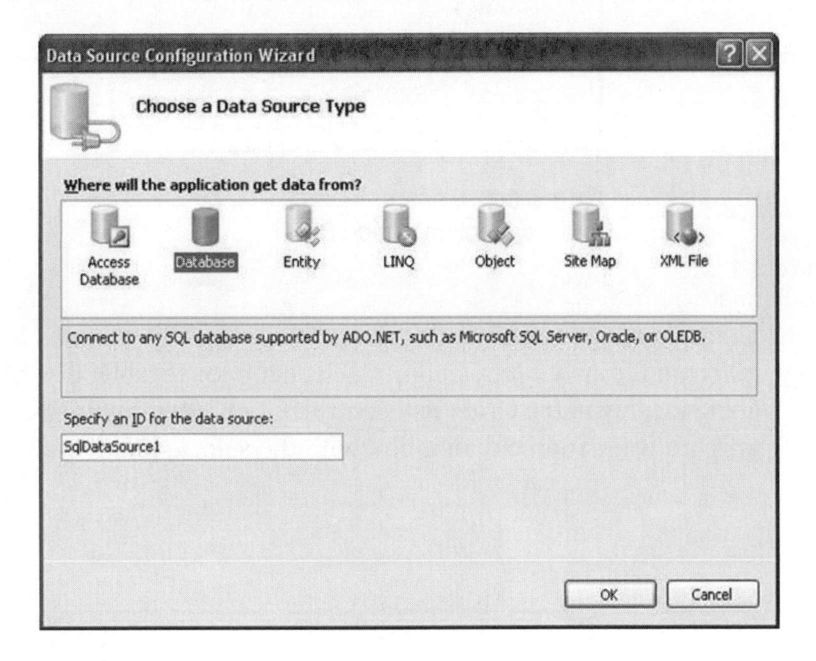

Figure 8-3
Data Source Configuration Wizard Dialog Box

8. Select New Connection. Select Microsoft SQL Server as Data Source and .NET Framework Data Provider for SQL Server as Data Provider.

On the Add Connection page under Server name enter . (dot). This populates the Select or enter a database name list with all the databases available in the SQL Server instance. Select pubs from the list, click OK. This takes you back to the main wizard page. Then click Next. Figure 8-4 shows the Add Connection dialog box with the specified values.

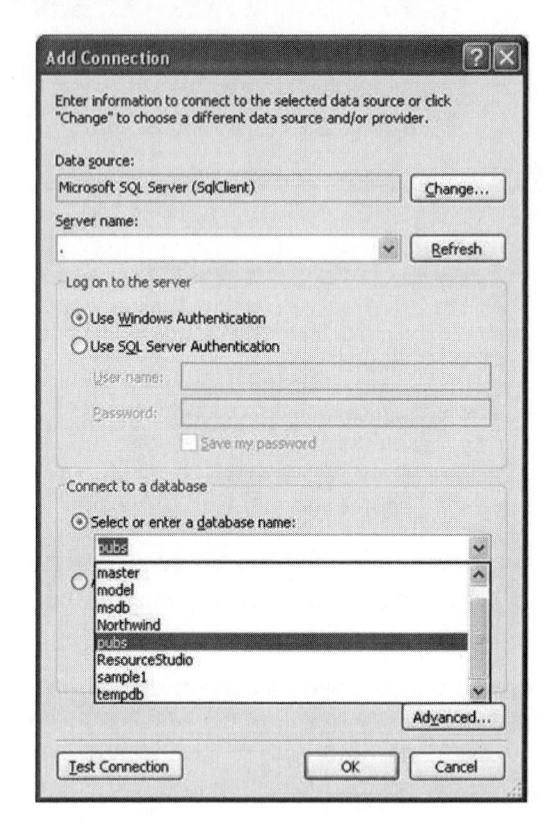

Figure 8-4
Add Connection Dialog Box

9. In the Configure Data Source dialog box, choose Specify columns from a table or view option and from the provided list, select employee table. Check the fields that you want to display in the GridView control. Click Next. Figure 8-5 shows the Configure Data Source dialog box with the selected table fields.

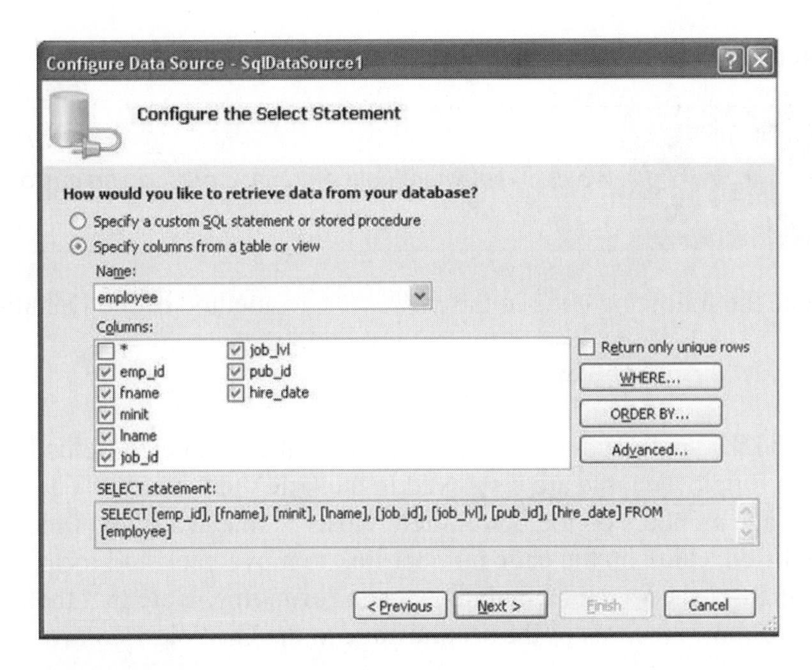

Figure 8-5
Configure Data Source Dialog Box

10. Click the Test Query button to ensure that the fields selected in Step 9 are displayed correctly in a result form. Then click Finish. Figure 8-6 shows the Configure Data Source dialog box displaying the result of the query statement.

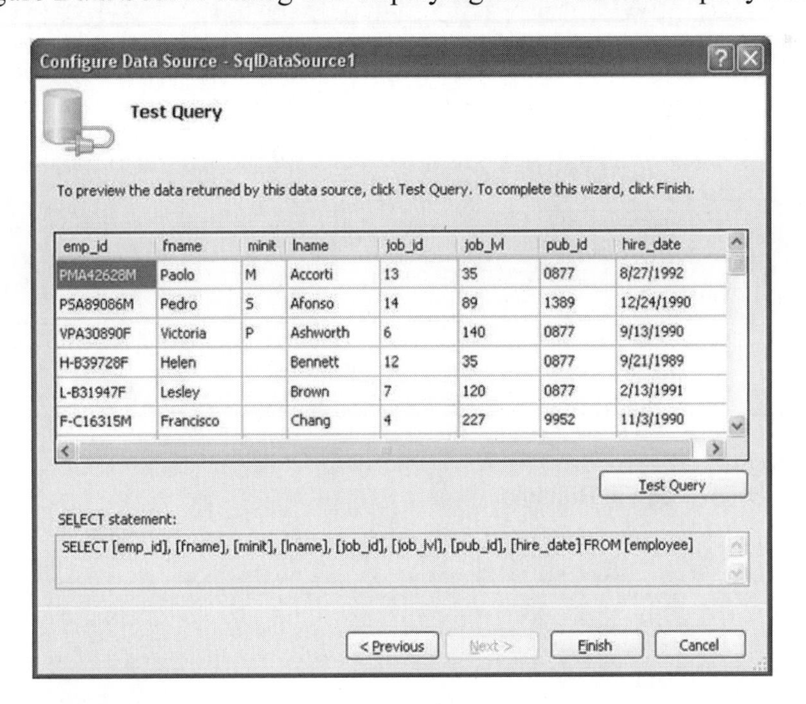

Figure 8-6
Configure Data Source Dialog Box Showing the Result of the Query

11. Check EnablePaging in the Smart Tag pane.

> **NOTE**
>
> *We can implement both automatic paging and custom paging.*

12. Place the following code in the `page_load` method of the Default.aspx page:

```
GridView1.DataBind();
```

13. Debug the application using F5. Observe that the selected fields from the Pubs.Employee table are displayed in the GridView control. The control displays the page numbers on the bottom left. Observe that at a given time only 10 records are listed. Click on the page number link to move back and forth to read the data. Figure 8-7 shows the Default.aspx page at runtime. Note that the page in the figure shows records of the second page in the GridView control.

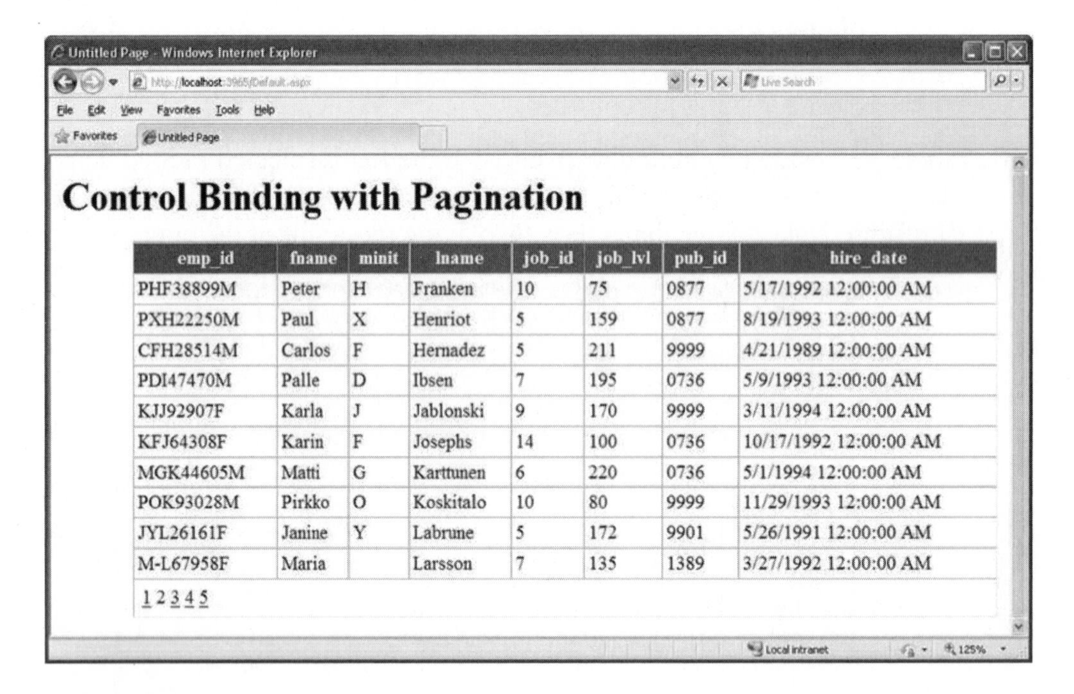

emp_id	fname	minit	lname	job_id	job_lvl	pub_id	hire_date
PHF38899M	Peter	H	Franken	10	75	0877	5/17/1992 12:00:00 AM
PXH22250M	Paul	X	Henriot	5	159	0877	8/19/1993 12:00:00 AM
CFH28514M	Carlos	F	Hernadez	5	211	9999	4/21/1989 12:00:00 AM
PDI47470M	Palle	D	Ibsen	7	195	0736	5/9/1993 12:00:00 AM
KJJ92907F	Karla	J	Jablonski	9	170	9999	3/11/1994 12:00:00 AM
KFJ64308F	Karin	F	Josephs	14	100	0736	10/17/1992 12:00:00 AM
MGK44605M	Matti	G	Karttunen	6	220	0736	5/1/1994 12:00:00 AM
POK93028M	Pirkko	O	Koskitalo	10	80	9999	11/29/1993 12:00:00 AM
JYL26161F	Janine	Y	Labrune	5	172	9901	5/26/1991 12:00:00 AM
M-L67958F	Maria		Larsson	7	135	1389	3/27/1992 12:00:00 AM

1 2 3 4 5

Figure 8-7
Default.aspx Page at Runtime

LAB REVIEW QUESTIONS

Completion time	15 minutes

1. What is the difference between `ExecuteNonQuery` and `ExecuteReader` methods?

2. Define the `DataFormatString` property of `GridView` control.

3. Consider the following setting in a web.config file. Write code to access the connection string defined in the web.config file:

```
<configuration>
<connectionStrings>
<add name="name" connectionString="Server=(local);Integrated
Security=True;Database=pubs;" providerName="System.Data.SqlClient" />
</connectionStrings>
</configuration>
```

LAB CHALLENGE 8.1: BINDING A DATA-BOUND CONTROL TO A STORED PROCEDURE

Completion time	15 minutes

Consider a database table named product that stores details about electrical products. Additionally assume that the database has a stored procedure called sp_product that retrieves values from the product table. Create an application in which a DataGrid control must be bound to the sp_product stored procedure rather than the product table.

LAB CHALLENGE 8.2: IMPLEMENTING PAGINATION USING A STORED PROCEDURE

Completion time	**20 minutes**

Consider that you have a database table named employee. You create an application that retrieves the records from the employee table and displays them in a GridView control. However, you want to implement pagination so that only records for the current page are retrieved instead of all records. How will you implement custom pagination at the data source using a stored procedure?

LAB 9
SOURCING DATA FROM DIFFERENT DATA SOURCES

This lab contains the following exercises and activities:

Exercise 9.1	Working with SQLDataSource Controls
Exercise 9.2	Working with ObjectDataSource Controls
Exercise 9.3	Working with XMLDataSource Controls
Exercise 9.4	Querying with LINQ to SQLDataSources
Exercise 9.5	Querying with LINQ to ObjectDataSources
Exercise 9.6	Querying with LINQ to XMLDataSources
Lab Review Questions	
Lab Challenge 9.1	Querying String Objects Using LINQ
Lab Challenge 9.2	Performing Database Interactions Using ObjectDataSource Control

BEFORE YOU BEGIN

Lab 9 assumes that the lab setup has been completed as specified in the setup document and that StudentXX-A, StudentXX-B, and StudentXX-C computers have Microsoft .NET Framework 3.5 and Microsoft Visual Studio 2008 installed.

NOTE	*In this lab, you will see the characters XX. When you see these characters, substitute the two-digit number assigned to your computer.*

SCENARIO

You are building an application for a company to manage its employee details. The company stores the employee details in data sources such as SQL Server database and XML files. You should query these data sources from your application and display the data in a data-bound control.

In this lab, you will learn to interact with various data sources such as a database and an XML file from .NET applications using different data source controls. Additionally, you will also learn to query these data sources using LINQ, a new feature introduced in .NET 3.5.

After completing this lab, you will be able to:

- Use SQLDataSource controls to query database data
- Use ObjectDataSource controls to query database data
- Use XMLDataSource controls to query XML data
- Implement LINQ to SQL
- Implement LINQ to objects
- Implement LINQ to XML

Estimated lab time: 150 minutes

Exercise 9.1	Working with SQLDataSource Controls
Overview	You are developing a web application for a company to manage its employee details. The application stores employee data in a SQL Server database. You want to display employee records in a GridView control according to the user's input. You use SQLDataSource control to interact with the database.

	In this lab exercise, you will use Microsoft Visual Studio 2008 and SQL Server database. This task is complete when you are able to retrieve data successfully from the database using the SQLDataSource control. To complete this lab exercise, all the student computers such as StudentXX-A and StudentXX-B must be started and must have network access.
Completion time	15 minutes

1. From the Start menu, select Microsoft Visual Studio 2008, and then select Microsoft Visual Studio 2008.

2. Select File → New Project → ASP.NET Web Site, and enter the name **SqlDataSource**. Visual Studio creates a new Web site that contains the Default.aspx page.

3. Add the controls given in Table 9-1 to the Default.aspx page.

Table 9-1
Controls in Default.aspx Page of SqlDataSource Application

Control	***ID***
SqlDataSource	`sourceEmpCity`
SqlDataSource	`SqlDataSource1`
GridView	`GridView1`
DropDownList	`DropDownList1`

4. Select `sourceEmpCity` control smart tag. Click Configure the `DataSource` property.

5. Configure the `sourceEmpCity` control to connect to the Employees table of the Northwind database by clicking on New Connection. In the Add Connection dialog box, click the Test Connection button and perform the following:

    a. Set the `DataSource` property to Microsoft SQL Server(SqlClient) as shown in Figure 9-1.

b. Set the Server Name to .(local) and the Database to Northwind as shown in Figure 9-1.

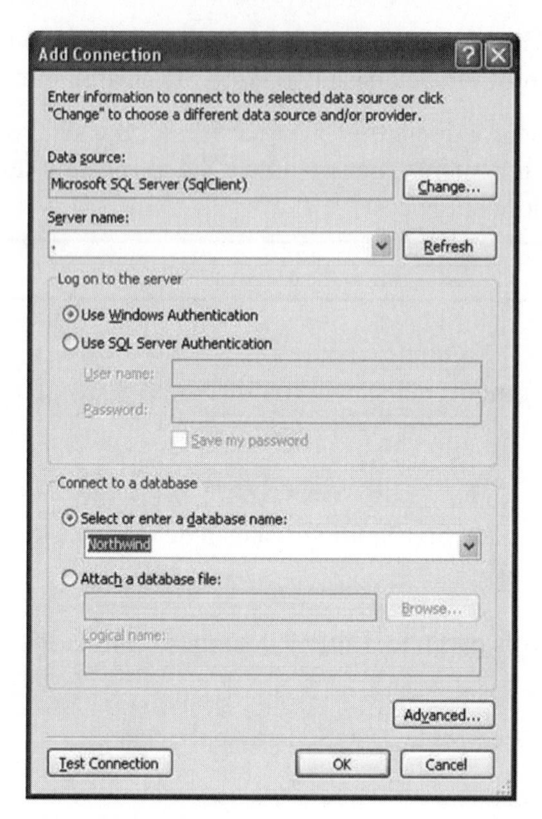

Figure 9-1
Add Connection Dialog Box

c. Click Ok → Next → Next → Choose the Specify Columns from a Table or View Radio button and select the * check box from the columns pane as shown in Figure 9-2. Click Next, and then click Finish. Note that all the columns pertaining to the Employees table are displayed.

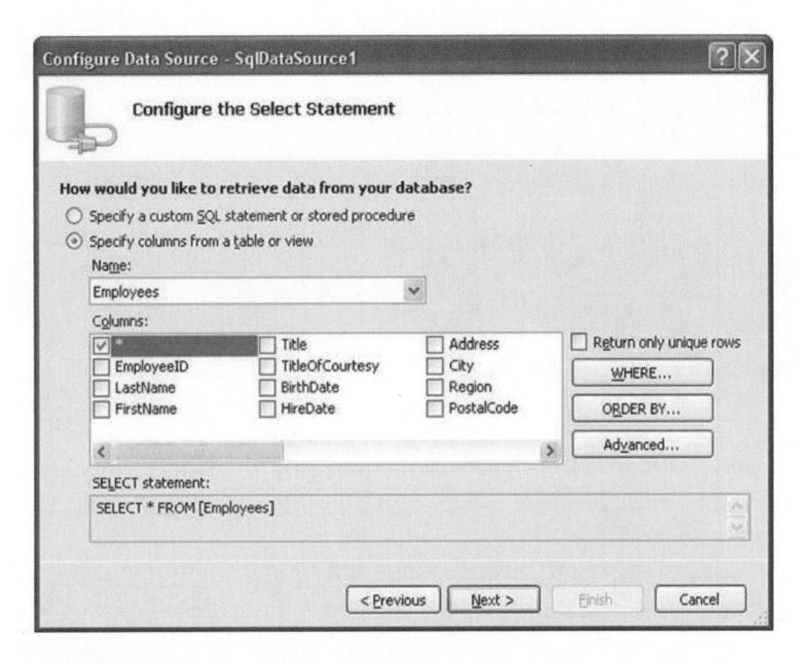

Figure 9-2
Configure Data Source Dialog Box

6. Choose the option Custom Sql Statement or Stored Procedure, and click Next.

7. Place the given query into the SELECT pane, and then click Next.

```
SELECT DISTINCT CITY FROM EMPLOYEES
```

8. Test the query, and then click Finish.

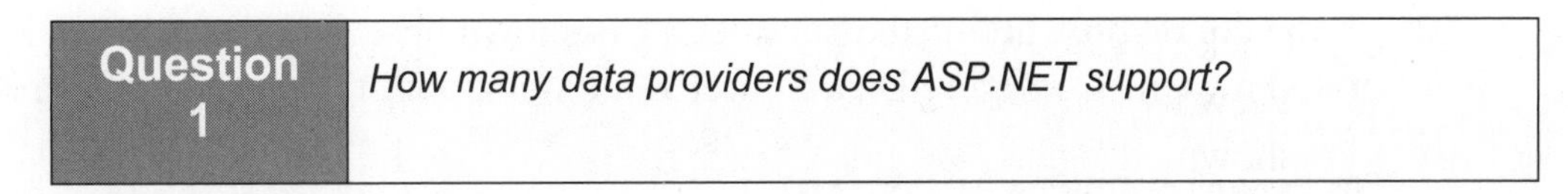

Question 1 *How many data providers does ASP.NET support?*

9. Bind the `DropDownList1` control with the `sourceEmpCity` control. To perform this:

   a. Click the `DropDownList1` control and click Smart Tag.

   b. At the Select data source drop down, choose `sourceEmpCity`. In the Data Source Configuration Wizard dialog box, configure the DropDownList display data field and the DropDownList value data field as shown in Figure 9-3.

   c. Click OK.

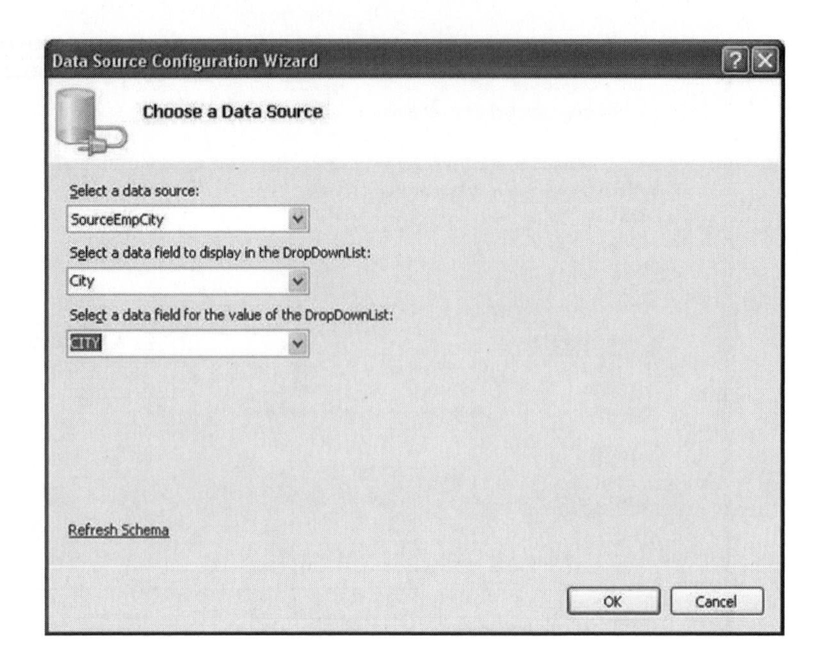

Figure 9-3
Data Source Configuration Wizard Dialog Box

10. Configure the `SqlDataSource1` control by repeating Steps 5 and 6.

11. Place the given query in the Select pane, and then click Next:

```
    SELECT EmployeeID, LastName, FirstName, Title, Address, City, Country
FROM Employees WHERE (City = @City)
```

12. In the dialog box, define the parameters as shown here, and then click OK. Figure 9-4 shows the Configure Data Source dialog box with the defined parameters:

```
Parameter Source = Control
ControlId = DropDownList1
DefaultView = blank
```

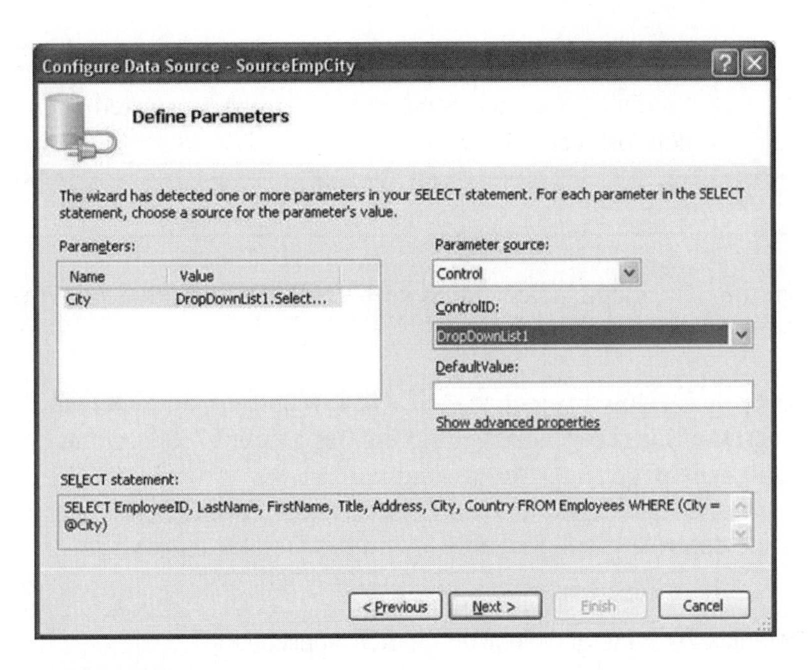

Figure 9-4
Configure Data Source Dialog Box with the Defined Parameters

13. Test the query, and then click Finish.

14. Set the `DataSource` property of `GridView1` to `SqlDataSource1`.

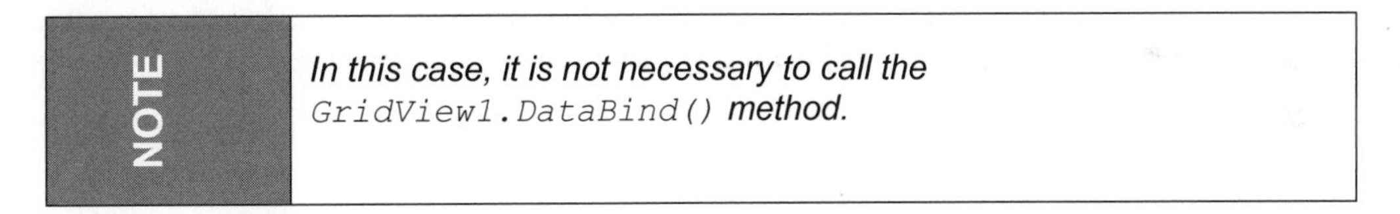

NOTE

In this case, it is not necessary to call the `GridView1.DataBind()` method.

15. Debug the application using F5. Observe that the DropDownList control lists the values of the city field. Select a city and observe the corresponding employee records displayed in the GridView control.

Exercise 9.2	Working with ObjectDataSource Controls
Overview	You are developing a web application for a company to manage its employee details. The application stores employee data in a SQL Server database. You want to display employee records in a GridView control. You use an ObjectDataSource control to interact with the database. In this lab exercise, you will use Microsoft Visual Studio 2008 and SQL Server database. This task is complete when you are able to retrieve data successfully from the database using ObjectDataSource control.

	To complete this lab exercise, all the student computers such as StudentXX-A and StudentXX-B must be started and must have network access.
Completion time	15 minutes

1. From the Start menu, select Microsoft Visual Studio 2008, and then select Microsoft Visual Studio 2008.

2. Select File → New Project → ASP.NET Web Site, and enter the name **ObjectDataSource**. Visual Studio creates a new Web site that contains the Default.aspx page.

3. Add the controls given in Table 9-2 to the Default.aspx page.

Table 9-2
Controls in Default.aspx Page of ObjectDataSource Application

Control	***ID***
ObjectDataSource	`ObjectDataSource1`
GridView	`GridView1`
DropDownList	`DropDownList1`

4. Add a class, **EmployeeDetails**, to the solution as shown:

```
public class EmployeeDetails
{
  private int empid;
  public int EmpID
 {
    get { return empid; }
    set { empid = value; }
 }
 private string fname;
 public string FName
 {
    get { return fname; }
    set { fname = value; }
 }
 private string lname;
 public string LName
```

```
        {
           get { return lname; }
           set { lname = value; }
        }
        private string title;
        public string Title
        {
           get { return title; }
           set { title = value; }
        }
        public EmployeeDetails(int id, string Fname, string Lname, string
title)
        {
           this.empid = id;
           this.fname = Fname;
           this.lname = Lname;
           this.title = title;
        }
      }
```

Question 2	*What is the significance of Refresh Schema in a smart tag ?*

5. Add a class, **EmployeeDB**, to the solution as shown:

```
      using System;
      using System.Data;
      using System.Data.SqlClient;
      using system.Collections.Generic;
      public class EmployeeDB
      {
        private string conString;
        public EmployeeDB()
        {
          // Define the connection string to connect to the Northwind
database.
          conString = "Data Source=.;Initial Catalog=Northwind;user
id=sa;password=sa";
        }
```

```
        // Create GetEmps method to return the employee details of all the
employees. This method returns List<EmployeeDetails>
        public List<EmployeeDetails> GetEmps()
        {
          SqlConnection con = new SqlConnection(conString);
          string qry = "select EmployeeID, FirstName, LastName,
TitleOfCourtesy from employees";
          SqlCommand cmd = new SqlCommand(qry, con);
          List<EmployeeDetails> employee = new List<EmployeeDetails>();
          try
          {
              con.Open();
              // Use DataReader to execute the query
              SqlDataReader sdr = cmd.ExecuteReader();
              // Read records from the result set
              while (sdr.Read())
              {
                  // Create an object of EmployeeDetails class and populate
its properties with the respective values in the result set.
                  EmployeeDetails emp = new
EmployeeDetails((int)sdr["EmployeeID"], (string)sdr["FirstName"],
(string)sdr["LastName"], (string)sdr["TitleOfCourtesy"]);
                  // Add the EmployeeDetails object to the list
                  employee.Add(emp);
              }
                  sdr.Close();
                  // Return the list
                  return employee;
          }
          catch (SqlException ex)
          {
              throw new ApplicationException("Data Error!");
          }
          finally
          {
              con.Close();
          }
      }
    }
```

6. In the design view, select `ObjectDataSource` control, and then click Smart Tag.

NOTE	*The classes, EmployeeDB.cs and EmployeeDetails.cs, must reside in the App_Code folder. The App_Code folder is an application folder that contains source code files such as .cs files, which you can compile as part of your application. Alternatively, you can also keep the compiled version of the Employee.cs and EmployeeDetails.cs files as assemblies in the Bin folder and reference these files in your application. To learn more about the App_Code folder and Bin folder, refer to the section ASP.NET Web Site Layout in the MSDN library.*

7. On the Choose Business Object page, select ObjectDataSource.EmployeeDB, and click Next.
8. On the Select tab, choose the GetEmps method, and then click Finish.
9. Set the `DataSource` property of the `GridView1` control to `ObjectDataSource1`. To do this, select GridView, right click on Smart Tag, and then, from the Choose Data Source drop down, select ObjectDataSource1.
10. Debug the application using F5. Observe that the employee records are displayed in the GridView control.

Exercise 9.3 Working with XMLDataSource Controls

Overview	You are creating a web application for an online movie rental store. The application stores movie details in an XML file. You display the available movies in a GridView control. You use XmlDataSource control to interact with the XML file. In this lab exercise, you will use Microsoft Visual Studio 2008. This task is complete when you are able to display available movies in a GridView control using XmlDataSource control. To complete this lab exercise, all the student computers such as StudentXX-A and StudentXX-B must be started and must have network access.
Completion time	20 minutes

1. From the Start menu, select Microsoft Visual Studio 2008, and then select Microsoft Visual Studio 2008.

2. Select File → New Project → ASP.NET Web Site, and enter the name **XmlDataSource**. Visual Studio creates a new Web site that contains the Default.aspx page.

3. Drag `XmlDataSource` control and `GridView` control to the Default.aspx page. Set the `ID` property of the XmlDataSource control to "sourceData."

4. Create an XML file as given:

```
<?xml version="1.0" encoding="utf-8" ?>
  <DvdList>
   <DVD id="1" Category="War"></DVD>
   <DVD id="2" Category="Commedy"></DVD>
   <DVD id="3" Category="Science Fiction"></DVD>
  <DVD id="4" Category="Thriller"></DVD>
  <DVD id="5" Category="Action"></DVD>
  <DVD id="6" Category="Epic"></DVD>
</DvdList>
```

5. Set the `DataFile` property of the `XmlDataSource` control to the name of the created XML file.

6. Set the `DataSource` property of the `GridView` control to the id of the `XmlDataSource` control, which is `sourceData` in this case.

7. Call the `GridView.DataBind` method in the `page_load` method of the Default.aspx page, as shown:

```
GridView1.DataBind();
```

Question 3	*Is it mandatory to call the `DataBind` method during page load? If yes, why?*

8. Debug the application using F5. Observe that the movie data from the XML file is displayed in the GridView control.

Exercise 9.4	Querying with LINQ to SQLDataSources
Overview	You are developing a web application for a company to manage its employee details. The application stores employee data in a SQL Server database. You want to display employee records in a GridView control. You use LINQ to SQL to interact with the database. In this lab exercise, you will use Microsoft Visual Studio 2008 and SQL Server database. This task is complete when you are able to display the required database data in a GridView control using LINQ to SQL. To complete this lab exercise, all the student computers such as StudentXX-A and StudentXX-B must be started and must have network access.
Completion time	15 minutes

1. From the Start menu, select Microsoft Visual Studio 2008, and then select Microsoft Visual Studio 2008.

2. Select File → New Project → ASP.NET Web Site, and enter the name **LinqtoSql**. Visual Studio creates a new Web site that contains the Default.aspx page.

Question 4	*What are Lambda Expressions?*

3. Place a GridView control on the Default.aspx page.

4. Add references to the following namespaces in the Default.aspx.cs file:

```
using System.Collections.Generic;
using System.Data.Linq.Mapping;
using Sytem.Data.Linq;
```

5. Add a class, **Employees**, in the Default.aspx.cs file as shown:

```
        // This entity class corresponds to the Employees table of the
Northwind database
         [Table(Name = "Employees")]
    public class Employees
    {
      [Column]
      public int EmployeeID { get; set; }
```

```
        [Column]
        public string FirstName { get; set; }
        [Column]
        public string LastName { get; set; }
        [Column]
        public string City { get; set; }
        [Column]
        public string Country { get; set; }
    }
```

6. Add the following code in the `page_load` method of the Default.aspx page:

```
    protected void Page_Load(object sender, EventArgs e)
    {
        // Define the connection string to connect to the Northwind
database.
        string connString ="Data Source=.;Initial
Catalog=Northwind;Integrated Security=SSPI";
        // Define a DataContext object that represent the database
connection.
        DataContext Northwind = new DataContext(connString);
        // Define a Table object that represent the Employees table of the
Northwind database.
        Table<Employees> emp = Northwind.GetTable<Employees>();
        // Define a LINQ query to retrieve employee records
           // In the query below "c" is a range variable of type Employees
          // Also variables EmpID, EmpFName, EmpLName, EmpCity, and
Country are of the same type as that of the corresponding properties of the
Employees class
        var custs = from c in emp
                    select new
                    {
                      EmpId = c.EmployeeID,
                      EmpFName = c.FirstName,
                      EmpLName = c.LastName,
                      EmpCity = c.City,
                      Country = c.Country
                   };
        GridView1.DataSource = custs;
        GridView1.DataBind();
    }
```

Question 5	*What is DataContext?*

7. Debug the application using F5. Observe that the respective fields from the Employees table are displayed in the GridView control.

Exercise 9.5	Querying with LINQ to ObjectDataSources
Overview	You are developing a web application for a company to manage its employee details. The application stores employee data in a SQL Server database. You want to display employee records in a GridView control. You query the database data using Standard LINQ. In this lab exercise, you will use Microsoft Visual Studio 2008 and SQL Server database. This task is complete when you are able to display the required database data in a GridView control using LINQ to SQL. To complete this lab exercise, all the student computers such as StudentXX-A and StudentXX-B must be started and must have network access.
Completion time	15 minutes

1. From the Start menu, select Microsoft Visual Studio 2008, and then select Microsoft Visual Studio 2008.

2. Select File → New Project → ASP.NET Web Site, and enter the name **LinqtoObject**. Visual Studio creates a new Web site that contains the Default.aspx page.

3. Place GridView and ObjectDataSource controls on the Default.aspx page.

4. Add a new file, **Employees.dbml**, by selecting LINQ to SQL classes. To achieve this, right click on Project, click Add, click New Item, select Linq to SQL classes, and then name it **Employees.dbml**.

NOTE	*DataContext keyword gets added to the .dbml class as a suffix automatically. In this case, we have the Employees.dbml class, which will then be modified automatically as EmployeesDataContext in the class file.*

5. Drag the Employee table from the Server Explorer into the Employees.dbml.

6. Add a new class file, **Employee.cs**, to the solution and add the following code:

```
using System.Collections.Generic;
using System.Linq;
using System.Data.Linq;
public partial class Employee
{
  public static IEnumerable<Employee> Select()
  {
    // Instantiate Employees.dbml
    EmployeesDataContext db = new EmployeesDataContext();
    // The given query extracts all the records pertaining to the
Employees table and orders them in ascending order by EmployeeID
    return db.Employees.OrderBy(e => e.EmployeeID);
  }
}
```

Question 6	*What is the DBML extractor?*

7. Set the `TypeName` property of the ObjectDataSource control to `LinqtoObject.Employee`.

8. Debug the application using F5. Observe that the GridView control has been populated with the Employees table records.

Exercise 9.6	Querying with LINQ to XMLDataSources
Overview	You are developing a web application for a company to manage its business contacts. Business contact details are stored in an XML file. You use GridView control to display the contact details from the XML file using LINQ to XML. In this lab exercise, you will use Microsoft Visual Studio 2008. This task is complete when you are able to display the data from the XML file in a GridView control using LINQ to XML. To complete this lab exercise, all the student computers such as StudentXX-A and StudentXX-B must be started and must have network access.
Completion time	15 minutes

1. From the Start menu, select Microsoft Visual Studio 2008, and then select Microsoft Visual Studio 2008.
2. Select File → New Project → ASP.NET Web Site, and enter the name **LinqtoXml**. Visual Studio creates a new Web site that contains the Default.aspx page.
3. Place a GridView control on the default.aspx page.
4. Create an XML file as shown:

```
<?xml version="1.0" encoding="utf-8" ?>
<contacts>
  <contact contactId="2">
    <firstName>Barney</firstName>
    <lastName>Gottshall</lastName>
  </contact>
  <contact contactId="3">
   <firstName>Armando</firstName>
   <lastName>Valdes</lastName>
 </contact>
 <contact contactId="4">
   <firstName>Adam</firstName>
  <lastName>Gauwain</lastName>
</contact>
</contacts>
```

Question 7	*What namespaces are required to use the functionality of DataContext class and LINQ statements?*

5. Add the following code in the `Page_Load` method of the Default.aspx page:

```
// Load the XML file to the memory
XDocument loaded = XDocument.Load(Server.MapPath("XMLFile1.xml"));
// Query the loaded xml data and select the sub elements of the node
<contact>
// The variable c in the code represents the element contact defined in the
Xml file
// Descendants specifies that the search includes the element's descendants
including children.
// q will have all the resultset of the next query
```

```
 var q = from c in loaded.Descendants("contact")
        select (string)c.Element("firstName") + ", " +
        (string)c.Element("lastName");
GridView1.DataSource = q;
GridView1.DataBind();
```

> **NOTE** *We can use `Server.MapPath` method to specify the proper physical address of the XML file located in the current project.*

6. Save the project and debug it using F5. Observe that the GridView control displays all the data from the XML file.

LAB REVIEW QUESTIONS

Completion time	**20 minutes**

1. What is LINQ to Object?
2. Differentiate between a SqlDataSource control and an ObjectDataSource control.
3. Write a sample code to extract the first name and the last name from the Employee table using LINQ.
4. Consider the following Dictionary object:

```
Dictionary<string, string> dict = new Dictionary<string, string>();
dict.Add("Child1", "Value1");
dict.Add("Child2", "Value2");
dict.Add("Child3", "Value3");
dict.Add("Child4", "Value4");
```

How can you generate an XML element from the given Dictionary object using LINQ to XML?

LAB CHALLENGE 9.1: QUERYING STRING OBJECTS USING LINQ

Completion time	**15 minutes**

You are programming a text editing tool in your application, which contains a search toolbar that provides quick text searching. Consider that one of the toolbar menus should provide a count of the occurrence of a given text in a given string. For example,

"Historically, the world of data and the world of objects have not been well integrated. Programmers work in C# or Visual Basic."

How will you find the count of the occurrence of the text "data" in the given string using Standard LINQ?

LAB CHALLENGE 9.2: PERFORMING DATABASE INTERACTIONS USING OBJECTDATASOURCE CONTROL

Completion time	**20 minutes**

Imagine that you are a programmer at ABC Solutions. You are assigned the task of implementing insert and update employee information into a SQL Server database table named Employee. Write the steps to achieve this task using ObjectDataSource control.

LAB 10
ENHANCING WEB APPLICATIONS

This lab contains the following exercises and activities:

Exercise 10.1	Using WCF Service Architecture
Exercise 10.2	Using ASMX Service Architecture
Exercise 10.3	Using REST Architecture
Exercise 10.4	Building Global Applications
Lab Review Questions	
Lab Challenge 10.1	Creating a WCF Service
Lab Challenge 10.2	Creating a Global Application

BEFORE YOU BEGIN

Lab 10 assumes that the lab setup has been completed as specified in the setup document and that StudentXX-A, StudentXX-B, and StudentXX-C computers have Microsoft .NET Framework 3.5 and Microsoft Visual Studio 2008 installed.

> NOTE
>
> *In this lab, you will see the characters XX. When you see these characters, substitute the two-digit number assigned to your computer.*

SCENARIO

You are building an application to perform mathematical calculations. You want to create web services to perform different functions and consume them in your application. In addition, you want to build a single application that different users can use with their choice of language.

In this lab, you will learn to create and consume web services using three different architectures: WCF, ASMX, and REST. In addition, you will learn to build a global web application.

In the Lab Challenges, you will create a WCF Web service. In addition, you will create a global application that can be localized to many languages.

After completing this lab, you will be able to:

- Create and consume a WCF service
- Create and consume a ASMX Web service
- Create and consume a REST service
- Create a global application

Estimated lab time: 145 minutes

Exercise 10.1	Using WCF Service Architecture
Overview	You want to develop a web service to calculate the area of a circle. In addition, you want to consume this web service from a Web site and display the result. In this lab exercise, you will use Microsoft Visual Studio 2008 to create and consume a web service using the WCF Service Architecture. This task is complete when you are able to successfully create and consume a web service. To complete this lab exercise, all the student computers such as StudentXX-A and StudentXX-B must be started and must have network access.
Completion time	30 minutes

1. From the Start menu, select Microsoft Visual Studio 2008, and then select Microsoft Visual Studio 2008.

2. Select File → New Project → WCF Service Application, and enter the name **WCFService**. Visual Studio adds a class file (.svc) and an interface file (.cs) automatically to the solution.

3. Rename the file named IService to **IArea.cs** and the file named Service1.svc to **AreaService.svc**.

4. Add a reference to the following namespaces in the IArea.cs file as shown:

```
using System.Runtime.Serialization;
using System.ServiceModel;
```

5. Erase all the existing code from IArea.cs and add the following code:

```
[ServiceContract]
public interface IArea
{
  [OperationContract]
  double CalculatePI(double value);
}
```

> **NOTE**
> *You must include the `[ServiceContract]`, `[OperationContract]` attributes in the interface. The `ServiceContract` attribute is used to define an interface or a class as a service contract. The `OperationContract` attribute is used on the class or interface methods to define the service contract operations.*

6. Open the AreaService.svc.cs file and inherit it to the IArea interface, and add code to define the service implementation:

```
public class AreaService : IArea
{
  double area;
  public double CalculatePI(double dc)
  {
    area = Convert.ToDouble(Math.PI * dc * dc);
    return area;
  }
}
```

7. In the Solution Explorer, right click on AreaService.svc, and select View Markup. Add the following code:

```
    <%@ ServiceHost Language="C#" Debug="true" Service="Sample.AreaService"
CodeBehind="AreaService.svc.cs" %>
```

NOTE	In this code, you are defining the correct namespace into the Service attribute and redirecting to the correct code behind the file. You must properly define the services into the SVC file with full naming convention.

8. Open the web.config file, erase the existing contents, and add the following code:

```
<?xml version="1.0"?>
<configuration>
   <system.serviceModel>
      <services>
            <service name="Sample.AreaService"
   behaviorConfiguration="areaBehavior">
                  <!-- This endpoint is exposed at the base address provided
   by host:
   http://localhost/servicemodelsamples/service.svc  -->
                  <endpoint address="" binding="wsHttpBinding"
   contract="Sample.IArea"/>

            </service>
      </services>
    <behaviors>
      <serviceBehaviors>
        <behavior name ="areaBehavior">
          <serviceMetadata httpGetEnabled ="true"/>
        </behavior>
      </serviceBehaviors>
    </behaviors>
   </system.serviceModel>
</configuration>
```

NOTE	*In this code, you have configured the following settings:* • *Defined the full name of the service (`Sample.AreaService`) into the `Service` attribute* • *Set the `behaviorConfiguration`* • *Mentioned the `contract` and `binding` in the `endpoint` tag* • *Added a custom `behavior` and set its `serviceMetadata` property `httpGetEnabled` to true*

Question 1	*What does the <endpoint> element specify?*

9. Build the application by clicking on the Build menu and choosing Build Solution (ctrl+shift+B). You will see an XML like file (WSDL file) in the browser, which assures that your service contract is defined properly.

Question 2	*What does WSDL stand for?*

10. In the Solution Explorer, add a new project, select ASP.NET Web Application, and enter the name **WcfSampleClient**. Visual Studio creates a new Web site that contains the Default.aspx page.

11. Add the controls given in Table 10-1 to the Default.aspx page.

Table 10-1
Controls in Default.aspx Page of WcfSampleClient Application

Control	***ID***	***Properties***
Label	Label1	Text = “”
TextBox	txtRadius	
Button	btnArea	Text = Area
Label	lblArea	Text = Result

12. In the Solution Explorer, right click on Reference, and select Add Service Reference.

13. Click on the Discovery button. The service you created appears.

14. Select the service, and click OK.

15. Add the reference to the web service namespace in the code behind page, default.aspx.cs, as shown:

```
using WcfSampleClient.ServiceReference1;
```

16. Add the following code to the `Click` event of the `btnArea` control:

```
protected void btnArea_Click(object sender, EventArgs e)
{
        try
        {
                double radius = Convert.ToDouble(txtRadius.Text);
                AreaClient proxy = new AreaClient("WSHttpBinding_IArea");
                lblArea.Text = Convert.ToString(proxy.CalculatePI(radius));
        }
        catch (Exception ex)
        {
                lblArea.Text = ex.StackTrace.ToString();
        }
}
```

> **NOTE**
> *You can get the `WSHttpBindingI_Area` value from the `name` attribute of the `endpoint` tag in the web.config file.*

17. Build the application by clicking on the Build menu and choosing Build Solution (ctrl+shift+B). You will see the interface.

18. Enter the value for radius and click the button. The code calculates and displays the area using the WCF service.

Exercise 10.2	Using ASMX Service Architecture
Overview	You want to develop a web service to calculate the square of a number. In addition, you want to consume this web service from a Web site and display the result. In this lab exercise, you will use Microsoft Visual Studio 2008 to create and consume a web service using the ASMX Architecture. This task is complete when you are able to create and consume a web service successfully. To complete this lab exercise, all the student computers such as StudentXX-A and StudentXX-B must be started and must have network access.
Completion time	15 minutes

1. From the Start menu, select Microsoft Visual Studio 2008, and then select Microsoft Visual Studio 2008.
2. Select File → New Project → Web Service, and enter the name **piService**. Visual Studio adds a .asmx file into the solution.
3. Rename this file to **CalculateService.asmx**.

Question 3	*Which namepsaces are mandatory to be included in a .asmx file?*

4. Open the CalculateService.asmx.cs file and replace the pre-added class and HelloWorld method code to appear as the following code:

```
public class CalculateService : System.Web.Services.WebService
{
  [WebMethod]
  public double piCal(double r)
  {
    return Math.PI*r*r;
  }
}
```

5. Build the application by clicking on the Build menu and choosing Build Solution (ctrl+shift+B). You will see the `pical` method declaration defined inside the web service. When you click the method definition, you are prompted to enter a value. You can enter a value and test the working of the service.

> **NOTE**
> *You can see the Web Service Description File by suffixing* `?wsdl` *after the service URL.*

6. In the Solution Explorer, add a new project, select ASP.NET Web Application, and enter the name **piClient**. Visual Studio creates a new Web site that contains the Default.aspx page.

7. In the Solution Explorer, right click on Reference, and select Add Web Reference. If you don't see Add Web Reference directly, select Add Service Reference, click the Advanced button, and then click on the Add Web Reference button. The Add Web Reference dialog box appears as shown in Figure 10-1.

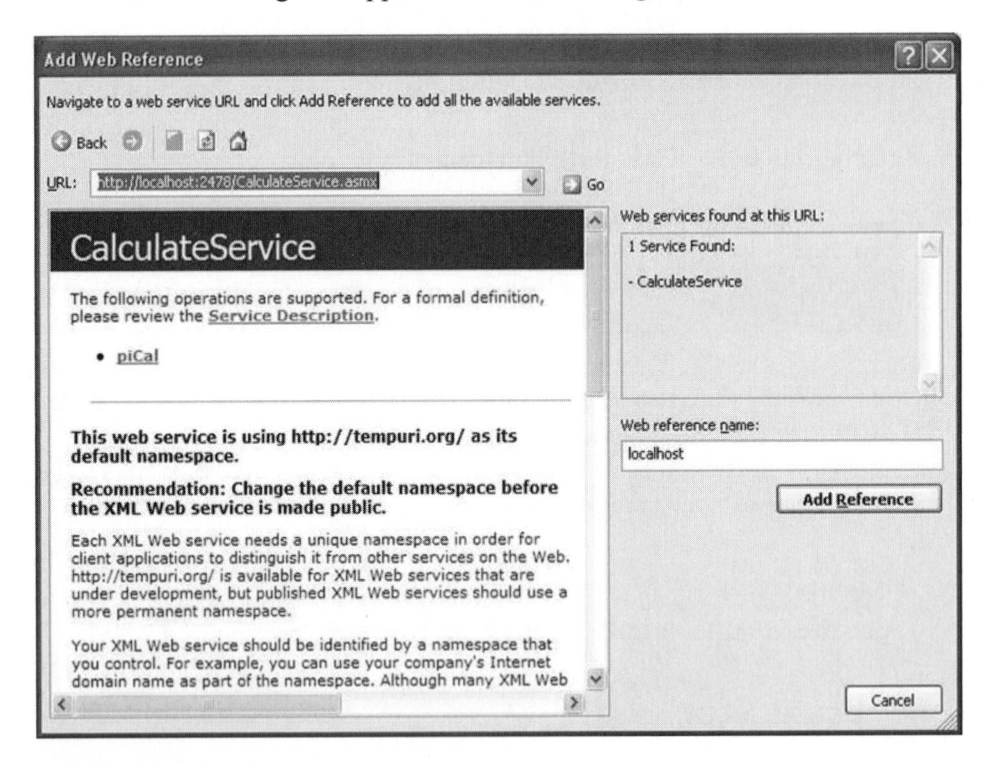

Figure 10-1
The Add Web Reference Dialog Box

8. In the Add Web Reference dialog box, specify the web service URL, and click OK. You can locate the web service URL by running the CalculateService.asmx created in Step 3 in a browser as shown in Figure 10-2. To perform this, select the CalculateService.asmx file, then right click, and choose View in Browser. Once you are ready to add the web service reference, rename its default name localhost to appear as myService.

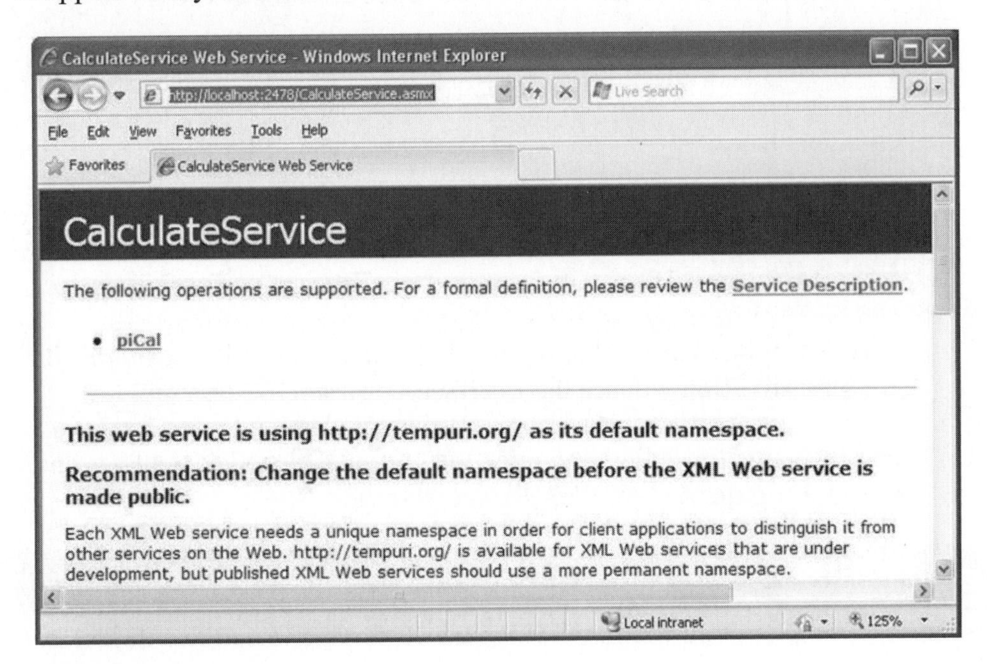

Figure 10-2
CalculateService Web Service

9. Add the controls given in Table 10-2 to the Default.aspx page.

Table 10-2
Controls in Default.aspx Page of piClient Application

Control	***ID***	***Properties***
Label	Label1	Text = “”
Text Box	txtRadius	
Button	btnPi	Text=Area
Label	lblResult	Text=Result

10. Add the reference to the Web service namespace in the code behind page, default.aspx.cs, as shown:

```
using piClient.myService;
```

11. Add the following code to the `Click` event of the `btnPi` control:

```
protected void btnPi_Click(object sender, EventArgs e)
{
    double r = Convert.ToDouble(txtRadius.Text);
    CalculateService obj = new CalculateService();
    lblResult.Text = obj.piCal(r).ToString() ;
}
```

NOTE	*You can configure the default page displayed using the Set as Start Page option from Solution Explorer.*

12. Build the application by clicking on the Build menu and choosing Build Solution (ctrl+shift+B). You will see the interface.

13. Enter the value for radius, and click the button. The code calculates and displays the area using the ASMX Web service.

Exercise 10.3	Using REST Service Architecture
Overview	You want to develop a web service to add two numbers. In addition, you want to consume this web service from a Web site and display the result. In this lab exercise, you will use Microsoft Visual Studio 2008 to create and consume a web service using the REST Service Architecture. This task is complete when you are able to create and consume a web service successfully. To complete this lab exercise, all the student computers such as StudentXX-A and StudentXX-B must be started and must have network access.
Completion time	30 minutes

NOTE	*Before starting this exercise, download the REST Starter Kit from http://aspnet.codeplex.com/Release/ProjectReleases.aspx?ReleaseId=24644. After installation, you can find the starter kit in the path "C:\Program Files\Microsoft WCF REST\WCF REST Starter Kit Preview 2."*

1. From the Start menu, select Microsoft Visual Studio 2008, and then select Microsoft Visual Studio 2008.

2. Select File → New Project → WCF Service, and enter the name **RestServicePublish**. Visual Studio adds a class file (.svc) and an interface file (.cs) to the solution automatically.

3. Rename the file named IService to **IRestService.cs** and the file named Service1.svc to **RestService.svc**.

Question 4	*What does REST stand for?*

4. Add a reference to the following namespaces in the IRestService.cs file as shown:

```
using System.Runtime.Serialization;
using System.ServiceModel;
```

5. Erase all existing code from IRestService.cs, and add the following code:

```
[ServiceContract]
public interface IRestService
{
    [OperationContract(Name = "ValueAddition")]
    [WebInvoke(UriTemplate = "/", Method = "POST")]
    int Add(AddService n1);
}
```

6. Open the RestService.svc.cs file and inherit it to the IRestService interface and add the following code to define the service implementation:

```
public class RestService : IRestService
{
    public int plus;

    public int Add(AddService ad)
    {
        plus = Convert.ToInt32(ad.x) + Convert.ToInt32(ad.y);
        return plus;
    }
}
```

7. In the Solution Explorer, right click on RestService.svc and select View Markup. Add the following code:

```
<%@ ServiceHost Language="C#" Debug="true"
Service="RestServiceServer.RestService" CodeBehind="RestService.svc.cs"
Factory="System.ServiceModel.Activation.WebServiceHostFactory"%>
```

Question 5	*Name the potential RESTful protocols.*

8. Add a new class library named **Extra** to the existing solution.

9. Open the class library, rename the class to **AddService**, and add the following code:

```
[Serializable]
public class AddService
{
  public int x { get; set; }
  public int y { get; set; }
}
```

NOTE	*You don't have to have the AddService Reference to a REST service implementation.*

10. Build the application by clicking on the Build menu and choosing Build Solution (ctrl+shift+B).

11. In the Solution Explorer, add a new project, select ASP.NET Web Application, and enter the name **RestClient**. Visual Studio creates a new Web site that contains the Default.aspx page.

12. Select the References folder in the project, right click and select Add Reference to add references of assemblies such as Microsoft.Http and Microsoft.Http.Extention. Note that these assemblies are located in the path C:\Program Files\Microsoft WCF REST\WCF REST Starter Kit Preview 2\Assemblies.

13. Add the controls given in Table 10-3 to the Default.aspx page.

Table 10-3
Controls in Default.aspx Page of RestClient Application

Control	*ID*	*Properties*
Label	Lbl1	Text = "Result(Addition)"
Label	Lbl2	Text = ""

14. Add the following references in the code behind page, default.aspx.cs, as shown:

```
using System.Collections.Generic;
using Microsoft.Http;
using System.Runtime.Serialization;
using Extra;
```

15. Declare a static string variable named uri inside the class to represent the address of your REST service:

```
static string uri;
```

> **NOTE**
> *You must define the variable uri as static type, so that it exists across instances of the class and can be accessed directly without creating an object of the class.*

16. Add the following code to the `Page_Load` method to define the uri, instantiate the `AddService` class, and pass this object to a user-defined method:

```
protected void Page_Load(object sender, EventArgs e)
{
    uri = "http://localhost:3602/RestService.svc/";
    AddService obj = new AddService() { x = 10, y = 15 };
    lbl2.Text = Implementation(obj);
}
```

> **NOTE**
> *You are not creating an interface to accept data, instead you are passing the values as 10 and 15.*
>
> *You will be implementing code for the `Implementation` method in the next step.*

17. Add the user-defined method named `Implementation` to the default.aspx.cs file as follows:

```
public static string Implementation(AddService obj)
{
    using (HttpResponseMessage response = new HttpClient().Post(uri,
HttpContentExtensions.CreateDataContract(obj)))
    {
        int plus = response.Content.ReadAsDataContract<int>();
        return plus.ToString();
    }
}
```

NOTE	*In this code, you have configured the following settings:* • *Defined a static type method with string return type* • *Instantiated the `HttpResponseMessage` class and passed the uri and data contract into the `post` method. This is because you have not manually included the service reference through Add Service Reference.* • *Retrieved the output using the `ReadAsDataContract` method and stored the result in a variable*

18. Configure the start page of the application.

19. Build the application by clicking on the Build menu and choosing Build Solution (ctrl+shift+B). You will see the result of addition displayed on a web page.

Exercise 10.4	Building Global Applications
Overview	You are developing an application that provides globalization in which English and German users can use a single application with language according to their choice. In this lab exercise, you will use Microsoft Visual Studio 2008 to create a global application. This task is complete when you are able to create and use a single application in two different languages successfully. To complete this lab exercise, all the student computers such as StudentXX-A and StudentXX-B must be started and must have network access.
Completion time	20 minutes

1. From the Start menu, select Microsoft Visual Studio 2008, and then select Microsoft Visual Studio 2008.

2. Select File → New Project → ASP.NET Web Application, and enter the name **GlobalApplication**.

3. Add the controls given in Table 10-4 to the Default.aspx page.

Table 10-4
Controls in Default.aspx Page of GlobalApplication Application

Control	*ID*	*Properties*
Label	Label1	Text = ""
Label	Label2	Text = ""
Label	Label3	
TextBox	TextBox1	
TextBox	TextBox2	
TextBox	TextBox3	
DropDownList	ddl	ListItem Value = "en-US" ListItem Value = "de-DE"

4. Right click on the project from Solution Explorer and add a system folder named **App_LocalResources**.

5. Right click on this folder, select Add New Item, and select Resource File. Name it **default.aspx.resx**.

NOTE	*The value for the "Name" field must be unique in all the resource files. If you try duplicating it, you will get an error "There is already another resource with the name '……..' "*

6. Open default.aspx.resx. You will see a table structure with column headings, Name and Value. Enter the values as shown in Table 10-5 for the English-speaking users. This file represents the content for English-speaking users.

Table 10-5
Content for English-Speaking Users

Name	*Value*
lblbith	BirthDate
lblfname	FirstName
lbllname	LastName

7. Add another resource file named **default.aspx.de.resx** for German-speaking users as shown in Table 10-6 and add the following content to this file.

Table 10-6
Content for German-Speaking Users

Name	*Value*
lblbith	Geburtsdatum
lblfname	Vorname
lbllname	Zuname

8. Save all files.

9. Open the default.aspx.cs file and add the following namespaces:

```
using System.Globalization;
using System.Threading;
```

Question 6	*What is implicit localization?*

10. Override the `InitializeCulture` method that lets you choose a culture from the drop-down list at runtime on the page:

```
protected override void InitializeCulture()
{
    if (Request.Form["ddl"] != null)
    {
        String selectedLanguage = Request.Form["ddl"];
        UICulture = selectedLanguage;
        Culture = selectedLanguage;
        Thread.CurrentThread.CurrentCulture =
            CultureInfo.CreateSpecificCulture(selectedLanguage);
        Thread.CurrentThread.CurrentUICulture = new
CultureInfo(selectedLanguage);
    }
    base.InitializeCulture();
}
```

11. Add the following code to the `Page_Load` method for binding the label control to the resource file:

```
protected void Page_Load(object sender, EventArgs e)
{
    Label1.Text = GetLocalResourceObject("lblfname").ToString();
    Label2.Text = GetLocalResourceObject("lbllname").ToString();
    Label3.Text = GetLocalResourceObject("lblbith").ToString();
}
```

Question 7	*How can you change language settings from Internet Explorer?*

12. Open the default.aspx file to source view and define the culture attributes as follows:

```
<%@PageLanguage="C#"AutoEventWireup="true" CodeBehind="Default.aspx.cs"
Inherits="WebApplication1.Default" UICulture="auto" Culture="auto:en-US"
%>
```

13. Build the application by clicking on the Build menu and choosing Build Solution (ctrl+shift+B). You can see the three label controls with English data by default. If you select German language from the drop-down list box, the changes will be shown immediately. Observe that the labels now display German data.

LAB REVIEW QUESTIONS

Completion time	**15 minutes**

1. How can you generate the proxy of a service from the command line?
2. What are WebMethods in a web service?
3. Define the advantages of REST over SOAP?
4. How can you enable globalization settings from the web.config file?

LAB CHALLENGE 10.1: CREATING A WCF SERVICE

Completion time	**15 minutes**

Create a Web site that provides online astrological services. As one of the requirements, you need a service that provides the number of days a person has liveed since his birth. How can you achieve this?

LAB CHALLENGE 10.2: CREATING A GLOBAL APPLICATION

Completion time	**20 minutes**

You want to create a global application common to multiple languages. How can you create this using the `CultureInfo` class?

LAB 11 DESIGNING SECURITY MEASURES

This lab contains the following exercises and activities:

Exercise 11.1	Implementing Security Using Memberships
Exercise 11.2	Implementing Security Using Roles
Exercise 11.3	Extending Custom Providers
Lab Review Questions	
Lab Challenge 11.1	Retrieving User Data
Lab Challenge 11.2	Implementing a Custom Data Provider

BEFORE YOU BEGIN

Lab 11 assumes that the lab setup has been completed as specified in the setup document and that StudentXX-A, StudentXX-B, and StudentXX-C computers have Microsoft .NET Framework 3.5 and Microsoft Visual Studio 2008 installed.

> NOTE
>
> *In this lab, you will see the characters XX. When you see these characters, substitute the two-digit number assigned to your computer.*

SCENARIO

You are building an application to perform mathematical calculations. You want to build security for this application with various authentication facilities such as memberships and roles.

In this lab, you will learn to secure your web application using memberships and roles. In addition, you will learn to extend data providers to create alternate data stores.

In the Lab Challenges, you will use membership objects to retrieve user data from the data store. In addition, you will implement custom data provider for an XML data store.

After completing this lab, you will be able to:

- Use Memberships
- Use Roles
- Extend Custom Providers

Estimated lab time: 140 minutes

Exercise 11.1	Implementing Security Using Memberships
Overview	You want to use membership authentication to secure your web application. To achieve this, you want to create a registration form that accepts user details and stores the data in a database. The form also provides login facilities to existing users. In this lab exercise, you will use Microsoft Visual Studio 2008. This task is complete when you are able to successfully implement security using membership authentication. To complete this lab exercise, all the student computers such as StudentXX-A and StudentXX-B must be started and must have network access.
Completion time	20 minutes

1. From the Start menu, select Microsoft Visual Studio 2008, and then select Microsoft Visual Studio 2008.

2. Select File → New Project → ASP.NET Web Application, and enter the name **Membership**.

3. Right click on your project in the Solution Explorer, select Add New Item, and add a web form. Name the form as **NewRegistration.aspx**.

4. Add the controls listed in Table 11-1 to the NewRegistration.aspx page.

Table 11-1
Controls in NewRegistration.aspx Page of Membership Application

Control	*ID*	*Properties*
TextBox	`Textbox1`	
TextBox	`Textbox2`	
Button	`Login`	Text = "Login"
Literal	`ErrorMessage`	Text = ""
TextBox	`UserName`	
TextBox	`Password`	
TextBox	`ConfirmPassword`	
TextBox	`Email`	
TextBox	`Question`	
TextBox	`Answer`	
Button	`Create`	Text = "Register"

5. Add reference to the Security namespace in the code behind page, NewRegistration.aspx.cs, as shown:

```
using System.Web.Security;
```

Question 1	*Is there any other way to implement membership?*

6. In the `Create_Click` method, add the following code:

```
protected void Create_Click(object sender, EventArgs e)
{
    try
    {
```

```
            /* Create an enumeration of type MembershipCreateStatus. The
MembershipCreateStatus describes the result returned by the
Membership.CreateUser method */
            MembershipCreateStatus Status;
            /* Call the Membership.CreateUser method to add a user and the
associated data to the data store. Note that the last parameter, Status,
holds the result returned by the CreateUser method */
            Membership.CreateUser(UserName.Text, Password.Text,
ConfirmPassword.Text, Email.Text, Answer.Text, true, out Status);
            ErrorMessage.Text = "User created successfully!";
        }
        catch (Exception ex)
        {
            ErrorMessage.Text = ex.Message.ToString();
        }
    }
```

> **NOTE** *In this code, you are creating a variable of type `MembershipCreateStatus` and calling the CreateUser static method of the `Membership` class with respective arguments.*

7. In the `Login_Click` method, add the following code:

```
protected void login_Click(object sender, EventArgs e)
 {
        /* Check if the user is a valid user by calling the
Membership.ValidateUser method */
        if (Membership.ValidateUser(TextBox1.Text, TextBox2.Text))
        {
            // Redirect the valid user to the default page.
            FormsAuthentication.RedirectFromLoginPage(TextBox1.Text,
false);
        }
        else
        {
            ErrorMessage.Text = "Invalid user credential";
        }
 }
```

Question 2	*How can you implement the status of the user into the current session?*

8. Enable membership to SqlServer using the aspnet_regsql tool as explained in these steps:

   a. Click Start → Programs → Microsoft Visual Studio 2008 → Visual Studio Tools → Visual Studio 2008 Command Prompt. A command prompt appears.

   b. Navigate to C:\WINDOWS\Microsoft.NET\Framework\v2.0.50727.

   c. Run the aspnet_regsql.exe from this location. A wizard opens as shown in Figure 11-1.

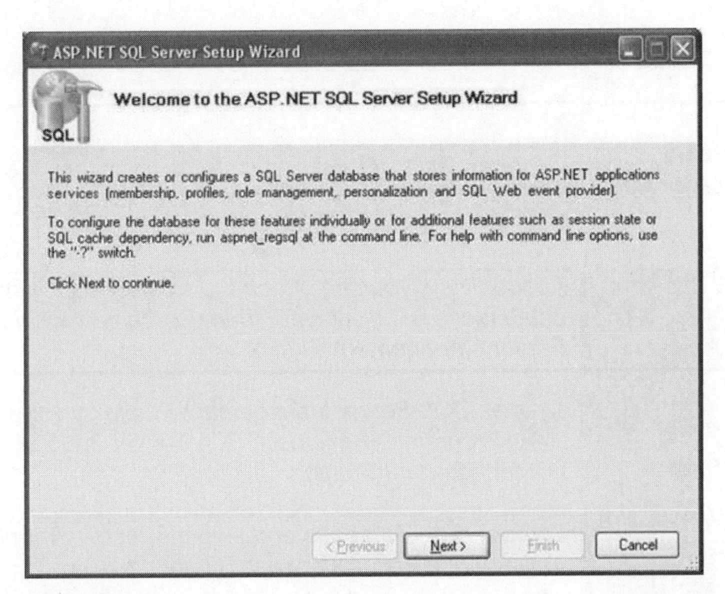

Figure 11-1
ASP.NET SQL Server Setup Wizard

   d. Choose default options. The wizard on completion creates an aspnetdb (SQL DB) for you. If you already have SQL Server 2005 Management Studio Express, open it and refresh the database node. You can see that the aspnetdb database is listed along with other databases. The aspnetdb database has some default tables in it, and these tables are empty by default. Figure 11-2 shows the SQL Server Management Studio.

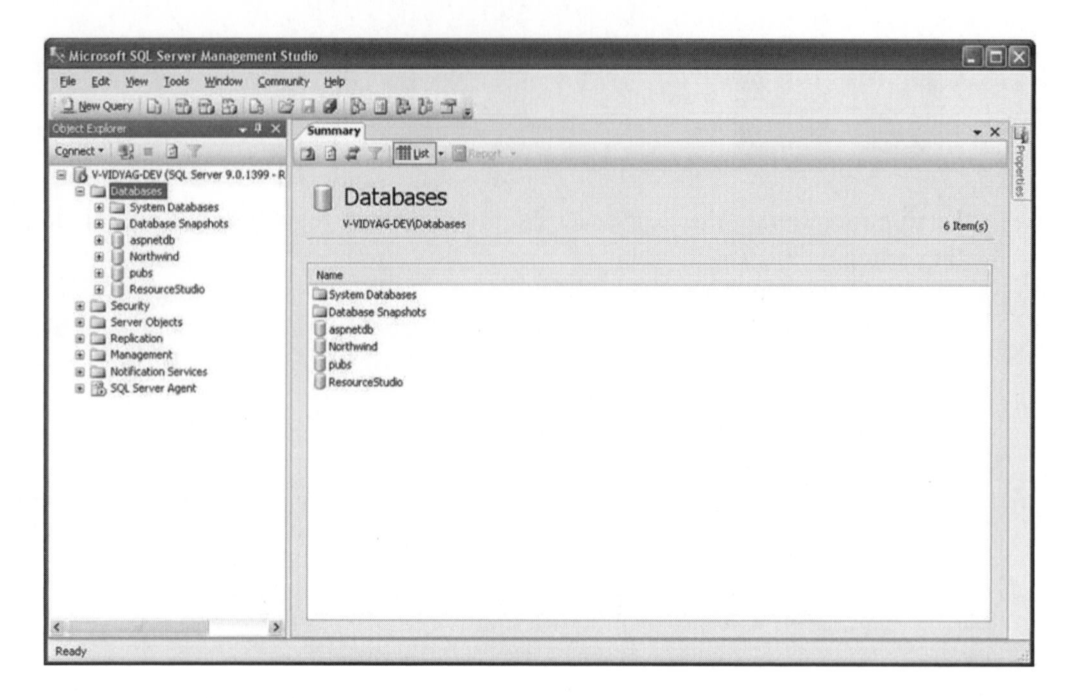

Figure 11-2
SQL Server Management Studio

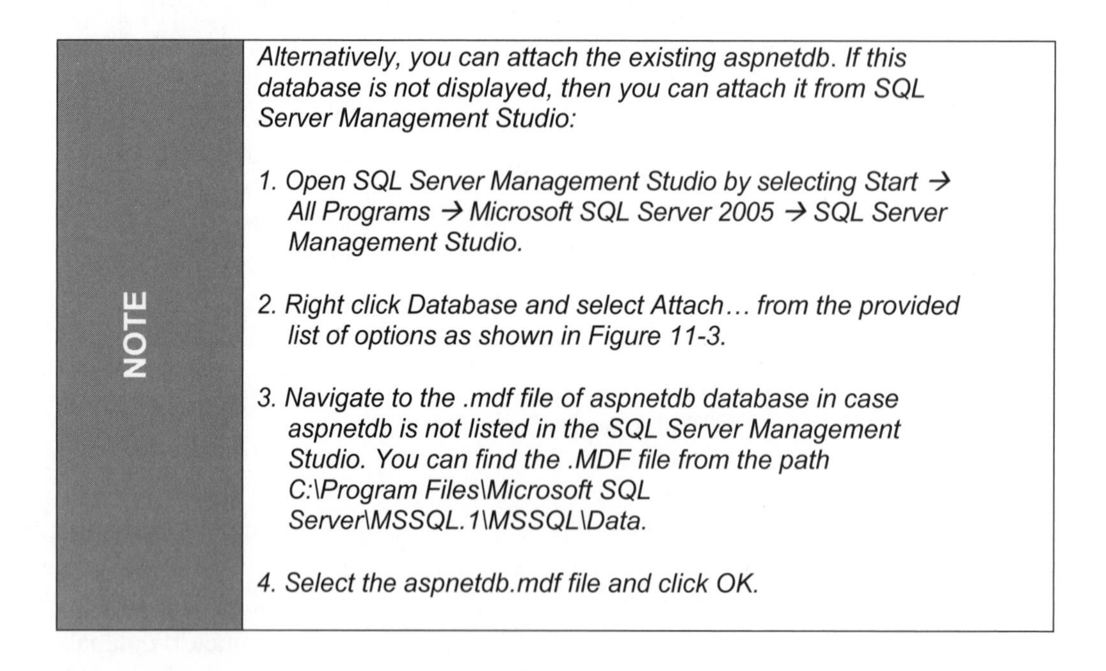

NOTE

Alternatively, you can attach the existing aspnetdb. If this database is not displayed, then you can attach it from SQL Server Management Studio:

1. *Open SQL Server Management Studio by selecting Start → All Programs → Microsoft SQL Server 2005 → SQL Server Management Studio.*
2. *Right click Database and select Attach… from the provided list of options as shown in Figure 11-3.*
3. *Navigate to the .mdf file of aspnetdb database in case aspnetdb is not listed in the SQL Server Management Studio. You can find the .MDF file from the path C:\Program Files\Microsoft SQL Server\MSSQL.1\MSSQL\Data.*
4. *Select the aspnetdb.mdf file and click OK.*

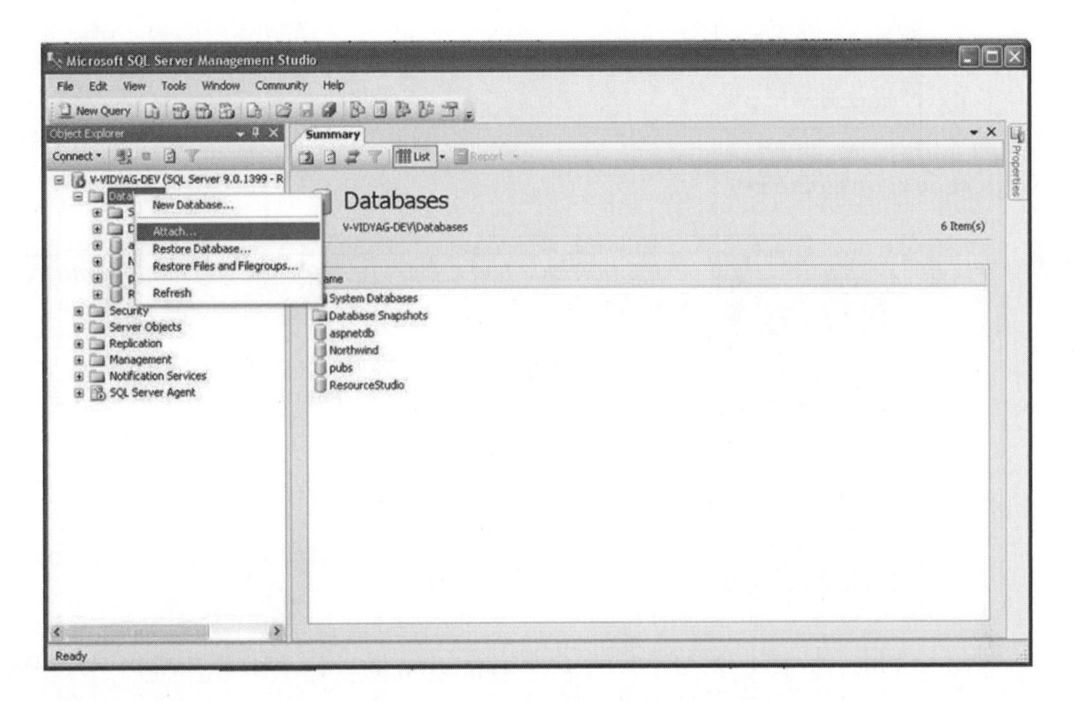

Figure 11-3
SQL Server Management Studio with the Attach Database Option Selected

9. Modify the configuration tag in the web.config file as shown:

```
<configuration>
  <appSettings/>
  <connectionStrings>
    <add name="MyMembershipConnString" connectionString="data
 source=(local);Integrated Security=SSPI;initial catalog=MyDatabase"/>
  </connectionStrings>
  <system.web>
    <compilation debug="true"/>
    <authentication mode="Forms">
      <forms loginUrl="Welcome.aspx" />
    </authentication>
    <membership defaultProvider="MyMembershipProvider">
      <providers>
        <add connectionStringName="MyMembershipConnString"
 applicationName="MyMembership"
        enablePasswordRetrieval="false" enablePasswordReset="true"
 requiresQuestionAndAnswer="true"
        requiresUniqueEmail="true" passwordFormat="Hashed"
 name="MyMembershipProvider"
        type="System.Web.Security.SqlMembershipProvider" />
```

```
      </providers>
    </membership>
  </system.web>
</configuration>
```

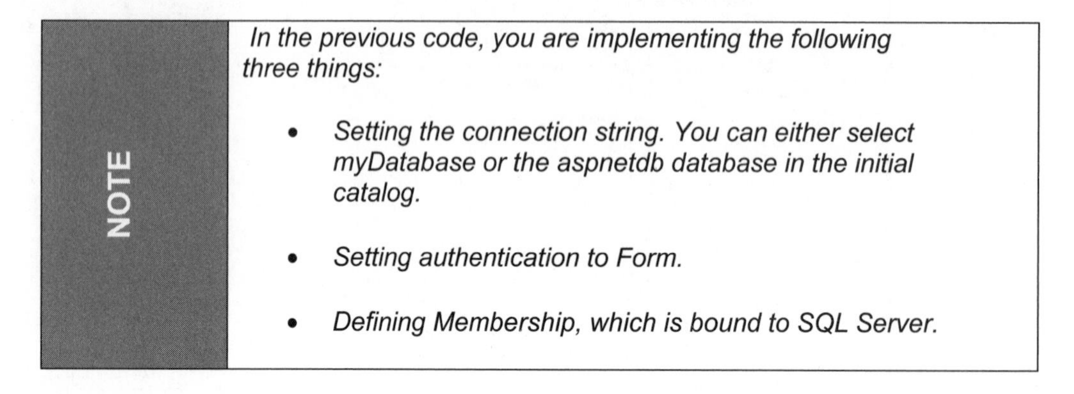

NOTE

In the previous code, you are implementing the following three things:

- Setting the connection string. You can either select myDatabase or the aspnetdb database in the initial catalog.
- Setting authentication to Form.
- Defining Membership, which is bound to SQL Server.

10. Select Project → ASP.NET Configuration as shown in Figure 11-4. A Web site Administration Tool web page appears as shown in Figure 11-5.

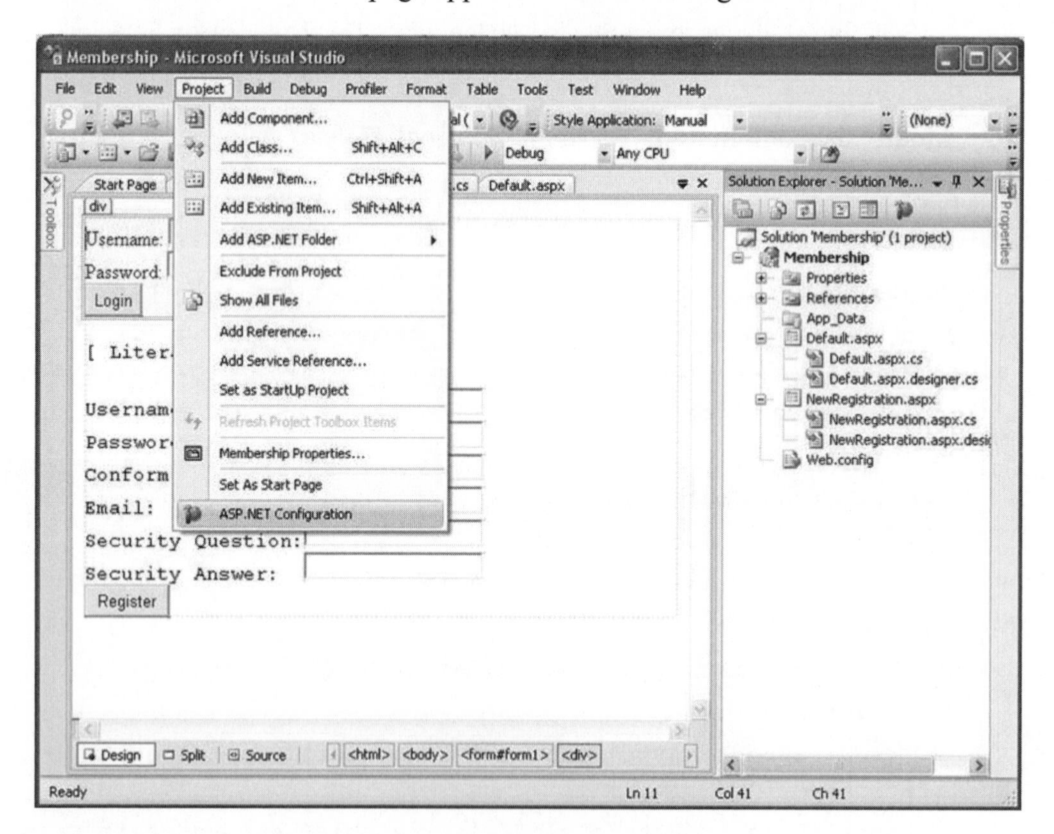

Figure 11-4
Project Menu with the ASP.NET Configuration Option Selected

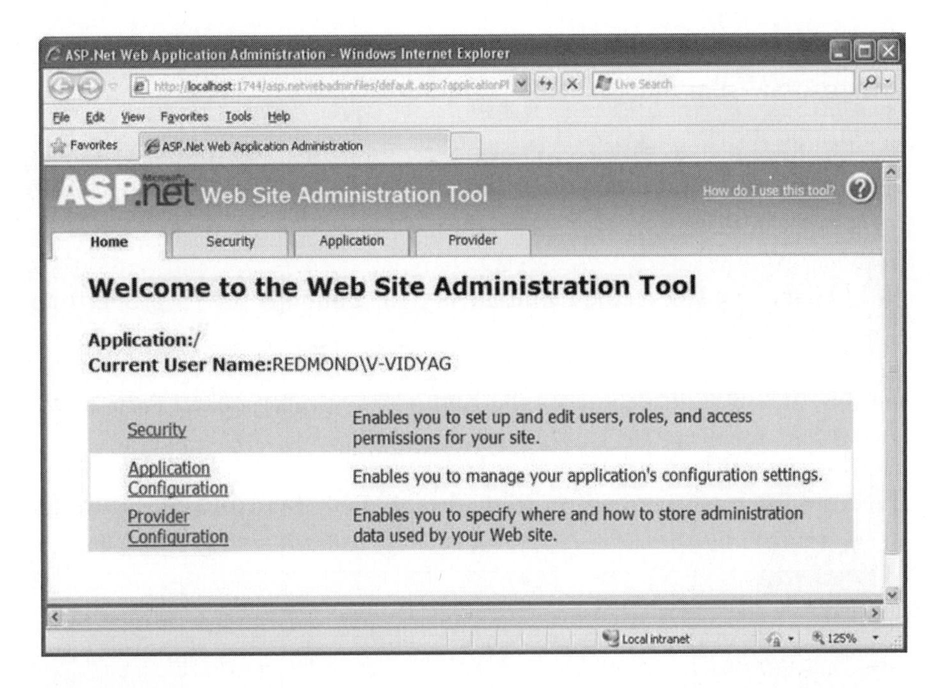

Figure 11-5
Web Site Administration Tool Web Page

11. In the Provider tab, select Advance Membership from the list.
12. Check the MyMembershipProvider radio button and click Test link.
13. Build the application by clicking on the Build menu and choosing Build Solution (ctrl+shift+B).
14. Create a new user and then use those credentials to log in.

Exercise 11.2	Implementing Security Using Roles
Overview	You are creating a web application and you want to secure it with roles authentication. In this lab exercise, you will use Microsoft Visual Studio 2008 to use roles authentication in your web application. This task is complete when you are able to implement roles authentication successfully. To complete this lab exercise, all the student computers such as StudentXX-A and StudentXX-B must be started and must have network access.
Completion time	20 minutes

1. From the Start menu, select Microsoft Visual Studio 2008, and then select Microsoft Visual Studio 2008.

2. Select File → New Project → ASP.NET Web Application, and enter the name **RoleSecurity**. Visual Studio creates a new Web site that contains the Default.aspx page.

3. Add a label control to the Default.aspx page and set its `ID` property to LabelRoleInformation.

4. Right click on your project in the Solution Explorer, select Add New Item, and add a web form named **Login.aspx**.

5. Add the Login server control to the Login.aspx page and configure its format.

Question 3	*How can you check the number of users online?*

6. Add a reference to the Security namespace in the code behind page, Default.aspx.cs, as shown:

```
using System.Web.Security;
```

7. In the `Page_Load` method, add the following code to define a `RolePrinciple` object, define a `StringBuilder` object, pass the entire properties pertaining to Role in the StringBuilder and print them one-by-one using a loop:

```
protected void Page_Load(object sender, EventArgs e)
{
    // Checks if the current user is an authenticated user
    if (User.Identity.IsAuthenticated)
    {
        /* Create a RolePrinciple object to represent the role
membership for the current user */
        RolePrincipal rp = (RolePrincipal)User;
        StringBuilder RoleInfo = new StringBuilder();
        /* Append the name of the current user to the StringBuilder
object */
        RoleInfo.AppendFormat("<h2>Welcome {0}</h2>",
rp.Identity.Name);
        /* Append the name of the role provider that stores and
retrieves the role information for the user */
```

```
            RoleInfo.AppendFormat("<b>Provider:</b> {0}<BR>",
rp.ProviderName);
            // Append the version number of the roles cookies
            RoleInfo.AppendFormat("<b>Version:</b> {0}<BR>", rp.Version);
            // Append the expiration date and time of the roles cookie
            RoleInfo.AppendFormat("<b>Expires at:</b> {0}<BR>",
rp.ExpireDate);
            RoleInfo.Append("<b>Roles:</b> ");
             /* Call the GetRoles method to get the list of role names
that the user is a member of */
            string[] roles = rp.GetRoles();
            /* Append the retrieved list of roles to the StringBuilder
object */
            for (int i = 0; i < roles.Length; i++)
            {
                if (i > 0) RoleInfo.Append(", ");
                RoleInfo.Append(roles[i]);
            }
            // Display the role information in the label control
            LabelRoleInformation.Text = RoleInfo.ToString();
        }
    }
```

> **NOTE**
> *You can view the existing provider setting from the Machine.Config file. However, you must not modify it.*

8. Modify the configuration tag in the web.config file as given here to add a new key and to define the connection string and role manager:

```
<configuration>
  <appSettings>
    <add key="EveryoneRoleName" value="Everyone" />
  </appSettings>
  <connectionStrings>
    <add name="MySqlStore" connectionString="data source=(local);Integrated
   Security=SSPI;initial catalog=MyDatabase"/>
  </connectionStrings>
  <system.web>
    <authorization>
      <deny users="?"/>
```

```
    </authorization>
    <roleManager enabled="true" cacheRolesInCookie="true"
  cookieName=".MyRolesCookie"
      defaultProvider="MySqlProvider">
      <providers>
        <add connectionStringName="MySqlStore" applicationName="RoleSecurity"
          name="MySqlProvider" type="System.Web.Security.SqlRoleProvider" />
      </providers>
    </roleManager>
    <authentication mode="Forms"/>
    <compilation debug="true">
      <assemblies>
        <add assembly="System.Configuration, Version=2.0.0.0, Culture=neutral,
  PublicKeyToken=B03F5F7F11D50A3A"/>
      </assemblies>
    </compilation>
  </system.web>
</configuration>
```

9. Select Project → ASP.NET Configuration (refer to Figure 11-4). A Web site Administration Tool web page appears (refer to Figure 11-5).

10. In the Provider tab, select the hyperlink "Select a different provider for each feature (advanced)" as shown in Figure 11-6.

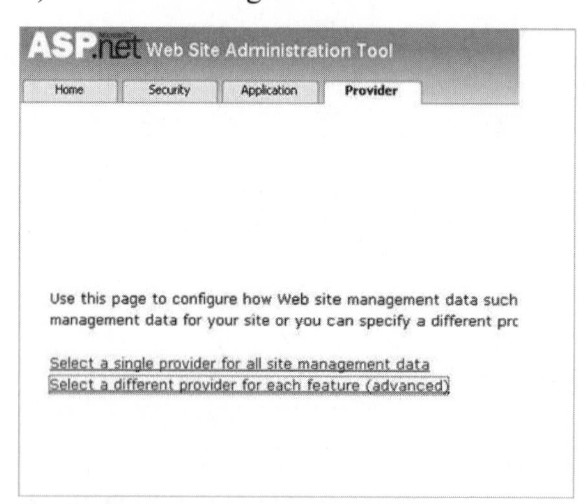

Figure 11-6
Provider Tab of the Web Site Administration Tool

11. Check the custom role provider "MySqlProvider" that you have defined in the web.config file and test it. Figure 11-7 shows the Provider tab with the MySqlProvider checked.

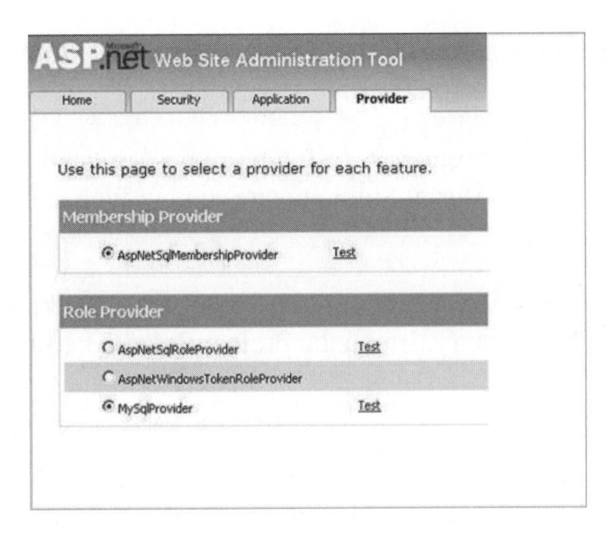

Figure 11-7
Provider Tab with the MySqlProvider Checked

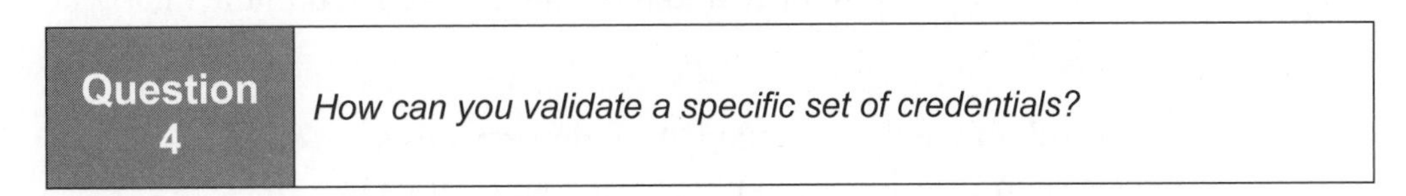

Question 4	*How can you validate a specific set of credentials?*

12. Build the application by clicking on the Build menu and choosing Build Solution (ctrl+shift+B).

13. Login with an existing user's credentials. You can use any of the user credentials created in the previous exercise. After authentication, you will be redirected to a welcome page with full specifications for this user.

Exercise 11.3	**Extending Custom Providers**
Overview	You are creating a web application in which you want to create a custom membership provider rather than storing the user credentials. In this lab exercise, you will use Microsoft Visual Studio 2008 to implement a custom membership provider. This task is complete when you are able to create a web application and implement custom membership providers to secure the application. To complete this lab exercise, all the student computers such as StudentXX-A and StudentXX-B must be started and must have network access.
Completion time	50 minutes

1. From the Start menu, select Microsoft Visual Studio 2008, and then select Microsoft Visual Studio 2008.

2. Select File → New Project → ASP.NET Web Application, and enter the name **CustomProviders**. Visual Studio creates a new Web site that contains the Default.aspx page.

3. Right click on your application in the Solution Explorer, select Add New Project which is a Class Library. Name the project **ProviderUtility**.

4. Add a reference to the System.Configuration dll to the class library. To perform this:

    a. In Solution Explorer, select the project, and right click on the References folder.

    b. Choose Add Reference and navigate to .NET tab in the dialog box that appears.

    c. Scroll down through the list of namespaces and select System.Configuration namespace and click OK.

5. Add a new class named **XmlMembershipProvider** into the ProviderUtility class library.

Question 5	*Why are you creating the `XmlMembershipProvider` class?*

6. In the XmlMembershipProvider.cs, add the following namespaces:

```
using System.Web.Security;
using System.Security.Permissions;
using ProviderUtility.utility;
```

NOTE	*You must derive the `XmlMembershipProvider` class from the MembershipProvider class to define a custom provider. When you derive from the `MembershipProvider` class, you must implement the required `MembershipProvider` members. To know which members need to be implemented in the derived class of the `MembershipProvider` class, refer to the section "Implementing a Membership Provider" in the MSDN library. This lab exercise contains the implementation of these members for a custom XmlMembership provider.*

7. Add the following code to the `XmlMembershipProvider` class:

```
public class XmlMembershipProvider : MembershipProvider
{
    // Declare the required class variables
    private string _Name;
    private string _FileName;
    private UserStore _CurrentStore = null;
    private string _ApplicationName;
    private bool _EnablePasswordReset;
    private bool _RequiresQuestionAndAnswer;
    private string _PasswordStrengthRegEx;
    private int _MaxInvalidPasswordAttempts;
    private int _MinRequiredNonAlphanumericChars;
    private int _MinRequiredPasswordLength;
    private MembershipPasswordFormat _PasswordFormat;
    private UserStore CurrentStore
    {
        get
        {
            if (_CurrentStore == null)
                _CurrentStore = UserStore.GetStore(_FileName);
            return _CurrentStore;
        }
    }
}
```

8. Override the `Initialize` method in the `XmlMembershipProvider` class using the following code to initialize the custom provider:

> **NOTE**
>
> *The following code example can be found on the Student Companion site to this book.*

```
public override void Initialize(string name,
 System.Collections.Specialized.NameValueCollection config)
{
    if (config == null)
    {
        throw new ArgumentNullException("config");
    }
    if (string.IsNullOrEmpty(name))
    {
        // Set the friendly name of the provider
        name = "XmlMembershipProvider";
    }
    if (string.IsNullOrEmpty(config["description"]))
    {          config.Remove("description");
        /* Add the new key value pair describing the custom provider to the
 configuration file */
        config.Add("description", "XML Membership Provider");
    }
    // Initialize the base class
    base.Initialize(name, config);
    // Initialize default values for the class properties
    _ApplicationName = "DefaultApp";
    _EnablePasswordReset = false;
    _PasswordStrengthRegEx = @"[\w| !§$%&/()=\-?\*]*";
    _MaxInvalidPasswordAttempts = 3;
    _MinRequiredNonAlphanumericChars = 1;
    _MinRequiredPasswordLength = 5;
    _RequiresQuestionAndAnswer = false;
    _PasswordFormat = MembershipPasswordFormat.Hashed;
    /* Now go through the settings in the configuration file and set the
 class properties accordingly */
    foreach (string key in config.Keys)
    {
```

```
    switch (key.ToLower())
    {
       case "name":
          _Name = config[key];
          break;
       case "applicationname":
          _ApplicationName = config[key];
          break;
       case "filename":
          _FileName = config[key];
          break;
       case "enablepasswordreset":
          _EnablePasswordReset = bool.Parse(config[key]);
          break;
       case "passwordstrengthregex":
          _PasswordStrengthRegEx = config[key];
          break;
       case "maxinvalidpasswordattempts":
          _MaxInvalidPasswordAttempts = int.Parse(config[key]);
          break;
       case "minrequirednonalphanumericchars":
          _MinRequiredNonAlphanumericChars = int.Parse(config[key]);
          break;
       case "minrequiredpasswordlength":
          _MinRequiredPasswordLength = int.Parse(config[key]);
          break;
       case "passwordformat":
          _PasswordFormat = (MembershipPasswordFormat)Enum.Parse(
                   typeof(MembershipPasswordFormat), config[key]);
          break;
       case "requiresquestionandanswer":
          _RequiresQuestionAndAnswer = bool.Parse(config[key]);
          break;
     }
  }
}
```

9. Define the following properties pertaining to the `Initialize` method:

> **NOTE**
> *The following code example can be found on the Student Companion site to this book.*

```
public override string ApplicationName
  {
      get
      {
          return _ApplicationName;
      }
      set
      {
          _ApplicationName = value;
          _CurrentStore = null;
      }
  }
  public override bool EnablePasswordReset
  {
      get { return _EnablePasswordReset; }
  }
  public override bool EnablePasswordRetrieval
  {
      get
      {
          if (this.PasswordFormat == MembershipPasswordFormat.Hashed)
              return false;
          else
              return true;
      }
  }
  public override int MaxInvalidPasswordAttempts
  {
      get { return _MaxInvalidPasswordAttempts; }
  }
  public override int MinRequiredNonAlphanumericCharacters
  {
      get { return _MinRequiredNonAlphanumericChars; }
```

```
}
public override int MinRequiredPasswordLength
{
    get { return _MinRequiredPasswordLength; }
}
public override int PasswordAttemptWindow
{
    get { return 20; }
}
public override MembershipPasswordFormat PasswordFormat
{
    get { return _PasswordFormat; }
}
public override string PasswordStrengthRegularExpression
{
    get
    {
        return _PasswordStrengthRegEx;
    }
}
public override bool RequiresQuestionAndAnswer
{
    get { return _RequiresQuestionAndAnswer; }
}
public override bool RequiresUniqueEmail
{
    get { return true; }
}
```

10. Define the following methods to create, delete, update, and get user details:

NOTE	*The following code example can be found on the Student Companion site to this book.*

```
    public override MembershipUser CreateUser(string username, string
password,
     string email, string passwordQuestion,
```

```
            string passwordAnswer, bool isApproved,
            object providerUserKey, out MembershipCreateStatus status)
        {
            try
            {
                // Validate the username and email
                if (!ValidateUsername(username, email, Guid.Empty))
                {
                    /* Set the status enumeration accordingly if the
validation fails */
                    status = MembershipCreateStatus.InvalidUserName;
                    return null;
                }
                // Raise the event before validating the password
                base.OnValidatingPassword(
                    new ValidatePasswordEventArgs(
                            username, password, true));
                // Validate the password
                if (!ValidatePassword(password))
                {
                    /* Set the status enumeration accordingly if the
validation fails */
                    status = MembershipCreateStatus.InvalidPassword;
                    return null;
                }
                // Everything is valid, create the user
                SimpleUser user = new SimpleUser();
                // Assign a unique key to the user
                user.UserKey = Guid.NewGuid();
                // Set the properties for the retrieved user object
                user.UserName = username;
                user.PasswordSalt = string.Empty;
                user.Password = this.TransformPassword(password, ref
user.PasswordSalt);
                user.Email = email;
                user.PasswordQuestion = passwordQuestion;
```

```
                user.PasswordAnswer = passwordAnswer;
                user.CreationDate = DateTime.Now;
                user.LastActivityDate = DateTime.Now;
                user.LastPasswordChangeDate = DateTime.Now;
                // Add the user to the store
                CurrentStore.Users.Add(user);
                CurrentStore.Save();
                status = MembershipCreateStatus.Success;
                return CreateMembershipFromInternalUser(user);
            }
            catch
            {
                throw;
            }
        }

        public override bool DeleteUser(string username, bool
deleteAllRelatedData)
        {
            try
            {
                // Retrieves the respective user from the store
                SimpleUser user = CurrentStore.GetUserByName(username);
                if (user != null)
                {
                    // If user exists delete the user from the store
                    CurrentStore.Users.Remove(user);
                    return true;
                }
                return false;
            }
            catch
            {
                throw;
            }
        }
```

```
    /* This method retrieves information for a specified username from the
data store */
    public override MembershipUser GetUser(string username, bool
userIsOnline)
    {
        try
        {
            // Create the user object for the specified user
            SimpleUser user = CurrentStore.GetUserByName(username);
            if (user != null)
            {
                // If user exists, check whether the user is online
                if (userIsOnline)
                {
                    /* Update the value of the LastActivityDate for the
user */
                    user.LastActivityDate = DateTime.Now;
                    // Save the changes to the store
                    CurrentStore.Save();
                }
                /* If user is not online, return a MembershipUser object
populated with current values from the store for the specified user */
                return CreateMembershipFromInternalUser(user);
            }
            else
            { /* If username not found in the data store, return a null
reference */
                return null;
            }
        }
        catch
        {
            throw;
        }
    }
    /* This method retrieves information from the data store for a user
based on the unique identifier of the membership user */
    public override MembershipUser GetUser(object providerUserKey, bool
userIsOnline)
```

```
        {
            try
            {
                // Create the user object for the specified user key
                SimpleUser user =
CurrentStore.GetUserByKey((Guid)providerUserKey);
                if (user != null)
                {
                    // If user exists, check whether the user is online
                    if (userIsOnline)
                    {
                        /* Update the value of the LastActivityDate for the
user */
                        user.LastActivityDate = DateTime.Now;
                        // Save the changes to the store
                        CurrentStore.Save();
                    }
                   /* If user is not online, return a MembershipUser object
populated with current values from the store for the specified user */
                    return CreateMembershipFromInternalUser(user);
                }
                else
                {
                  /* If username not found in the data store, return a null
reference */
                    return null;
                }
            }
            catch
            {
                throw;
            }
        }
        /* Get the username associated with the specified email address */
        public override string GetUserNameByEmail(string email)
        {
            try
            {
```

```
                /* Create the user object for the user associated with the
specified email address */
                SimpleUser user = CurrentStore.GetUserByEmail(email);
                              if (user != null)
                    // If user exists return the username
                    return user.UserName;
                else
                    // Else return a null reference
                    return null;
            }
            catch
            {
                throw;
            }
        }
        /* This method updates information for a specified user in the data
store */
        public override void UpdateUser(MembershipUser user)
        {
            try
            {
                // Create the user object for the specified user key
                SimpleUser suser =
CurrentStore.GetUserByKey((Guid)user.ProviderUserKey);
                if (suser != null)
                {   /* If user exists validate the user information and throw
exception accordingly */
                    if (!ValidateUsername(suser.UserName, suser.Email,
suser.UserKey))
                        throw new ArgumentException("Username and / or email
are not unique!");
                    /* If user information is valid, set the respective
properties with the supplied values */
                    suser.Email = user.Email;
                    suser.LastActivityDate = user.LastActivityDate;
                    suser.LastLoginDate = user.LastLoginDate;
                    suser.Comment = user.Comment;
                    // Save the updated information to the data store
                    CurrentStore.Save();
```

```
            }
            else
            {
                throw new ProviderException("User does not exist!");
            }
        }
        catch
        {
            throw;
        }
    }
    /* This method verifies that the specified username and password
exists in the data store */
    public override bool ValidateUser(string username, string password)
    {
        try
        {
           // Create the user object for the specified user
            SimpleUser user = CurrentStore.GetUserByName(username);
            // If user does not exist return false
            if (user == null)
                return false;
            if (ValidateUserInternal(user, password))
            {
                /* Set the LastLoginDate and LastActivityDate value for
the user */
                user.LastLoginDate = DateTime.Now;
                user.LastActivityDate = DateTime.Now;
                // Save the modified information to the data store
                CurrentStore.Save();
                return true;
            }
            else
            {
                return false;
            }
        }
        Catch
```

```
            {
                throw;
            }
        }
        // This method updates the password for a specified user
        public override bool ChangePassword(string username, string
    oldPassword, string newPassword)
        {
            try
            {
                // Get the user from the store
                SimpleUser user = CurrentStore.GetUserByName(username);
                if (user == null)
                    throw new Exception("User does not exist!");
                /* Verify whether the user's existing password matches with
    the supplied oldPassword value */
                if (ValidateUserInternal(user, oldPassword))
                {
                    // Raise the event before validating the password
                    base.OnValidatingPassword(
                        new ValidatePasswordEventArgs(
                                username, newPassword, false));
                    /* Validate whether the newPassword supplied meets the
    specified requirements */
                    if (!ValidatePassword(newPassword))
                        throw new ArgumentException("Password doesn't meet
    password strength requirements!");
                    user.PasswordSalt = string.Empty;
                    user.Password = TransformPassword(newPassword, ref
    user.PasswordSalt);
                    user.LastPasswordChangeDate = DateTime.Now;
                    // Save the new password in the store
                    CurrentStore.Save();
                    return true;
                }
                return false;
            }
            catch
            {
```

```
            throw;
        }
    }
    /* This method updates the password question and answer for a
specified user */
    public override bool ChangePasswordQuestionAndAnswer(string username,
string password, string newPasswordQuestion, string newPasswordAnswer)
    {
        try
        {
            // Get the user from the store
            SimpleUser user = CurrentStore.GetUserByName(username);
            if (ValidateUserInternal(user, password))
            {
               // Set the password question and answer for the user
                user.PasswordQuestion = newPasswordQuestion;
                user.PasswordAnswer = newPasswordAnswer;
                // Save the changes in the data store
                CurrentStore.Save();
                return true;
            }
            return false;
        }
        catch
        {
            throw;
        }
    }
    /* This method returns a list of membership users where the user's e-
mail address matches the supplied email address */
    public override MembershipUserCollection FindUsersByEmail(string
emailToMatch, int pageIndex, int pageSize, out int totalRecords)
    {
        try
        {
            /* Create a List object to store the list of users from the
store */
            List<SimpleUser> matchingUsers =
                CurrentStore.Users.FindAll(delegate(SimpleUser user)
```

```
                    {
                        return user.Email.Equals(emailToMatch,
StringComparison.OrdinalIgnoreCase);
                    });
                totalRecords = matchingUsers.Count;
                // Return the collection of matching users list
                return
CreateMembershipCollectionFromInternalList(matchingUsers);
            }
            catch
            {
                throw;
            }
        }
       /* This method returns a list of membership users where the username
matches the supplied usernameToMatch */
        public override MembershipUserCollection FindUsersByName(string
usernameToMatch, int pageIndex, int pageSize, out int totalRecords)
        {
            try
            {
                /* Create a List object to store the list of users from the
store */
                List<SimpleUser> matchingUsers =
                    CurrentStore.Users.FindAll(delegate(SimpleUser user)
                    {
                        return user.UserName.Equals(usernameToMatch,
StringComparison.OrdinalIgnoreCase);
                    });
                totalRecords = matchingUsers.Count;
                //Return the collection of matching users list
                return
CreateMembershipCollectionFromInternalList(matchingUsers);
            }
            catch
            {
                throw;
            }
        }
```

```
     /* This method returns a list of all of the users from the data store
*/
     public override MembershipUserCollection GetAllUsers(int pageIndex,
int pageSize, out int totalRecords)
     {
          try
          {
               totalRecords = CurrentStore.Users.Count;
               // Return the collection of users list
               return
CreateMembershipCollectionFromInternalList(CurrentStore.Users);
          }
          catch
          {
               throw;
          }
     }
     /* This method retrieves the number of users currently accessing the
application */
     public override int GetNumberOfUsersOnline()
     {
          // Declare an integer to track the number of online users
          int ret = 0;
          foreach (SimpleUser user in CurrentStore.Users)
          {
               // Check whether the LastActivityDate for this user is greater
than the current date and time minus the UserIsOnlineTimeWindow
               if (user.LastActivityDate.AddMinutes(
                        Membership.UserIsOnlineTimeWindow) >= DateTime.Now)
               {
                    // If the above condition is yes, increment the user
counter
                    ret++;
               }
          }
          return ret;
     }
     /* This method retrieves the password for the specified user from the
data store */
```

```
    public override string GetPassword(string username, string answer)
    {
        try
        {
            // Check if EnablePasswordRetrieval flag is true
            if (EnablePasswordRetrieval)
            {
                // Get the user from the store
                SimpleUser user = CurrentStore.GetUserByName(username);
                // Check the password answer with the supplied value
                if (answer.Equals(user.PasswordAnswer,
StringComparison.OrdinalIgnoreCase))
                {
                    // If the answer matches, return the user password
                    return user.Password;
                }
                else
                {
                    throw new
System.Web.Security.MembershipPasswordException();
                }
            }
            else
            {
                throw new Exception("Password retrieval is not enabled!");
            }
        }
        catch
        {
            throw;
        }
    }
    /* This method resets the password for a specified user in the data
store */
    public override string ResetPassword(string username, string answer)
    {
        try
        {
```

```
            // Get the user from the data store
            SimpleUser user = CurrentStore.GetUserByName(username);
            // Check the password answer with the supplied value
            if (user.PasswordAnswer.Equals(answer,
StringComparison.OrdinalIgnoreCase))
            {
                byte[] NewPassword = new byte[16];
                RandomNumberGenerator rng =
RandomNumberGenerator.Create();
                rng.GetBytes(NewPassword);
                string NewPasswordString =
Convert.ToBase64String(NewPassword);
                user.PasswordSalt = string.Empty;
                user.Password = TransformPassword(NewPasswordString, ref
user.PasswordSalt);
                // Save the new password in the data store
                CurrentStore.Save();
                return NewPasswordString;
            }
            else
            {
                throw new Exception("Invalid answer entered!");
            }
        }
        catch
        {
            throw;
        }
    }
    public override bool UnlockUser(string userName)
    {
        // This provider doesn't support locking
        return true;
    }
```

11. Define the following helper methods such as validate user, validate password, lock, password reset, and so on to provide additional functionalities as follows:

```
 /* This method transform user's password in the format as specified in
the MembershipPasswordFormat */
```

```
        private string TransformPassword(string password, ref string salt)
        {
            string ret = string.Empty;
            switch (PasswordFormat)
            {
                case MembershipPasswordFormat.Clear:
                    ret = password;
                    break;
                case MembershipPasswordFormat.Hashed:
                    // Generate the salt if not passed in
                    if (string.IsNullOrEmpty(salt))
                    {
                        byte[] saltBytes = new byte[16];
                        RandomNumberGenerator rng =
    RandomNumberGenerator.Create();
                        rng.GetBytes(saltBytes);
                        salt = Convert.ToBase64String(saltBytes);
                    }
                    // Hash the password with salt
                    ret =
    FormsAuthentication.HashPasswordForStoringInConfigFile(
                                                    (salt + password), "SHA1");
                    break;
                case MembershipPasswordFormat.Encrypted:
                    // Encrypt the password with UTF8 encoding
                    byte[] ClearText = Encoding.UTF8.GetBytes(password);
                    byte[] EncryptedText = base.EncryptPassword(ClearText);
                    ret = Convert.ToBase64String(EncryptedText);
                    break;
            }
            return ret;
        }
        // This method validates the specified user information
        private bool ValidateUsername(string userName, string email, Guid
    excludeKey)
        {
            bool IsValid = true;
            // Get the custom store
```

```
        UserStore store = UserStore.GetStore(_FileName);
        foreach (SimpleUser user in store.Users)
        {
            if (user.UserKey.CompareTo(excludeKey) != 0)
            {
                // Check if the specified username exists
                if (string.Equals(user.UserName, userName,
StringComparison.OrdinalIgnoreCase))
                {
                    IsValid = false;
                    break;
                }
                // Check if the user email address exists
                if (string.Equals(user.Email, email,
StringComparison.OrdinalIgnoreCase))
                {
                    IsValid = false;
                    break;
                }
            }
        }
        return IsValid;
    }
    /* This method validates whether the user's password is in a valid
format */
    private bool ValidatePassword(string password)
    {
        bool IsValid = true;
        Regex HelpExpression;
        // Validate simple properties
        IsValid = IsValid && (password.Length >=
this.MinRequiredPasswordLength);
        // Validate nonalphanumeric characters
        HelpExpression = new Regex(@"\W");
        IsValid = IsValid && (HelpExpression.Matches(password).Count >=
this.MinRequiredNonAlphanumericCharacters);
        // Validate regular expression
        HelpExpression = new
Regex(this.PasswordStrengthRegularExpression);
```

```
            IsValid = IsValid && (HelpExpression.Matches(password).Count > 0);
            return IsValid;
        }
        /* This method checks the password for the specified user, stored in
the data store with the supplied password */
         private bool ValidateUserInternal(SimpleUser user, string password)
        {
            if (user != null)
            {
                // Transform the supplied password in the specified format
                string passwordValidate = TransformPassword(password, ref
user.PasswordSalt);
                /* Compare the transformed password with the user's password
stored in the data store */
                if (string.Compare(passwordValidate, user.Password) == 0)
                {
                    return true;
                }
            }
            return false;
        }
        /* This method returns a MembershipUser object populated with
information for the specified user */
        private MembershipUser CreateMembershipFromInternalUser(SimpleUser
user)
        {
            MembershipUser muser = new MembershipUser(base.Name,
                user.UserName, user.UserKey, user.Email,
user.PasswordQuestion, string.Empty, true, false, user.CreationDate,
user.LastLoginDate, user.LastActivityDate, user.LastPasswordChangeDate,
DateTime.MaxValue);
            return muser;
        }
        // This method returns a MembershipUserCollection object
        private MembershipUserCollection
CreateMembershipCollectionFromInternalList(List<SimpleUser> users)
        {
            MembershipUserCollection ReturnCollection = new
MembershipUserCollection();
            foreach (SimpleUser user in users)
```

```
        {
            ReturnCollection.Add(CreateMembershipFromInternalUser(user));
        }
        return ReturnCollection;
    }
```

12. Build the application by clicking on the Build menu and choosing Build Solution (ctrl+shift+B).

Question 6	*Is there any serialization happening when you develop a custom provider? If yes, then specify the type of serialization?*

13. Add a folder named **utility** to the ProviderUtility class library and add two class files named **SimpleUser.cs** and **UserStore.cs** inside the Utility folder.

14. Open the SimpleUser.cs class and add the following code that defines some variables:

```
namespace ProviderUtility.utility
{
  public class SimpleUser
  {
    public Guid UserKey = Guid.Empty;
    public string UserName = "";
    public string Password = "";
    public string PasswordSalt = "";
    public string Email = "";
    public DateTime CreationDate = DateTime.Now;
    public DateTime LastActivityDate = DateTime.MinValue;
    public DateTime LastLoginDate = DateTime.MinValue;
    public DateTime LastPasswordChangeDate = DateTime.MinValue;
    public string PasswordQuestion = "";
    public string PasswordAnswer = "";
    public string Comment;
  }
}
```

15. Open the UserStore.cs class and add the following code:

> **NOTE**
> *The following code example can be found on the Student Companion site to this book.*

```
Namespace ProviderUtility.utility
{
 public class UserStore
 {
     private string _FileName;
     private List<SimpleUser> _Users;
     private XmlSerializer _Serializer;
     #region "Singleton implementation"
     private static Dictionary<string, UserStore> _RegisteredStores;
     // Constructor
     private UserStore(string fileName)
     {
         _FileName = fileName;
         _Users = new List<SimpleUser>();
         _Serializer = new XmlSerializer(typeof(List<SimpleUser>));
         LoadStore(_FileName);
     }
     // This method returns the store
     public static UserStore GetStore(string fileName)
     {
         // Create the registered stores
         if (_RegisteredStores == null)
             _RegisteredStores = new Dictionary<string, UserStore>();
         // Now return the approprate store
         if (!_RegisteredStores.ContainsKey(fileName))
         {
             _RegisteredStores.Add(fileName, new UserStore(fileName));
         }
         return _RegisteredStores[fileName];
     }
     #endregion
     #region "Private Helper Methods"
     // This method loads the specified XML file
```

```
    private void LoadStore(string fileName)
    {
        try
        {
            if (System.IO.File.Exists(fileName))
            {
                using (XmlTextReader reader = new XmlTextReader(fileName))
                {
                    _Users =
(List<SimpleUser>)_Serializer.Deserialize(reader);
                }
            }
        }
        catch (Exception ex)
        {
            throw new Exception(
                string.Format("Unable to load file {0}", fileName), ex);
        }
    }
    // This method saves the file
    private void SaveStore(string fileName)
    {
        try
        {
            if (System.IO.File.Exists(fileName))
                System.IO.File.Delete(fileName);
            using (XmlTextWriter writer = new XmlTextWriter(fileName,
Encoding.UTF8))
            {
                _Serializer.Serialize(writer, _Users);
            }
        }
        catch (Exception ex)
        {
            throw new Exception(
                string.Format("Unable to save file {0}", fileName), ex);
        }
    }
```

```
        #endregion
        public List<SimpleUser> Users
        {
            get { return _Users; }
        }

        public void Save()
        {
            SaveStore(_FileName);
        }
        // This method returns a matching SimpleUser object
        public SimpleUser GetUserByName(string name)
        {
            return _Users.Find(delegate(SimpleUser user)
                    {
                        return string.Equals(name, user.UserName);
                    });
        }
        /* This method returns a matching SimpleUser object for the specified
    email address */
        public SimpleUser GetUserByEmail(string email)
        {
            return _Users.Find(delegate(SimpleUser user)
                    {
                        return string.Equals(email, user.Email);
                    });
        }
        /* This method returns a matching SimpleUser object for the specified
    user key */
        public SimpleUser GetUserByKey(Guid key)
        {
            return _Users.Find(delegate(SimpleUser user)
            {
                return (user.UserKey.CompareTo(key) == 0);
            });
        }
     }
    }
```

16. Build the whole class library and save the library.

> **NOTE**
> *You have to create another project to test the custom provider created earlier.*

17. Right click on your application in the Solution Explorer, select Add New Project, and name the project **TestXMLProvider**.

18. Add the following code to the design view of the Default.aspx page in the TestXMLProvider project.

19. Open the default.aspx.cs code behind file and add code to the `PostBackCommand_OnClick` event handler as follows:

```
protected void PostbackCommand_OnClick(object sender, EventArgs e)
{
    ResultsLabel.Text = DateTime.Now.ToLongTimeString();
}
```

20. Right click on the TestXmlProvider project and add a new web form named **CreateTest.aspx**.

21. Open the CreateTest.aspx page in design mode and drag a `CreateUserWizard` web server control and provide the settings as given:

> **NOTE**
> *The following code example can be found on the Student Companion site to this book.*

```
  <asp:CreateUserWizard ID="CreateUserWizard1" runat="server"
LoginCreatedUser="False"
OnContinueButtonClick="CreateUserWizard1_ContinueButtonClick">
        <WizardSteps>
            <asp:CreateUserWizardStep ID="CreateUserWizardStep1"
runat="server">
                <ContentTemplate>
                    <table border="0">
                        <tr>
                            <td style="background-color:red"
align="center" colspan="2">
```

```
                                    Sign Up for Your New Account</td>
                            </tr>
                            <tr>
                                <td align="right">
                                    <asp:Label ID="UserNameLabel"
runat="server" AssociatedControlID="UserName">User
                                    Name:</asp:Label>
                                </td>
                                <td>
                                    <asp:TextBox ID="UserName"
runat="server"></asp:TextBox>
                                    <asp:RequiredFieldValidator
ID="UserNameRequired" runat="server"
                                        ControlToValidate="UserName"
ErrorMessage="User Name is required."
                                        ToolTip="User Name is required."
ValidationGroup="CreateUserWizard1">*</asp:RequiredFieldValidator>
                                </td>
                            </tr>
                            <tr>
                                <td align="right">
                                    <asp:Label ID="PasswordLabel"
runat="server" AssociatedControlID="Password">Password:</asp:Label>
                                </td>
                                <td>
                                    <asp:TextBox ID="Password" runat="server"
TextMode="Password"></asp:TextBox>
                                    <asp:RequiredFieldValidator
ID="PasswordRequired" runat="server"
                                        ControlToValidate="Password"
ErrorMessage="Password is required."
                                        ToolTip="Password is required."
ValidationGroup="CreateUserWizard1">*</asp:RequiredFieldValidator>
                                </td>
                            </tr>
                            <tr>
                                <td align="right">
                                    <asp:Label ID="ConfirmPasswordLabel"
runat="server"
```

```
AssociatedControlID="ConfirmPassword">Confirm Password:</asp:Label>
                                </td>
                                <td>
                                    <asp:TextBox ID="ConfirmPassword"
runat="server" TextMode="Password"></asp:TextBox>
                                    <asp:RequiredFieldValidator
ID="ConfirmPasswordRequired" runat="server"
                                        ControlToValidate="ConfirmPassword"
                                        ErrorMessage="Confirm Password is
required."
                                        ToolTip="Confirm Password is
required."
ValidationGroup="CreateUserWizard1">*</asp:RequiredFieldValidator>
                                </td>
                            </tr>
                            <tr>
                                <td align="right">
                                    <asp:Label ID="EmailLabel" runat="server"
AssociatedControlID="Email">E-mail:</asp:Label>
                                </td>
                                <td>
                                    <asp:TextBox ID="Email"
runat="server"></asp:TextBox>
                                    <asp:RequiredFieldValidator
ID="EmailRequired" runat="server"
                                        ControlToValidate="Email"
ErrorMessage="E-mail is required."
                                        ToolTip="E-mail is required."
ValidationGroup="CreateUserWizard1">*</asp:RequiredFieldValidator>
                                </td>
                            </tr>
                            <tr>
                                <td align="right">
                                    <asp:Label ID="QuestionLabel"
runat="server" AssociatedControlID="Question">Security
                                    Question:</asp:Label>
                                </td>
                                <td>
```

```
                                    <asp:TextBox ID="Question"
runat="server"></asp:TextBox>
                                    <asp:RequiredFieldValidator
ID="QuestionRequired" runat="server"
                                        ControlToValidate="Question"
ErrorMessage="Security question is required."
                                        ToolTip="Security question is
required."
ValidationGroup="CreateUserWizard1">*</asp:RequiredFieldValidator>
                                </td>
                            </tr>
                            <tr>
                                <td align="right">
                                    <asp:Label ID="AnswerLabel" runat="server"
AssociatedControlID="Answer">Security
                                    Answer:</asp:Label>
                                </td>
                                <td>
                                    <asp:TextBox ID="Answer"
runat="server"></asp:TextBox>
                                    <asp:RequiredFieldValidator
ID="AnswerRequired" runat="server"
                                        ControlToValidate="Answer"
ErrorMessage="Security answer is required."
                                        ToolTip="Security answer is required."
ValidationGroup="CreateUserWizard1">*</asp:RequiredFieldValidator>
                                </td>
                            </tr>
                            <tr>
                                <td align="center" colspan="2">
                                    <asp:CompareValidator ID="PasswordCompare"
runat="server"
                                        ControlToCompare="Password"
ControlToValidate="ConfirmPassword"
                                        Display="Dynamic"
                                        ErrorMessage="The Password and
Confirmation Password must match."

ValidationGroup="CreateUserWizard1"></asp:CompareValidator>
                                </td>
                            </tr>
```

```
                        <tr>
                            <td align="center" colspan="2"
style="color:Red;">
                                <asp:Literal ID="ErrorMessage"
runat="server" EnableViewState="False"></asp:Literal>
                            </td>
                        </tr>
                    </table>
                </ContentTemplate>
            </asp:CreateUserWizardStep>
            <asp:CompleteWizardStep ID="CompleteWizardStep1"
runat="server">
            </asp:CompleteWizardStep>
        </WizardSteps>
    </asp:CreateUserWizard>
```

22. Switch to the CreateTest.aspx.cs code behind file and add a `ContinueButtonClick` handler for the wizard control as follows:

```
 protected void CreateUserWizard1_ContinueButtonClick(object sender,
EventArgs e)
 {
     // Redirect the user to the CreateTest.aspx page
     Response.Redirect("CreateTest.aspx");
 }
```

23. Open the web.config file and add this code below the `<system.web>` node as follows:

```
 <membership defaultProvider="XmlMembership">
         <providers>
                <add name="XmlMembership" applicationName="MyTestApp"
fileName="MyTestApp_Users.config"
type="ProviderUtility.XmlMembershipProvider, ProviderUtility"
requiresQuestionAndAnswer="true"/>
         </providers>
   </membership>
```

24. Build the entire solution once again, and then set the CreateTest.aspx page as the start page. Create a new user.

25. Reset the start page to Default.aspx. View the login box, enter the user credentials, and verify the output.

LAB REVIEW QUESTIONS

Completion time	**15 minutes**

1. What is the difference between authentication and authorization?
2. How are roles cached?
3. How is a custom data provider class used?

LAB CHALLENGE 11.1: RETRIEVING USER DATA

Completion time	**15 minutes**

Create an application to retrieve the details of all members from a sqlserver store and display them in a grid view.

LAB CHALLENGE 11.2: IMPLEMENTING A CUSTOM DATA PROVIDER

Completion time	**20 minutes**

Consider that you must implement a custom provider to store user credentials in an XML data store. You want to manipulate records stored in an XML file by searching, deleting users, and so on. How will you implement this?

LAB 12
PROTECTING WEB APPLICATIONS

This lab contains the following exercises and activities:

Exercise 12.1	Configuring Security
Exercise 12.2	Protecting Web Applications from Vulnerabilities
Exercise 12.3	Protecting Sensitive Information
Lab Review Questions	
Lab Challenge 12.1	Implementing a Custom Authentication Scheme
Lab Challenge 12.2	Manipulating Authentication Settings

BEFORE YOU BEGIN

Lab 12 assumes that the lab setup has been completed as specified in the setup document and that StudentXX-A, StudentXX-B, and StudentXX-C computers have Microsoft .NET Framework 3.5 and Microsoft Visual Studio 2008 installed.

> **NOTE**
> *In this lab, you will see the characters XX. When you see these characters, substitute the two-digit number assigned to your computer.*

SCENARIO

You are building an application to perform mathematical calculations. You want to configure security for this application.

In this lab, you will learn to configure security for your web application to protect your application from security vulnerabilities and intruders.

In the Lab Challenges, you will create a custom authentication scheme. In addition, you will manipulate authentication settings.

After completing this lab, you will be able to:

- Configure security
- Protect web applications from vulnerabilities
- Protect sensitive information
- Manipulate authentication settings

Estimated lab time: 95 minutes

Exercise 12.1	Configuring Security
Overview	You want to authenticate user credentials in your web application using forms authentication. In this lab exercise, you will use Microsoft Visual Studio 2008. This task is complete when you are able to successfully authenticate users of your web application using forms authentication. To complete this lab exercise, all the student computers such as StudentXX-A and StudentXX-B must be started and must have network access.
Completion time	15 minutes

1. From the Start menu, select Microsoft Visual Studio 2008, and then select Microsoft Visual Studio 2008.
2. Select File → New Project → ASP.NET Web Application, and enter the name **ConfigurationSecurity**.

3. Right click on your project in the Solution Explorer, select Add a New Item, and add a web form named **Login.aspx**.

4. Add the controls given in Table 12-1 to the Login.aspx page.

Table 12-1
Controls in Login.aspx Page of ConfigurationSecurity Application

Control	*ID*	*Properties*
TextBox	Textbox1	
TextBox	Textbox2	
Button	Button1	Text = Login

5. Add a reference to the Security namespace in the code behind pages, login.aspx.cs, and Default.aspx.cs, as shown:

```
using System.Web.Security;
```

6. Add a reference to the `System.Security.Principal` namespace in the Default.aspx.cs file as shown:

```
using System.Security.Principal;
```

7. Add the following code to the `Click` events handler of the Button1 button control to validate the user credentials:

```
protected void Button1_Click(object sender, EventArgs e)
{
        // Check if the supplied username and password are valid
        if (FormsAuthentication.Authenticate(TextBox1.Text,
TextBox2.Text))
        {
            // If the credentials are valid, redirect the logged in user to
the default URL as specified in the web.config file
            FormsAuthentication.RedirectFromLoginPage(TextBox1.Text, true);
        }
        else
        {
            // If the credentials are invalid, display a suitable message
to the user
            Response.Write("Invalid credentials");
```

```
        }
    }
```

8. Open the Default.aspx page in the design mode. Drag a label and button control to the form and set their ID properties to Label1 and SignOut, respectively.

9. In the `Click` handler for the SignOut button control in the Default.aspx page, add the following code to log the user out:

```
protected void SignOut_Click(object sender, EventArgs e)
{
    // Call the SignOut method to clear the forms authentication
ticket information
    FormsAuthentication.SignOut();
    // Redirect the user to the login page
    FormsAuthentication.RedirectToLoginPage();
}
```

10. In the `Load` handler for the Default.aspx page, add the following code to display various information about the Windows identity for the current user:

```
protected void Page_Load(object sender, EventArgs e)
{
    // Display the name of the currently logged in user in the Label1
label control
    Label1.Text = User.Identity.Name.ToString();
    // Get the Windows identity for the current user
    WindowsIdentity AuthUser = WindowsIdentity.GetCurrent();
    // Display the authentication type used to identify the current
user; the impersonation level for the current user; whether the user
account is an anonymous account, guest account, or system account and is
authenticated by Windows and the user's Windows log on name
    Response.Write(AuthUser.AuthenticationType.ToString() + "<br>" +
AuthUser.ImpersonationLevel.ToString() + "<br>" +
AuthUser.IsAnonymous.ToString() + "<br>" +
AuthUser.IsAuthenticated.ToString() + "<br>" +
AuthUser.IsGuest.ToString() + "<br>" +
AuthUser.IsSystem.ToString() + "<br>" +
AuthUser.Name.ToString());
}
```

> **NOTE**
> *You must define the authentication mode as Forms in the web.config file as shown next.*

11. Open the web.config file and add the given setting just below the `<Compilation>` tag to enable forms authentication to log users into the application. Note that the authorization element in the given setting specifies that user Steve is allowed access to resources in this application and user Bill is denied access to resources in this application:

```
<authentication mode="Forms">
<forms
   name=".ASPXAUTH"
   loginUrl="Login.aspx"
   defaultUrl="default.aspx"
   protection="All"
   timeout="30"
   path="/"
   requireSSL="false"
   slidingExpiration="true"
   cookieless="UseDeviceProfile" domain=""
   enableCrossAppRedirects="false">
  <credentials passwordFormat="Clear">
    <user name="Bill" password="Gates" />
    <user name="Steve" password="Balmer" />
  </credentials>
</forms>

</authentication>
<authorization>
    <deny users ="Bill" />
    <allow users="Steve" />
</authorization>
```

> **Question 1**
> *Define the meaning of "*" and "?" in allow and deny tags.*

12. Build the application by clicking on the Build menu and choosing Build Solution (ctrl+shift+B).

13. Enter a user ID and password configured in the web.config file and see the result displayed in the Default.aspx page. If you enter a valid username and password as specified in the web.config file, the page will successfully postback. On the other hand, if you enter credentials other than the ones specified in the web.config file, you will see the message "Invalid credentials."

> **NOTE**
> *You can bar all users from using the application:*
>
> ```
> <deny users = "*">
> ```

Exercise 12.2	Protecting Web Applications from Vulnerabilities
Overview	You want to protect your web application from vulnerability or security exploits executed by an intruder. In this lab exercise, you will use Microsoft Visual Studio 2008 to protect a web application from security vulnerabilities. This task is complete when you are able to secure your application from intruders successfully. To complete this lab exercise, all the student computers such as StudentXX-A and StudentXX-B must be started and must have network access.
Completion time	15 minutes

1. From the Start menu, select Microsoft Visual Studio 2008, and then select Microsoft Visual Studio 2008.

2. Select File → New Project → ASP.NET Web Application, and enter the name **VulProtection**. Visual Studio creates a new Web site that contains the Default.aspx page.

3. Add the controls given in Table 12-2 to the Default.aspx page.

Table 12-2
Controls in Default.aspx Page of VulProtection Application

Control	*ID*	*Properties*
TextBox	txtZip	
RegularExpressionValidator	RegularExpressionValidator1	ControlToValidate = "txtZip" ValidationExpression = "\d{5}" Display = "Static" EnableClientScript = "false" ErrorMessage = "ZIP Code must be 5 numeric digits"
Button	show	Text = Show
Label	lblOutput	Autoassociateid = "txtZip"
GridView	GridView1	

> **NOTE** *Because this application retrieves data from the database, it is prone to SQL injection attacks. To avoid injection attacks, you should use an ASP.NET validator control such as the RegularExpressionValidator control to constrain input in the txtZip field. The RegularExpressionValidator control in this case, restricts the zip code field to contain only 5 digit values.*

4. Add references to the various namespaces in the code behind page Default.aspx.cs as shown:

```
using System.Web.Security;
using System.Security.Cryptography;
using System.Web.Configuration;
using System.Data.SqlClient;
```

5. Add the following code to the `Page_Load` method of the default.aspx.cs file to secure the sensitive data using GUID and encryption:

```
protected void Page_Load(object sender, EventArgs e)
{
    if (!Page.IsPostBack)
    {
        // Store the guid in the view state
        ViewState["token"] = new Guid();
```

```
                // Open the Web application configuration file using the
ASP.NET application's virtual application root path on the server
                Configuration config =
WebConfigurationManager.OpenWebConfiguration(Request.ApplicationPath);
                // Get the connection strings section
                ConfigurationSection section =
config.GetSection("connectionStrings");
                // Check whether the connection strings section is protected
                if (section != null &&
!section.SectionInformation.IsProtected)
                {
                    // If the section is not protected, encrypt the section to
protect the connection details from unauthorized access
                    section.SectionInformation.ProtectSection
("DataProtectionConfigurationProvider");
                    // Save the section
                    config.Save();
                }
            }
        }
```

NOTE

The value you pass for the `GetSection` method must be the same as in the corresponding web.config file entry.

6. In the `show_Click` method, add the functionality to retrieve data from the database as follows:

```
protected void show_Click(object sender, EventArgs e)
{
    if (Page.IsValid)
    {
        // HtmlEncode the supplied zip code to limit the user input by
converting the characters such as blanks and punctuation if any, into
character entity equivalents. Also convert the single quotation mark into
double quotes in the supplied value. This avoids any malicious SQL command
to be executed against the database.
        string
inputZip=System.Web.HttpUtility.HtmlEncode(txtZip.Text.Replace("'","''"));
        // Get the connection string from the web.config file
```

```
            string ConectionString =
WebConfigurationManager.ConnectionStrings["conString"].ConnectionString;
            // Create a SqlConnection object for the specified connection
string
            SqlConnection con = new SqlConnection(ConectionString);
            try
            {
                // Create a SQL query string to retrieve all the authors
residing in the supplied zip code
                string query = "Select * from authors where zip=@zip";
                // Create a command object
                SqlCommand cmd = new SqlCmmand(query, con);
                // Add the supplied parameter value to the command object.
Note that use of the parameters collection can avoid SQL injection attacks
because a parameter is treated as a literal value and not as executable
code
                cmd.Parameters.AddWithValue("@zip", inputZip);
                // Open the database connection
                con.Open();
                // Create a DataReader object by executing the SQL command
                SqlDataReader reader = cmd.ExecuteReader();
                // Bind the DataReader object with the GridView control
                GridView1.DataSource = reader;
                GridView1.DataBind();
            }
            finally
            {
                // Close the connection
                con.Close();
            }
        }
    }
```

Question 2	*What is the purpose of the `HtmlEncode` method?*

7. Edit the web.config file by adding the following setting, which adds the connection string that specifies the authentication mode and specifies that a custom error page will be shown if any error occurs in the application. By

showing a custom error page, you can limit the amount of error information to be displayed and can hide the detailed error message from the user that can reveal valuable information such as the connection string, SQL Server name, and database naming conventions:

```
<connectionStrings>
  <add name ="conString" connectionString ="Data Source=.;Integrated Security=SSPI;Initial Catalog=pubs"/>
</connectionStrings>
<authentication mode="Windows"/>
<customErrors mode="RemoteOnly" defaultRedirect="GenericErrorPage.htm">
        <error statusCode="403" redirect="NoAccess.htm" />
</customErrors>
```

8. Add a web form to the application by right clicking on the project in the solution explorer. Name the form **GenericErrorPage.htm**.

9. Type the following text inside the GenericErrorPage.htm file:

```
    <html>
  <head>
  <title>
   Generic Error Page
  </title>
 </head>
 <body>
  An error has occurred in the application.
 </body>
</html>
```

10. Add another web form to the application by right clicking on the project in the solution explorer. Name the form **NoAccess.htm**.

11. Type the following text inside the NoAccess.htm file:

```
    <html>
  <head>
  <title>
   Error Page
  </title>
 </head>
 <body>
```

```
  Access Denied.
 </body>
</html>
```

12. Build the application by clicking on the Build menu and choosing Build Solution (ctrl+shift+B).

13. You can see that a save change alert from an outside source is prompted in the web.config file as shown in Figure 12-1. A text box for zip code and a button control appear as shown in Figure 12-2. After entering the input, click the button to see the records in the grid view as shown in Figure 12-3.

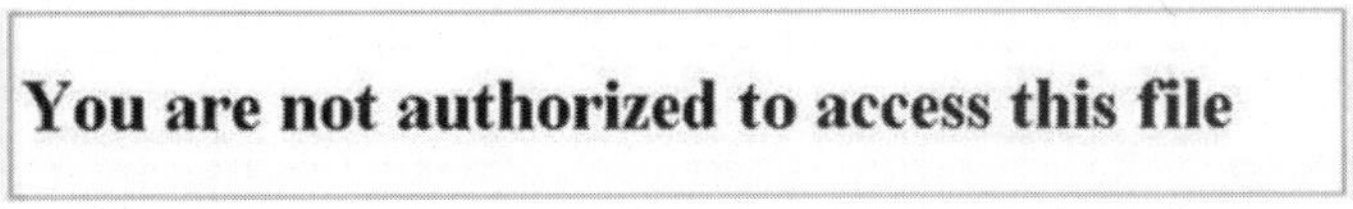

You are not authorized to access this file

Figure 12-1
Alert Box

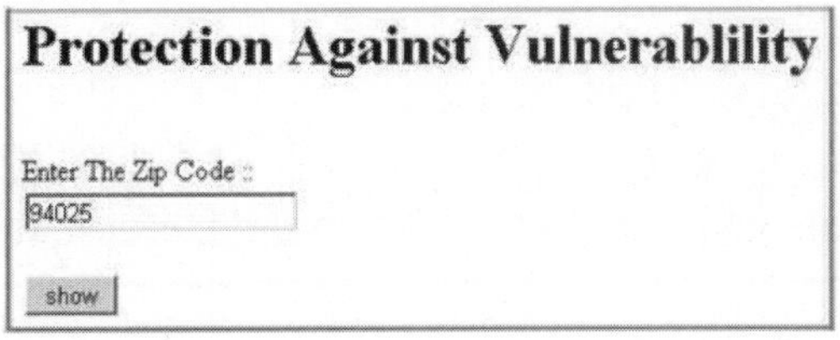

Protection Against Vulnerablility
Enter The Zip Code ::
94025
show

Figure 12-2
Default.aspx Page with Input Control

Protection Against Vulnerablility
Enter The Zip Code ::
94025
show
au_id au_lname au_fname phone address city state zip contract
172-32-1176 White Johnson 408 496-7223 10932 Bigge Rd. Menlo Park CA 94025

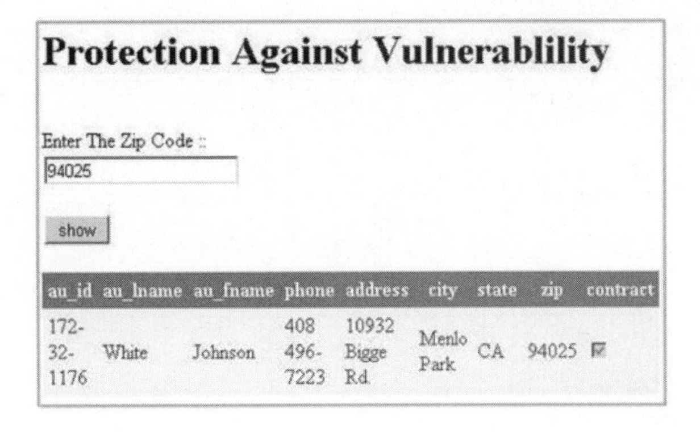

Figure 12-3
Default.aspx Page Displaying Author Details

Exercise 12.3	Protecting Sensitive Information
Overview	You want to encrypt and decrypt sensitive configuration information for your web application. In this lab exercise, you will use Microsoft Visual Studio 2008 to encrypt and decrypt sensitive information. This task is complete when you are able to protect and unprotect the configuration information of your application. To complete this lab exercise, all the student computers such as StudentXX-A and StudentXX-B must be started and must have network access.
Completion time	15 minutes

1. From the Start menu, select Microsoft Visual Studio 2008, and then select Microsoft Visual Studio 2008.

2. Select File → New Project → ASP.NET Web Application, and enter the name **ProtectSensitiveInfo**. Visual Studio creates a new Web site that contains the Default.aspx page.

3. Add the controls given in Table 12-3 to the Default.aspx page.

Table 12-3
Controls in Default.aspx Page of ProtectSensitiveInfo Application

Control	*ID*	*Properties*
Button	btnEncrypt	Text = "Encrypt"
Label	Label1	
Button	btnDecrypt	Text = "Decrypt"

4. Add references to the various namespaces in the code behind page Default.aspx.cs as shown:

```
using System.Web.Security;
using System.Security.Cryptography;
using System.Web.Configuration;
```

Question 3	*How can you protect resources that are not part of web pages?*

5. In the `btnEncrypt_Click` method, add the functionality to encrypt configuration information as follows:

```
protected void btnEncrypt_Click(object sender, EventArgs e)
{
    // Call the ProtectSection method to encrypt the authentication
section of the web.config file
    ProtectSection("authentication",
"DataProtectionConfigurationProvider");
    // Call the ProtectSection method to encrypt the connectionStrings
section of the web.config file
    ProtectSection("connectionStrings",
"DataProtectionConfigurationProvider");
    // Display a status message
    Label1.Text = "Data Encryption Successful";
}
```

6. Add code to the `ProtectSection` method to encrypt the specified section with the specified protection provider as shown:

```
private void ProtectSection(string sectionName, string provider)
{
    // Open the web application configuration file using the ASP.NET
application's virtual application root path on the server
    Configuration config =
WebConfigurationManager.OpenWebConfiguration(Request.ApplicationPath);
    // Get the specified section
    ConfigurationSection section = config.GetSection(sectionName);
    // Check whether the specified section is encrypted
    if (section != null && !section.SectionInformation.IsProtected)
    {
        // If the specified section is not encrypted, encrypt the
section with the specified protection provider
        section.SectionInformation.ProtectSection(provider);
        // Save the section
        config.Save();
    }
}
```

> **NOTE**
> *You must always encryt the most sensitive data only. Encrypting data adds an extra overhead to the application because ASP.NET must automatically decrypt the accessed configuration section each time.*

7. In the `btnDecrypt_Click` method, add the functionality to decrypt configuration information as follows:

```
protected void btnDecrypt_Click(object sender, EventArgs e)
{
    // Call the UnProtectSection method to decrypt the authentication
section of the web.config file
    UnProtectSection("authentication");
    // Call the UnProtectSection method to decrypt the
connectionStrings section of the web.config file
    UnProtectSection("connectionStrings");
    // Display a status message
    Label1.Text = "Data Decryption Successful";
}
```

8. Add code to the `UnProtectSection` method as follows:

```
private void UnProtectSection(string sectionName)
{
    // Open the web application configuration file using the ASP.NET
application's virtual application root path on the server
    Configuration config =
WebConfigurationManager.OpenWebConfiguration(Request.ApplicationPath);
    // Get the section
    ConfigurationSection section = config.GetSection(sectionName);
    // Check whether the specified section is encrypted
    if (section != null && section.SectionInformation.IsProtected)
    {
        // If the specified section is encrypted, decrypt the section
        section.SectionInformation.UnprotectSection();
        // Save the section
        config.Save();
    }
}
```

9. Edit the web.config file and add the following settings for the connectionStrings section:

```
<connectionStrings>
  <add name="conString" connectionString="Data Source=.;Integrated
Security=SSPI;Initial Catalog=pubs" />
  <add name="MyMembershipConnString" connectionString="data
source=(local);Integrated Security=SSPI;initial catalog=aspnetdb" />
</connectionStrings>
```

10. Build the application by clicking on the Build menu and choosing Build Solution (ctrl+shift+B).

11. Open the web.config file and view the connectionStrings tag. You will be able to read the data. Close the web.config file.

12. Click on the encrypt button. Open the web.config file and view the connectionStrings tag. You will notice that the data is not readable. Close the web.config file.

13. Click on the decrypt button. Open the web.config file and view the connectionStrings tag. You will be able to read the data. Close the web.config file.

LAB REVIEW QUESTIONS

Completion time	**15 minutes**

1. How can you encrypt passwords when using Forms authentication?
2. What is impersonation and why do you use it?
3. How can you configure custom handler settings into the web.config file?
4. How can you encrypt a query string?

LAB CHALLENGE 12.1: IMPLEMENTING A CUSTOM AUTHENTICATION SCHEME

Completion time	**15 minutes**

You want to implement a custom authentication scheme where the credentials are confirmed from a database. How can you achieve this?

LAB CHALLENGE 12.2: MANIPULATING AUTHENTICATION SETTINGS

Completion time	**20 minutes**

You have created a web application that authenticates users using persistent cookies. However, you want to limit the life span of cookies to ten days. How can you achieve this?

LAB 13
CONFIGURING AND DEPLOYING WEB APPLICATIONS

This lab contains the following exercises and activities:

Exercise 13.1	Configuring Applications through Configuration Files
Exercise 13.2	Exploring Configuration File Hierarchy
Exercise 13.3	Accessing Configuration Settings Programmatically
Exercise 13.4	Deploying Web Applications
Lab Review Questions	
Lab Challenge 13.1	Deploying Applications

BEFORE YOU BEGIN

Lab 13 assumes that the lab setup has been completed as specified in the setup document and that StudentXX-A, StudentXX-B, and StudentXX-C computers have Microsoft .NET Framework 3.5 and Microsoft Visual Studio 2008 installed.

> **NOTE**
>
> *In this lab, you will see the characters XX. When you see these characters, substitute the two-digit number assigned to your computer.*

SCENARIO

You are developing web applications for your clients. You want to configure your application settings through configuration files. Additionally, you are required to deploy the application using IIS Web Server.

After completing this lab, you will be able to:

- Configure Applications through Configuration Files
- Deploy Web Applications

Estimated lab time: 140 minutes

Exercise 13.1	Configuring Applications through Configuration Files
Overview	You want to include a tracing feature in your web application to view the most recent activities. The trace information should be displayed on the web page. Additionally, you do not want remote computers to access your application's trace information, and you want your server to store only ten trace requests. You should achieve this by altering the application's web.config file. In this lab exercise, you will use Microsoft Visual Studio 2008. This task is complete when you are able to display successfully the trace messages through your application. To complete this lab exercise, all the student computers such as StudentXX-A and StudentXX-B must be started and must have network access.
Completion time	15 minutes

NOTE	*In this lab, you will configure tracing through the configuration file for the TraceLab application developed in Lab Exercise 7.1.*

1. In Visual Studio, open the TraceLab application.

2. Open the Default.aspx and set the `Trace` attribute of the `@Page` directive to `false`.

3. Open the web.config file. Place the following setting under the `<authentication>` section:

```
<trace enabled="true" localOnly="true" mostRecent="true"
pageOutput="true" requestLimit="10" traceMode="SortByTime"
   writeToDiagnosticsTrace="true"/>
```

NOTE	*The following points describe the given setting:* *enabled = "true"—Enables tracing* *localOnly = "true"—Disables tracing information being visible to remote computers* *mostRecent = "true"—Displays most recent tracing activity* *pageOutput = "true"—Sets tracing output to be shown on the page* *requestLimit = "10"—Number of trace requests to be stored on the server* *traceMode = "SortByTime"—Sets the mode of trace information being displayed in time order* *writeToDiagnosticsTrace = "true"—Sends the trace messages to `System.Diagnostics.Trace` class*

4. Save the application and debug it using F5.

5. Enter a number in the text box and click the Square Root button. Find the trace log information being displayed at the bottom of the page. Note that the trace log shows various information grouped into different sections. For example, the Request Details section includes the session ID, the time you made the web request, and the type of web request and encoding. The Trace Information section displays the various processing stages that the requested page went through. Additionally, note that it also includes the trace messages that you added to display the result and the value of the Page.IsPostBack property in red.

Exercise 13.2	**Exploring Configuration File Hierarchy**
Overview	You are creating a web application for an e-commerce company. You keep related web pages in individual subdirectories. You maintain multiple web.config files—one in the application root directory and the remaining in each of the subdirectories. When a page is requested, and if that page is not found, your application displays an error page depending on the setting in the `<customErrors>` element of the respective web.config file. In this lab exercise, you will use Microsoft Visual Studio 2008. This task is complete when your application displays an error page by applying the setting in the configuration files sequentially. To complete this lab exercise, all the student computers such as StudentXX-A and StudentXX-B must be started and must have network access.
Completion time	45 minutes

1. From the Start menu, select Microsoft Visual Studio 2008, and then select Microsoft Visual Studio 2008.

2. Select File → New Website →ASP.NET Web Application. Enter the name **ConfigHierarchy**.

3. In the Default.aspx page, add a HyperLink control and set its `NavigationUrl` property to **NonexistentPage.aspx**. Set the Default.aspx page as the start page of the application.

4. Open the machine.config file from the path "x:\<windows>\Microsoft.NET\Framework\ v2.0.50727\config\machine.config." Scroll to the `<customErrors>` element.

NOTE	*The `mode` attribute of the `<customErrors>` element specifies whether custom errors are enabled, disabled, or shown only to remote clients. The default value of this attribute is RemoteOnly. This value indicates that custom errors are displayed only to remote clients and the detailed ASP.NET errors are displayed to the local host.*

5. Double click the application's root web.config file and modify the default setting in the <customErrors> element as shown here. Note that the value of the mode attribute is set to the value "On" in the given setting. This indicates that custom errors are enabled. Additionally, these custom errors are shown both to remote clients and to the local host. The <error> element specifies the custom error page for the given status code:

```
<customErrors mode="On">
  <error statusCode="404" redirect="Custom404.aspx" />
</customErrors>
```

6. Add a web form to the application by right clicking on the project in the solution explorer. Name the form **Custom404.aspx**.

7. Type the following text inside the <form> element of the Custom404.aspx page:

```
<form id="form1" runat="server">
  <div>
    <h1>The Page that you were trying to open was not found</h1>
  </div>
</form>
```

8. Run the project using F5. Click the hyperlink that is displayed on the page. Note that the Custom404.aspx page appears on the browser. When the application runs, the settings in the <customErrors> element of the web.config file override the settings in the <customErrors> element of the machine.config file. Therefore, the Custom404.aspx page defined in the application's root web.config file is displayed.

9. Add a new folder by performing the following: select the project, right click and select Add, and then choose the "Add New Folder" option. Name the folder **SubDir**.

10. Right click the folder SubDir and add a new web form to the folder. Place a HyperLink control to the web form and set its NavigationUrl property to **NonexistentPage.aspx**. Set this page as the start page of the application.

11. Run the project using F5. Click the hyperlink. Notice that the Custom404.aspx page is displayed. Again, the settings in the web.config file of the application's root directory are applied.

12. Stop the project. Right click the folder SubDir and add a new web.config file. Modify the <customErrors> element in the new web.config file as shown

here. Note that in the given setting, the mode value of the `<customErrors>` element is set to the value "Off." This indicates that the custom errors are disabled and the detailed ASP.NET errors are shown both to remote clients and to the local host:

```
<configuration>
  <system.web>
    <customErrors mode ="Off "/>
  </system.web>
</configuration>
```

13. Run the project again using F5. Click the hyperlink displayed on the page. Notice that instead of the Custom404.aspx page, the default error page is displayed when the settings in the `<customErrors>` element of the web.config file residing in the subdirectory "SubDir," override the settings in the `<customErrors>` element of the application's root web.config file.

Exercise 13.3	**Accessing Configuration Settings Programmatically**
Overview	You are creating a web application in which you store the details of a page's banner in your application's configuration file. You need to programmatically access the configuration file and display the setting information of the banner in a TextBox control. In this lab exercise, you will use Microsoft Visual Studio 2008. This task is complete when you are able to access the banner's information stored in the application's configuration file successfully. To complete this lab exercise, all the student computers such as StudentXX-A and StudentXX-B must be started and must have network access.
Completion time	20 minutes

1. From the Start menu, select Microsoft Visual Studio 2008, and then select Microsoft Visual Studio 2008.

2. Select File → New Website → ASP.NET Web Application. Enter the name **ReadConfigSettings**.

3. In the Default.aspx page, add a TextBox control inside the <form> element as shown:

```
        <form id="form1" runat="server">
<div>
 Banner Text::<br />
 <asp:TextBox ID="txtRead" runat="server" Width="183px"></asp:TextBox>
</div>
</form>
```

4. Add the following using statement in the Default.aspx.cs file:

```
using System.Web.Configuration;
```

5. In the application's web.config file, include the information about the page banner in the <appSettings> element, by using <add> element and specifying a key-value pair as simple strings, as shown:

```
<appSettings>
  <add key="Banner" value ="Sample Banner Text"/>
</appSettings>
```

6. In the Default.aspx.cs file, add the following code in the Page_Load method:

```
protected void Page_Load(object sender, EventArgs e)
 {
   txtRead.Text                                          =
ConfigurationManager.AppSettings["Banner"].ToString();
 }
```

7. Set the Default.aspx page as the start page of the application.

8. Run the project using F5. Observe that the value of the Banner key stored in the <appSettings> element is displayed in the TextBox control.

Exercise 13.4 Deploying Web Applications

Overview	You are developing a web application to display customer details. You deploy the directory structure of your application using IIS Web Server.

	In this lab exercise, you will use Microsoft Visual Studio 2008, SQL Server database, and IIS Web Server. This task is complete when you are able to deploy your application successfully using IIS Web Server. To complete this lab exercise, all the student computers such as StudentXX-A and StudentXX-B must be started and must have network access.
Completion time	30 minutes

1. From the Start menu, select Microsoft Visual Studio 2008, and then select Microsoft Visual Studio 2008.

2. Select File → New Project → ASP.NET Web Site, and enter the name **DeployApplication**. Visual Studio creates a new Web site that contains the Default.aspx page.

3. Add the controls given in Table 13-1 to the Default.aspx page.

Table 13-1
Controls in Default.aspx Page of DeployApplication Application

Control	***ID***
GridView	`GridView1`
SqlDataSource	`SqlDataSource1`

4. Open the configuration file and modify the `<compilation>` section as shown:

```
<compilation debug="false">
```

5. Select the SqlDataSource control and click on its Smart Tag. Choose Configure Data Source. In the open dialog box, click on New Connection and perform the following:

   a. In the Server Name text box, type a . (dot) indicating the local server as shown in Figure 13-1.

b. From the Select or enter a database name dropdown, choose Northwind as shown in Figure 13-1 and click OK. Notice that a connection string has been built. Click Next.

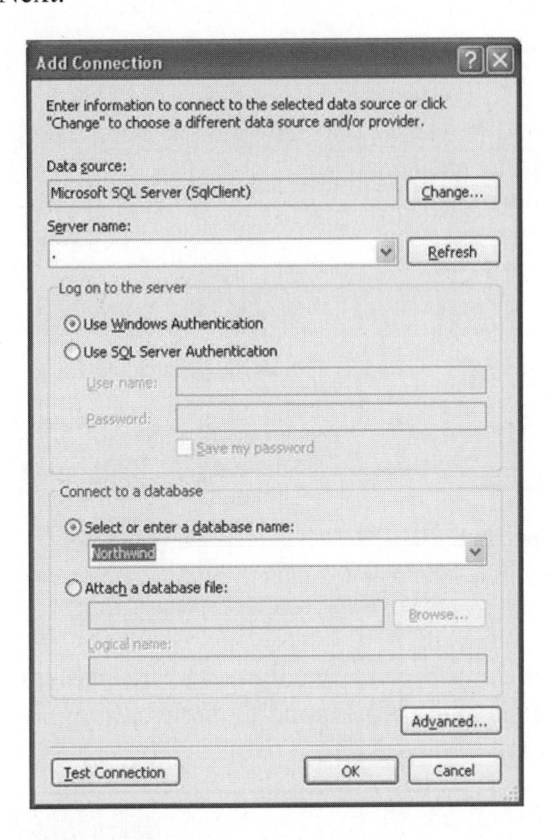

Figure 13-1
Add Connection Dialog Box

c. Save the connection string in the configuration file by checking the given check box and supplying a name for the connection string as shown in Figure 13-2. Click Next.

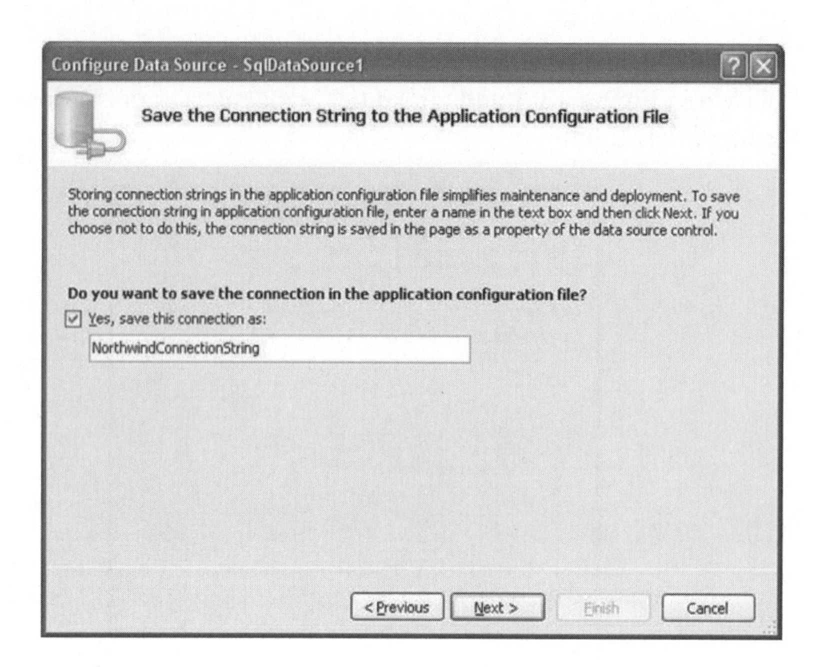

Figure 13-2
Saving the Connection String

d. Choose the option Specify columns from a table or view. Choose the table Customers and the corresponding table columns as shown in Figure 13-3. Click Next.

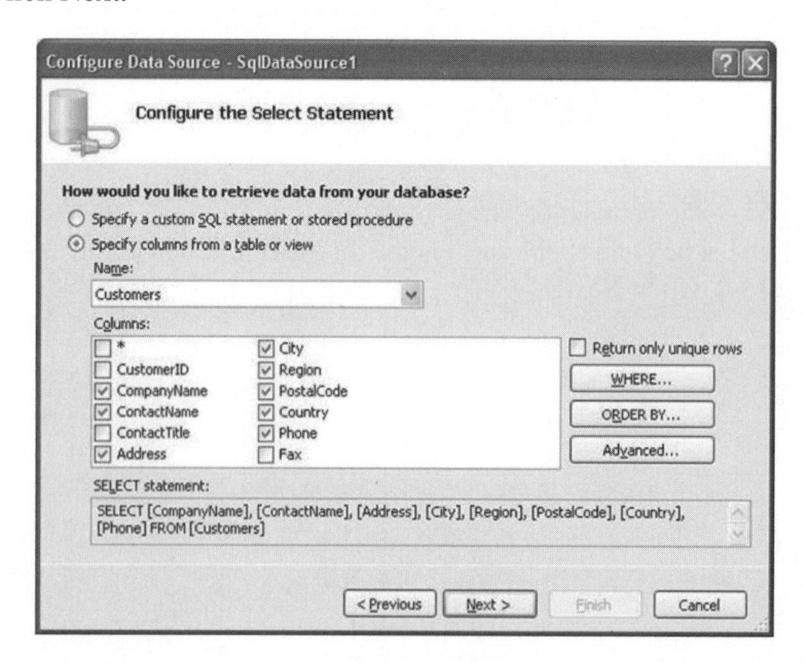

Figure 13-3
Configuring the Select Statement

e. Click the Test Query button. Observe that the data is populated from the Customers table for the selected column as shown in Figure 13-4. Click Finish.

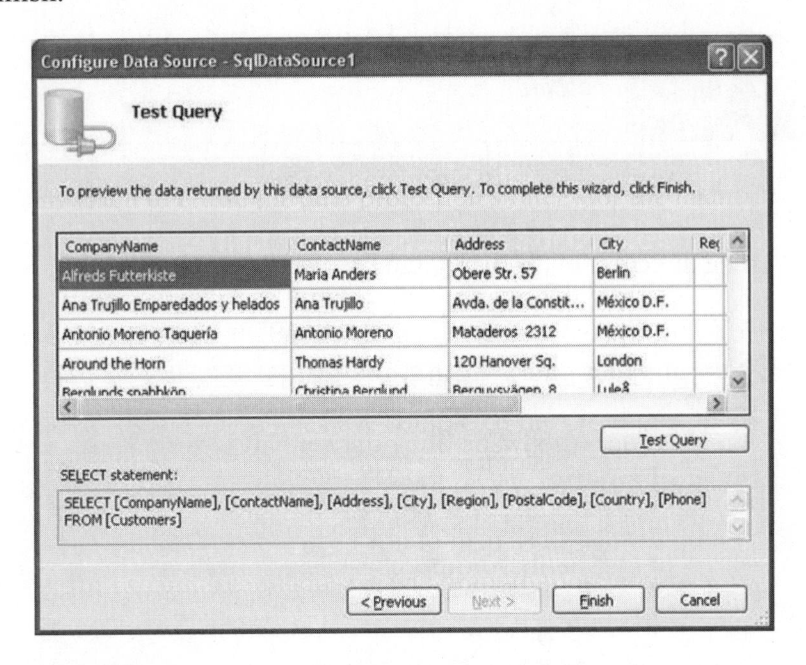

Figure 13-4
Testing the Query

6. Select the GridView and click its Smart Tag. Select the Choose Data Source dropdown and choose SqlDataSource1 as its data source.

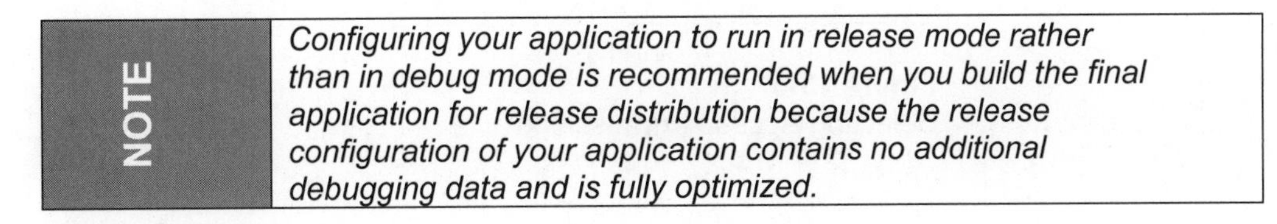

NOTE
Configuring your application to run in release mode rather than in debug mode is recommended when you build the final application for release distribution because the release configuration of your application contains no additional debugging data and is fully optimized.

7. Set the Release mode from the solution configuration and rebuild the entire solution.

8. Go to Build → Publish DeployApplication. Select the path (such as c:\abc) in which you want to store the deployment files. Click OK.

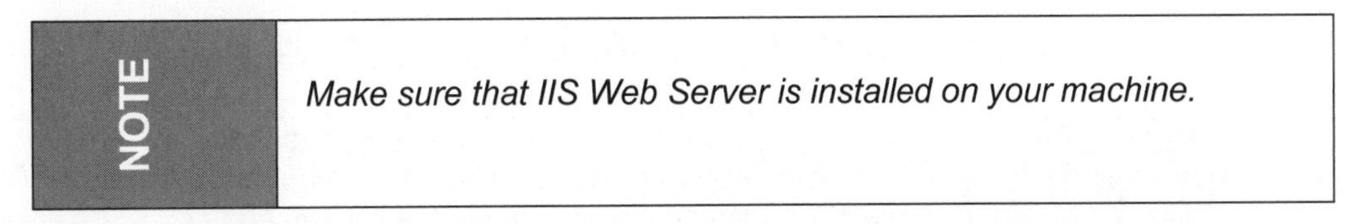

NOTE
Make sure that IIS Web Server is installed on your machine.

9. Open the IIS Web Server.

10. Go to IIS → Local → Web sites → Default Web Sites.

11. Right click on Default Web Sites, select New, and then select Virtual Directory.

Question 1	*How can you check whether IIS is configured on your machine?*

12. Enter the virtual alias name as **DeployApplication** and click Next.

13. Select the directory c:\abc using the browse tab and click Next.

14. Uncheck all the check boxes except the Read check box as shown in Figure 13-5. Click Next and then click Finish.

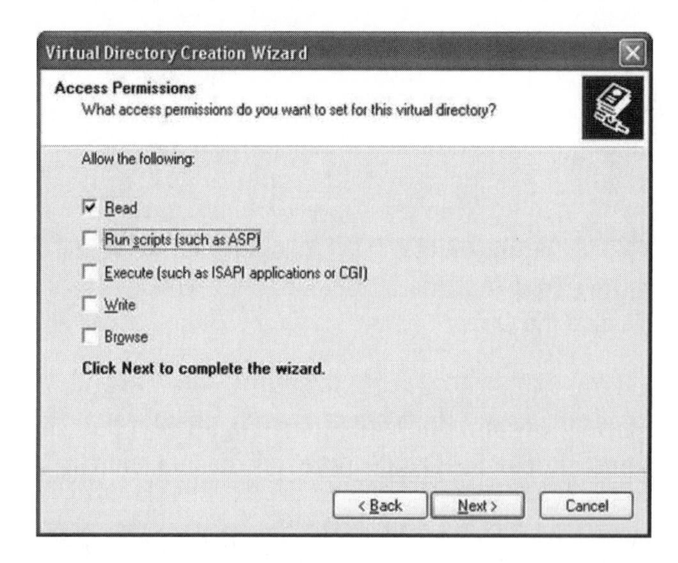

Figure 13-5
Selecting Access Permissions

15. Expand Default Web Sites. Locate the virtual directory DeployApplication.

16. Right click on DeployApplication and select properties.

17. Go to the Document tab and remove all the default content pages from the list box.

18. Click on Add and enter Default.aspx in the text box. Click Ok.

Question 2	*What command line tool can you use to copy your application files from the development computer to the production web server that hosts your application?*

19. Open the browser and type the following URL:

```
http://localhost/DeployApplication
```

20. Observe that the GridView control on the page displays all the customer records.

LAB REVIEW QUESTIONS

Completion time	**15 minutes**

1. List the files of a web application that are necessary during deployment.
2. How can we implement event logging through the web.config file?

LAB CHALLENGE 13.1: DEPLOYING APPLICATIONS

Completion time	**15 minutes**

Consider that you want to deploy your web application on a target machine using a web setup. How can you achieve this task?

APPENDIX: LAB SETUP GUIDE

The *Designing and Developing ASP.NET Applications Using the Microsoft .NET Framework 3.5* title of the Microsoft Official Academic Course (MOAC) series includes two books: a textbook and a lab manual. The exercises in the lab manual are designed for classroom use under the supervision of an instructor or a lab aide.

CLASSROOM SETUP

This course should be taught in a classroom containing networked or stand-alone computers where students can develop their skills through hands-on experience with Microsoft Visual Studio 2008. The exercises in the lab manual require the computers to be installed and configured in a specific manner. Failure to adhere to the setup instructions in this document can produce unanticipated results when the students perform the exercises.

Classroom Configuration

The following configurations and naming conventions are used throughout the course and are required for completing the labs as outlined in the lab manual:

- Active Directory Domain Services domain controller
- The student computers must run Windows XP.
- Each student computer is to be named Computer##, where ## is a unique number assigned to each computer by the instructor.

Student Computer Requirements

Each student computer requires the following hardware and software:

Hardware Requirements

- Processor: 1 GHz (minimum); 2 GHz or faster (recommended)
- RAM: 512 MB (minimum); 2 GB or more (recommended)
- First hard drive: 50+ GB, sufficient disk space for one 40 GB system partition and at least 10 GB of unpartitioned space
- Second hard drive: 10+ GB with no partitions

- DVD-ROM drive
- Super VGA (800 X 600) or higher-resolution monitor
- Keyboard and mouse (or other pointing device)
- One network interface adapter

Software Requirements

- IIS 7.0 must be installed and running on the computer.

INSTALLING SQL SERVER 2005 EXPRESS ON A STUDENT COMPUTER

Installing SQL Server 2005 Express	
Overview	Using the following procedure, install SQL Server 2005 Express on a student computer.
Completion time	15 minutes

1. Open Internet Explorer and type **http://www.microsoft.com/Sqlserver/2005/en/us/express-down.aspx** in the **Address** box. The page to download and install Microsoft SQL Server 2005 appears.

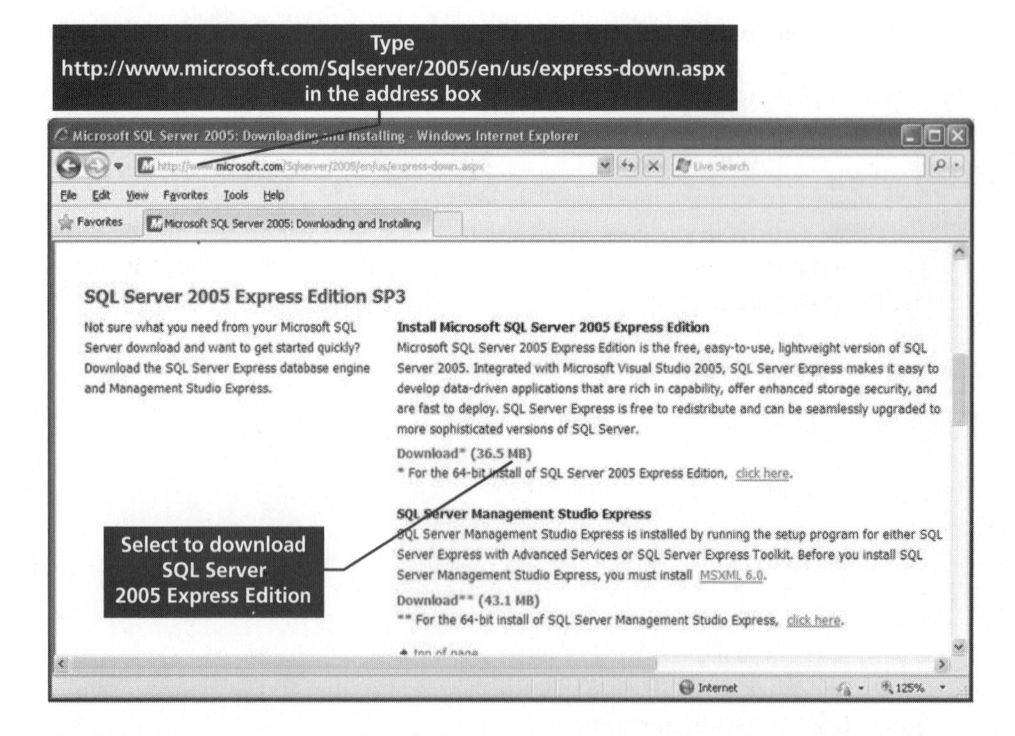

Figure 1
Download Page of Microsoft SQL Server 2005

2. On the page that opens, under the section **Install Microsoft SQL Server 2005 Express Edition**, click the **Download** link. A dialog box appears with **Run** and **Save** options.

3. In the dialog box, click the Run option if you want to run the SQLServer2005_SSMSEE.msi file directly.

   OR

   Click the Save option to save the file on the disk and then execute it later from the saved location.

4. After clicking **Run**, a page showing the *End User License Agreement* appears. Read the licensing terms, select the check box beside the **I accept the licensing terms and conditions** option, and then click **Next**.

NOTE	*You can click Cancel to abort all changes and go to the previous page.*

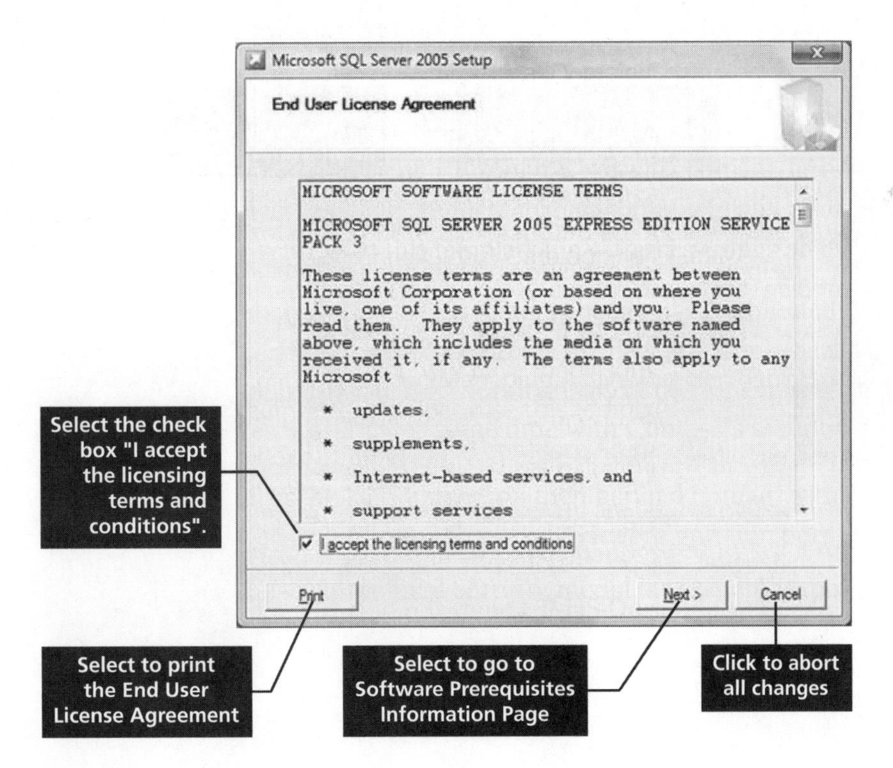

Figure 2
End User License Agreement Page

5. After accepting the license, an *Installing Prerequisites* page appears that displays the list of software components that are required before installing SQL Server Express.

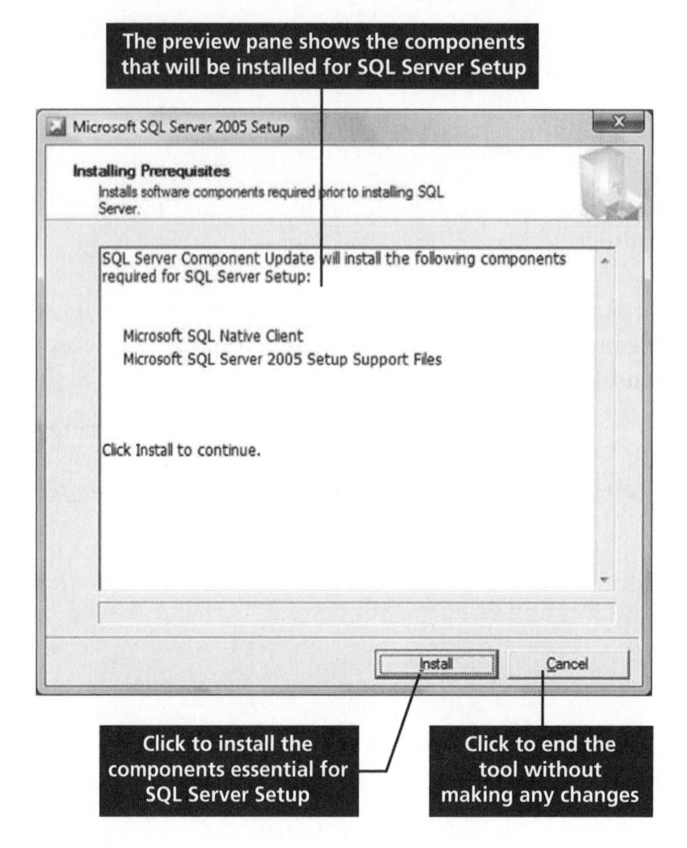

Figure 3
Software Prerequisites Information Page

6. After viewing the components that are essential for SQL Server Setup, click **Install**.

   The *Installing Prerequisites* page highlights the successful installation of the software components.

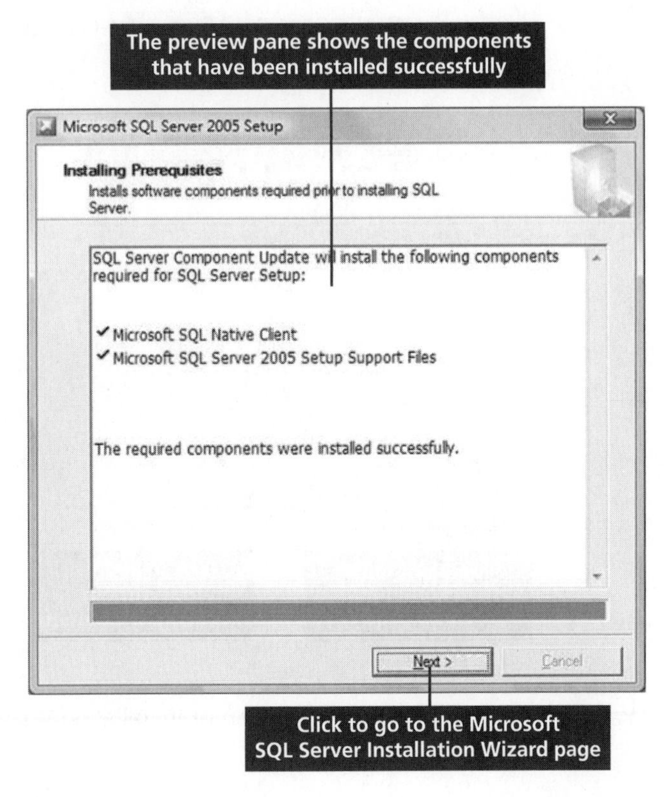

Figure 4
Successful Installation of the Prerequisite Components

7. A dialog box appears that informs you that a system check is in progress; it will close after it is complete. After a few seconds, the *Microsoft SQL Server Installation Wizard* appears.

Figure 5
Welcome Page of Microsoft SQL Server Installation Wizard

8. On the welcome page of the Microsoft SQL Server Installation wizard, click **Next**.

   The *System Configuration Check* page appears.

   The *System Configuration Check* page lists the components that are successfully installed for the installation of SQL Server.

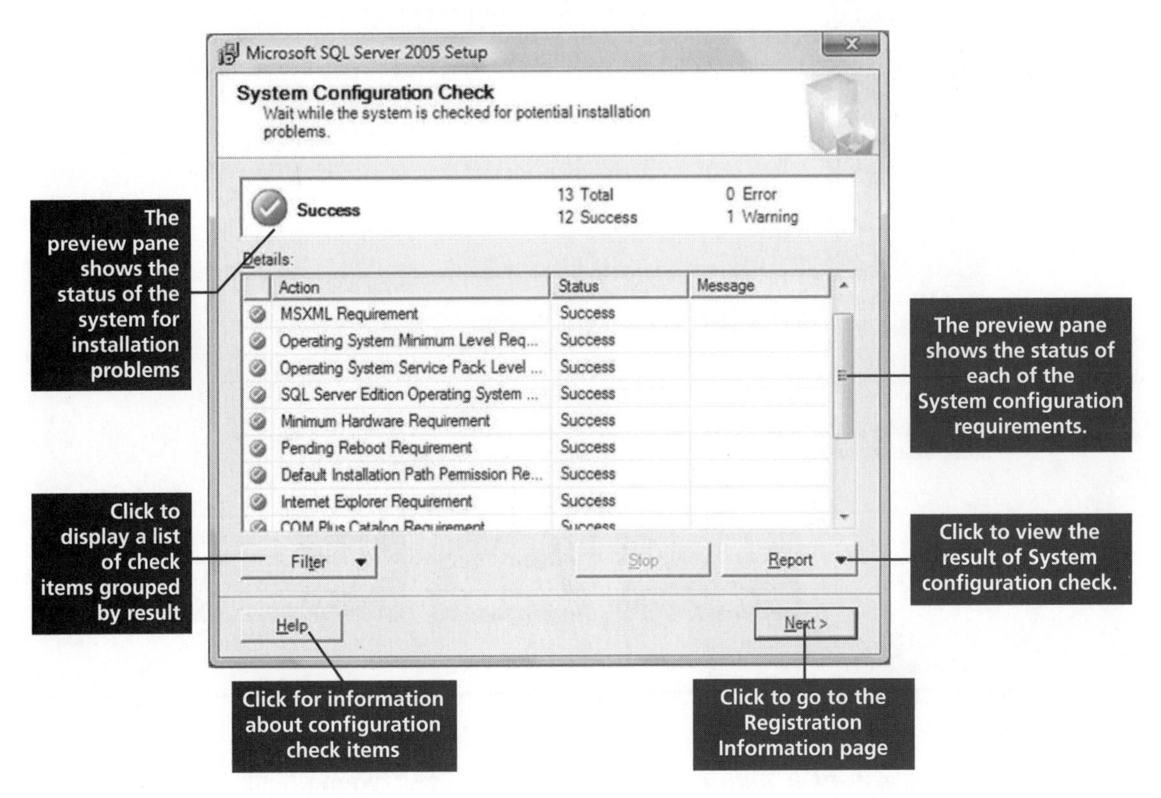

Figure 6
System Configuration Check Page

9. On the *System Configuration Check* page, click **Next**.

   The Registration Information page appears.

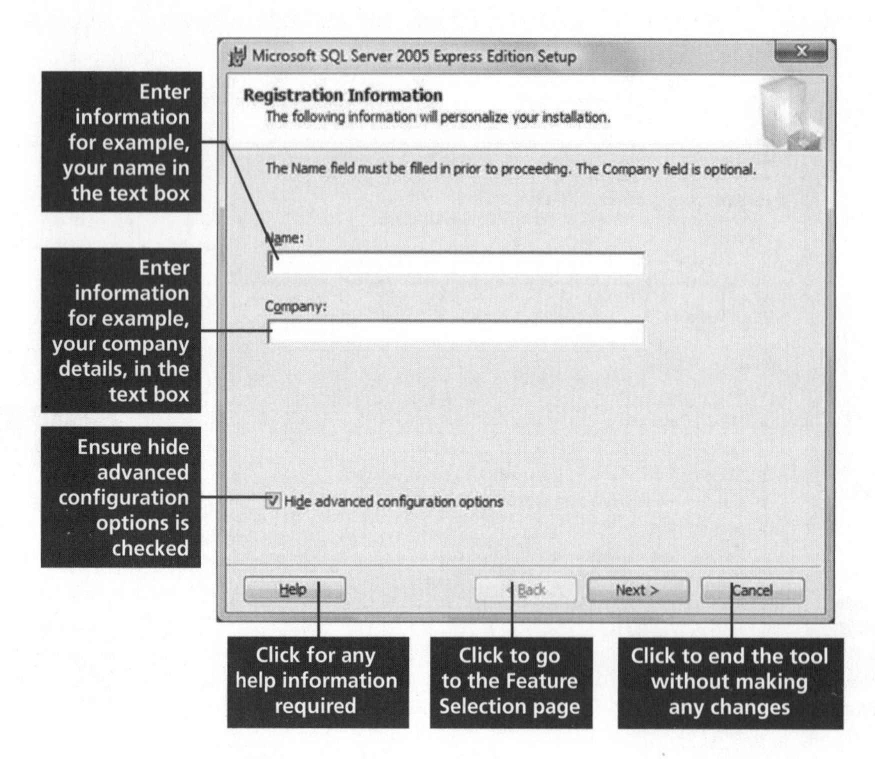

Figure 7
Registration Information Page

10. On the *Registration Information* page, enter your **Name** and **Company** information in the respective boxes, and click **Next**. The *Feature Selection* page appears.

NOTE	*It is mandatory to fill in the Name field; the Company field is optional.*

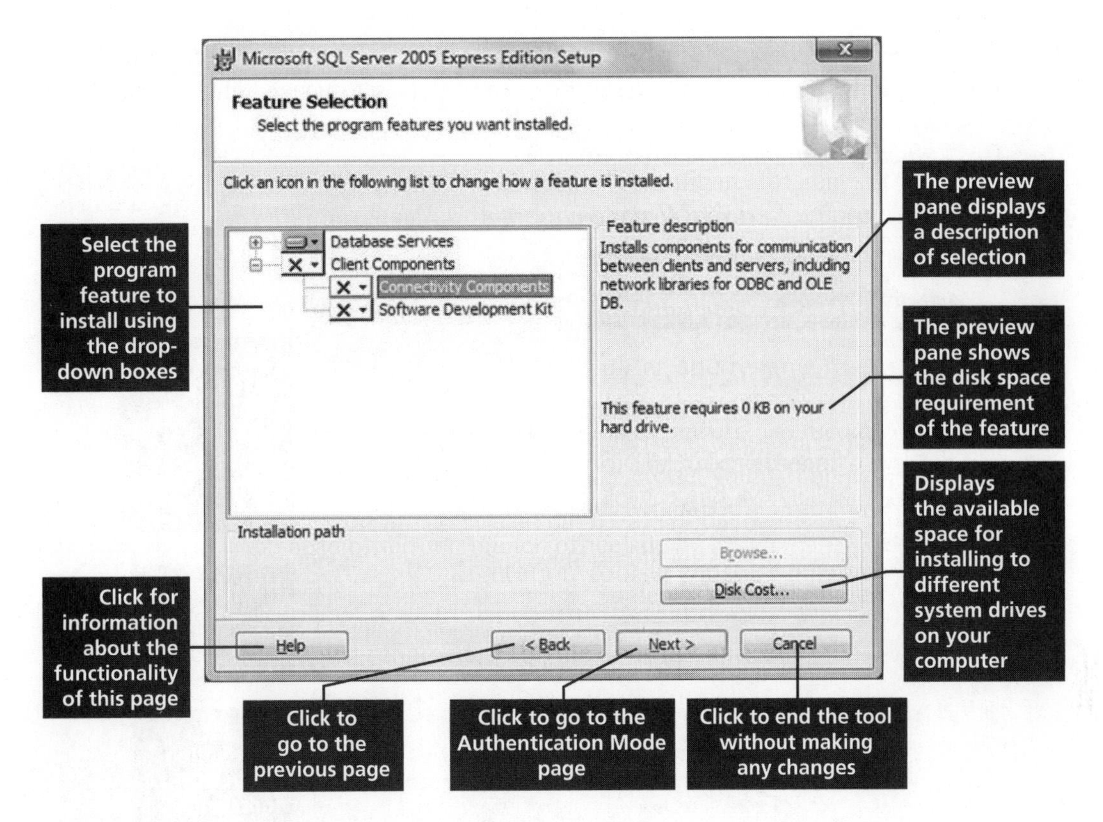

Figure 8
Feature Selection Page

11. The *Feature Selection* page shows the default settings. There is no need to make any changes with respect to these settings. View these settings and click **Next**.

    The *Authentication Mode* page appears.

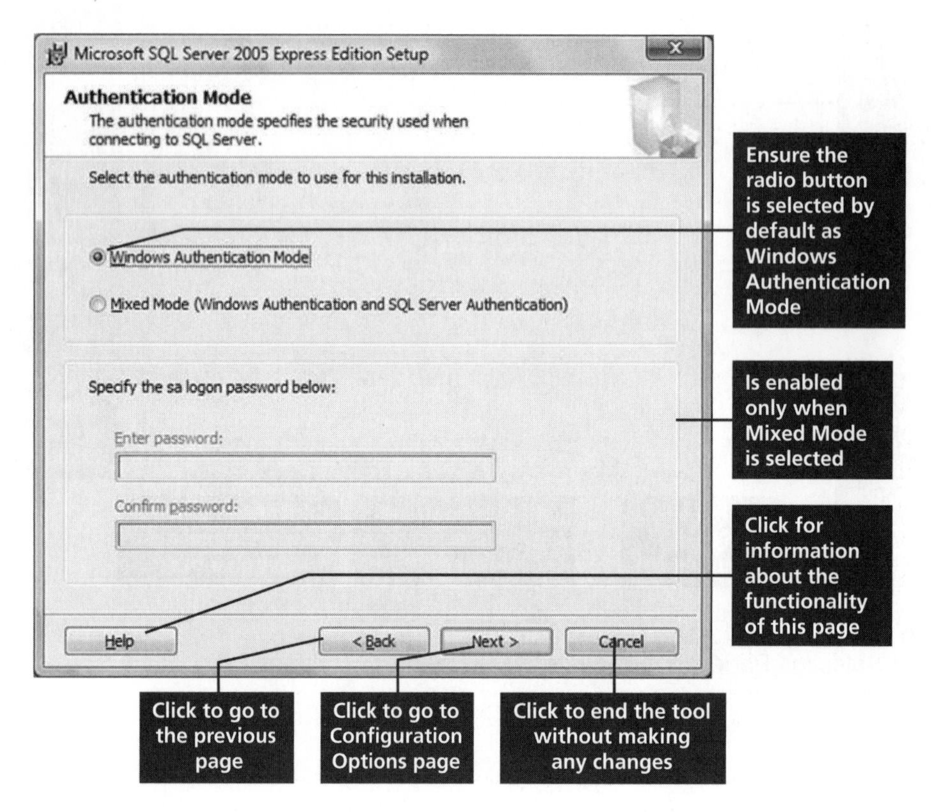

Figure 9
Authentication Mode Page

12. On the *Authentication Mode* page, the **Windows Authentication Mode** option is preselected. There is no need to change this option. Click **Next**.

    The *Configuration Options* page appears.

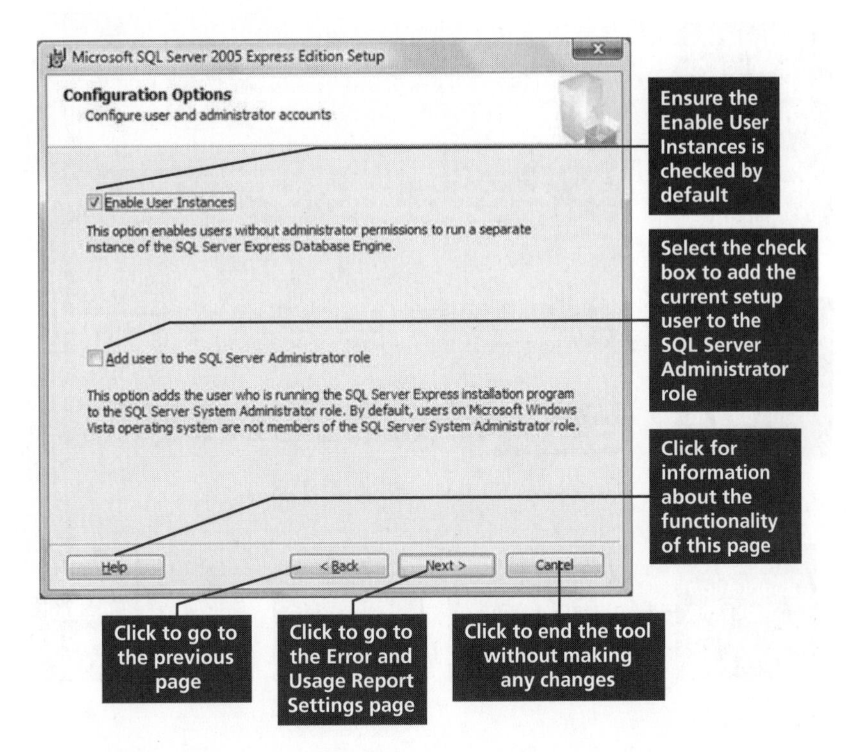

Figure 10
Configuration Options Page

13. On the *Configuration Options* page, retain the default settings and click **Next**.

    The *Error and Usage Report Settings* page appears.

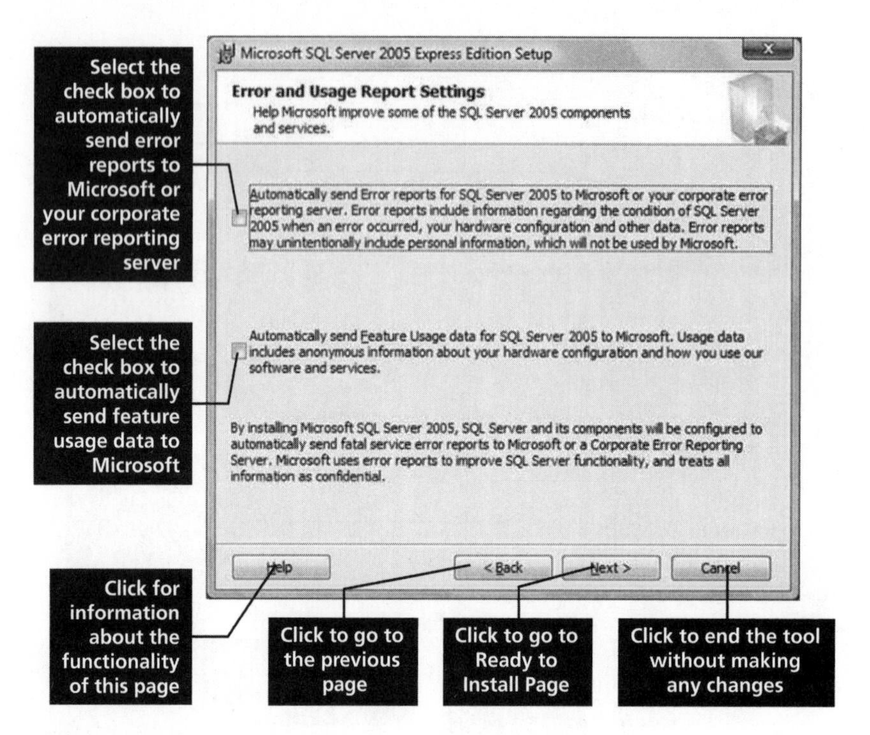

Figure 11
Error and Usage Settings Page

14. On the *Error and Usage Settings* page, click **Next** without selecting any options.

    The *Ready to Install* page appears.

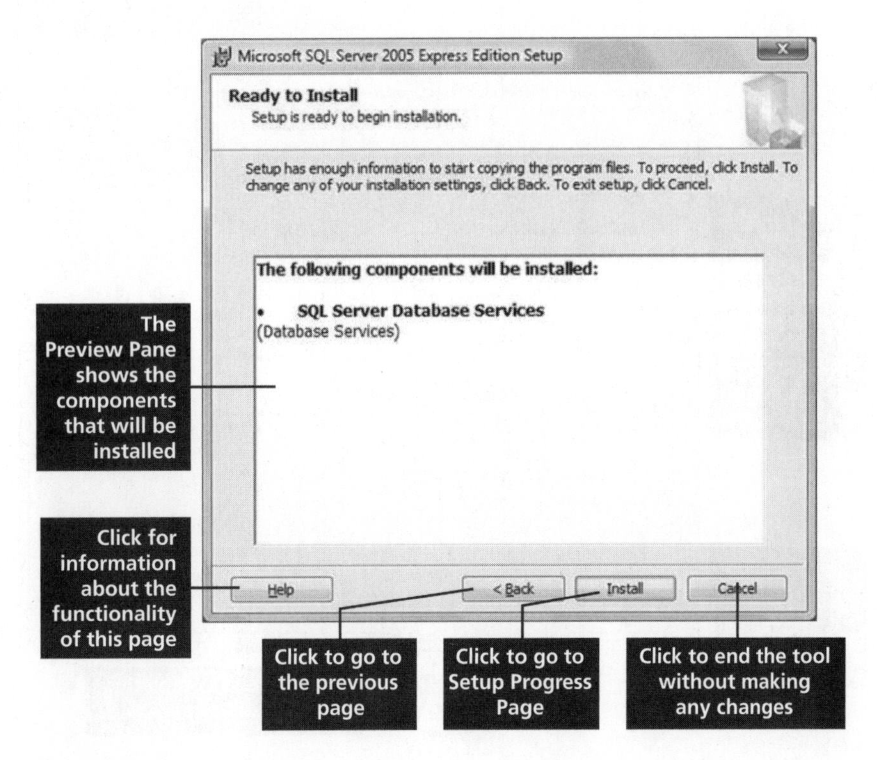

Figure 12
Ready to Install Page

15. On the *Ready to Install* page, click **Install**.

    The *Setup Progress* page appears.

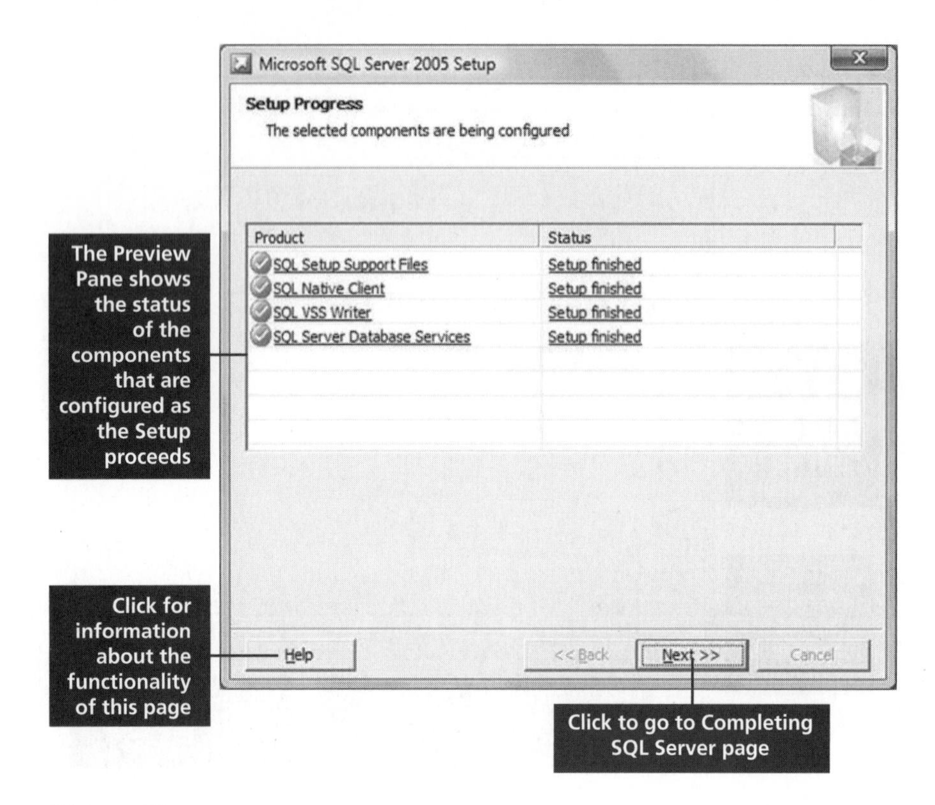

Figure 13
Setup Progress Page

The *Setup Progress* page displays the components that are being configured along with their setup status.

16. On the *Setup Progress* page, click **Next**.

The *Completing Microsoft SQL Server 2005 Setup* page appears.

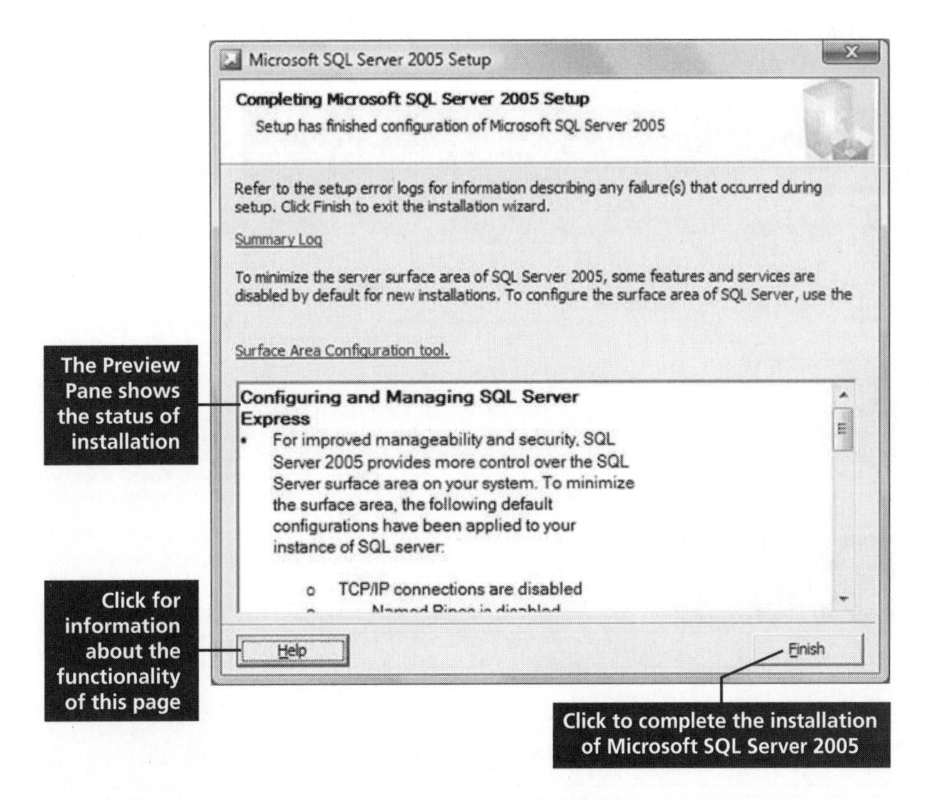

Figure 14
Completing Microsoft SQL Server 2005 Setup Page

The *Completing Microsoft SQL Server 2005 Setup* page confirms completion of the configuration of Microsoft SQL Server 2005.

17. On the Completing Microsoft SQL Server 2005 Setup page, click **Finish**.

This completes the installation of Microsoft SQL Server 2005.

INSTALLING SQL SERVER MANAGEMENT STUDIO 2005 EXPRESS ON A STUDENT COMPUTER

Installing SQL Server 2005 Express	
Overview	Using the following procedure, install SQL Server Management Studio 2005 Express on a student computer.
Completion time	15 minutes

1. Open your Internet Explorer and type http://www.microsoft.com/Sqlserver/2005/en/us/express-down.aspx in the Address box.

   The page to download and install *Microsoft SQL Server 2005 Express Edition* appears.

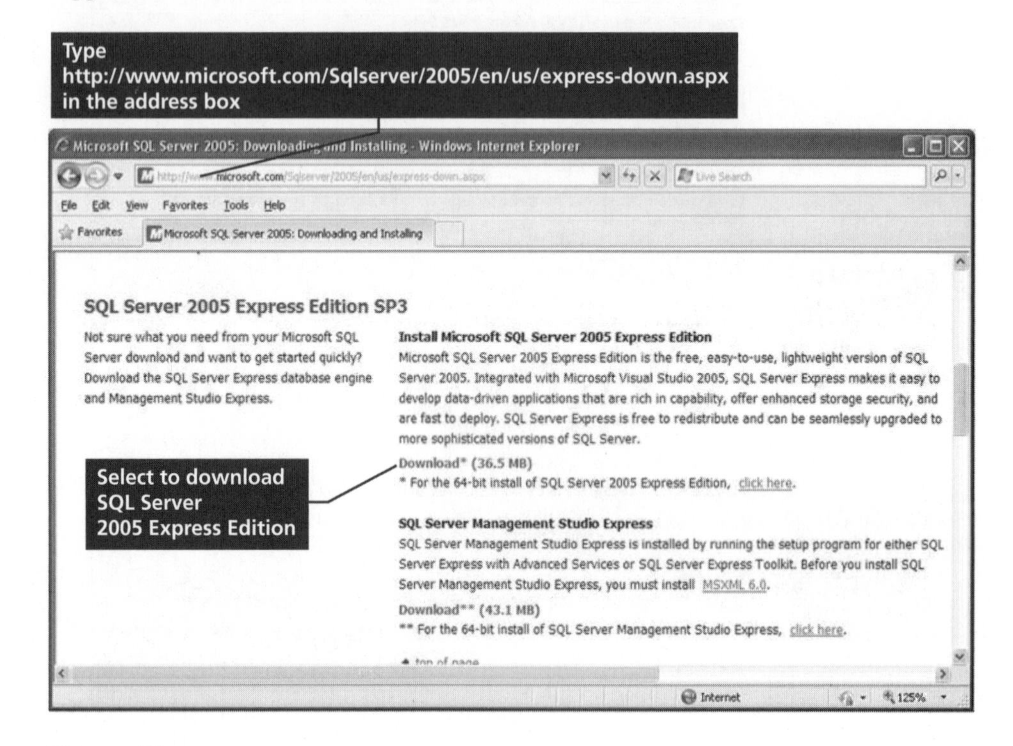

Figure 15
Download Page of Microsoft SQL Server 2005

2. On the page that opens, under the section *Install Microsoft SQL Server 2005 Express Edition*, click the **Download** link.

   A dialog box with **Run** and **Save** options appears.

3. In the dialog box, click the **Run** option if you want to run the SQLServer2005 SSMSEE.msi file directly.

   OR

   Click the Save option to save the file on the disk and then execute it later from the saved location.

4. After clicking **Run**, the *Welcome to Microsoft SQL Server Management Studio Express Setup* page appears.

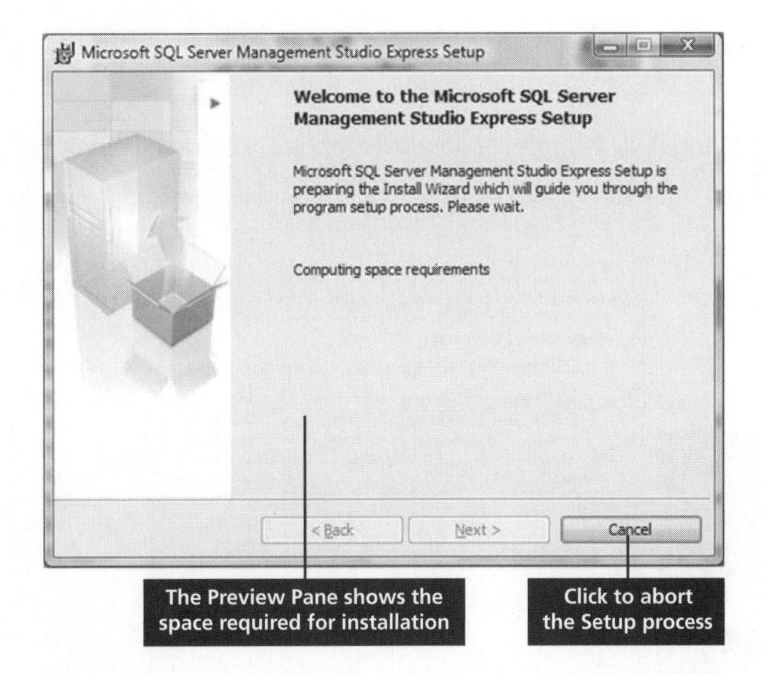

Figure 16
Welcome Page of Microsoft SQL Server Management Studio Express Setup

5. On the Welcome to Microsoft SQL Server Management Studio Express Setup page, click **Next**.

   A page showing the License Agreement appears.

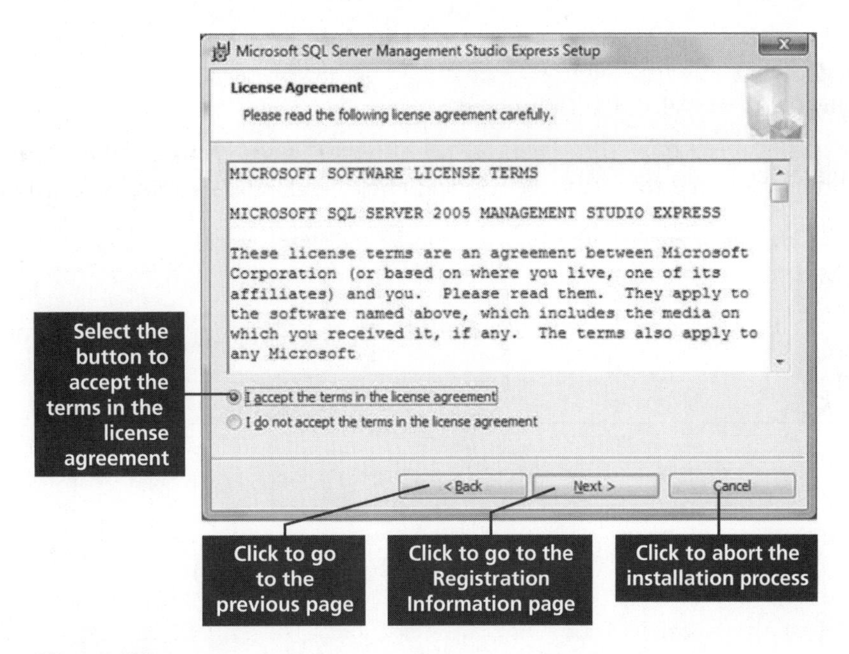

Figure 17
License Agreement Page

6. On the *License Agreement* page, read the license agreement, select the check box beside the **I accept the terms in the license agreement** option, and then click **Next**.

   The *Registration Information* page appears.

NOTE	*You can click Cancel to abort all changes and go to the previous page.*

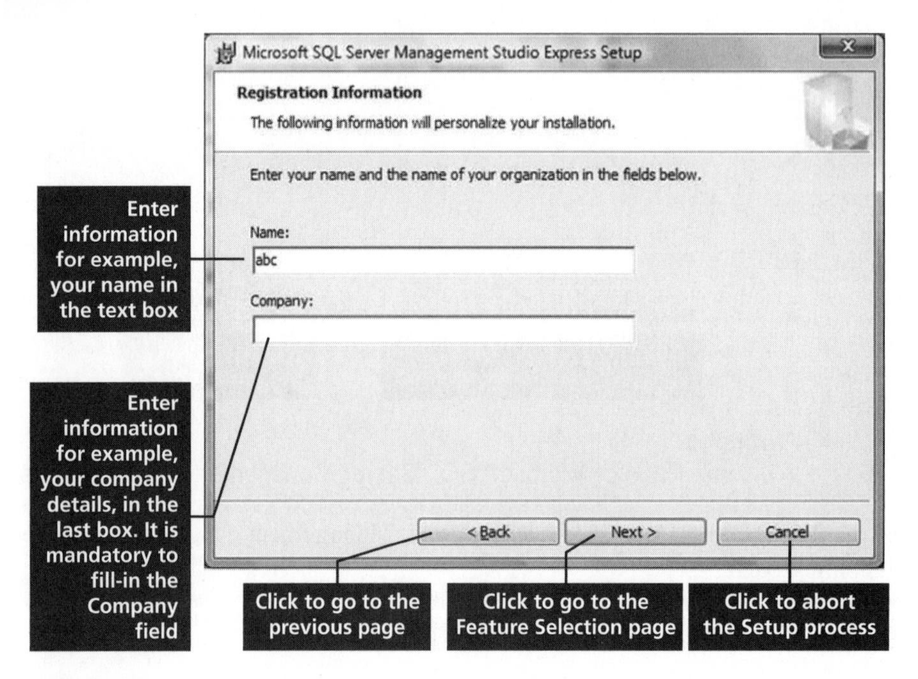

Figure 18
Registration Information Page

7. On the *Registration Information* page, enter your **Name** and **Company** information in the respective boxes, and click **Next**. The *Feature Selection* page appears.

NOTE	*It is mandatory to fill in the Name field; the Company field is optional.*

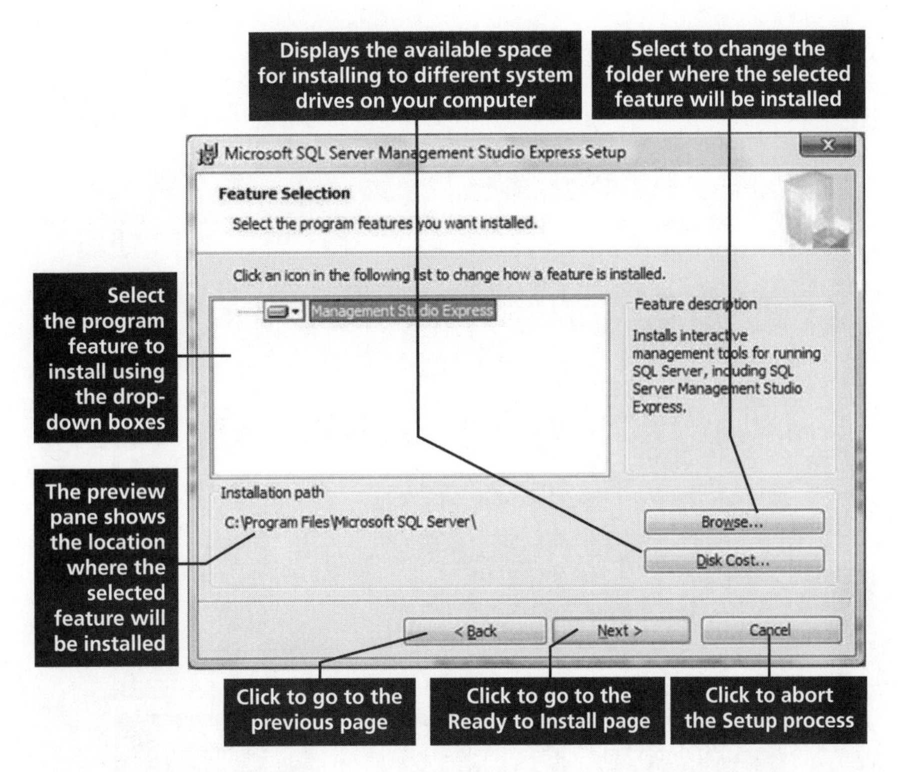

Figure 19
Feature Selection Page

8. The *Feature Selection* page shows the default settings. There is no need to make any changes with respect to these settings. View these settings and click **Next**.

The *Ready to Install the Program* page appears.

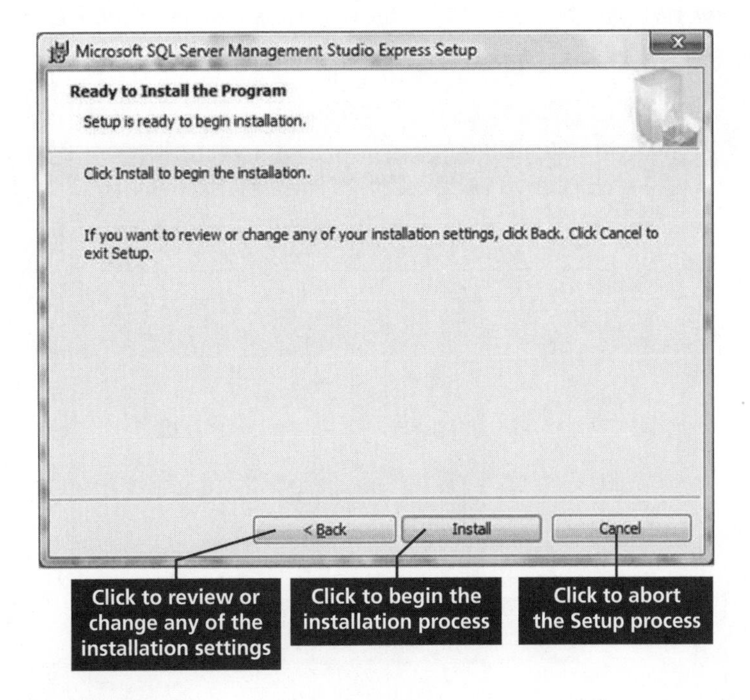

Figure 20
Ready to Install the Program Page

9. On the *Ready to Install the Program* page, click **Install**.

   The Installing Microsoft SQL Server Management Studio Express page appears.

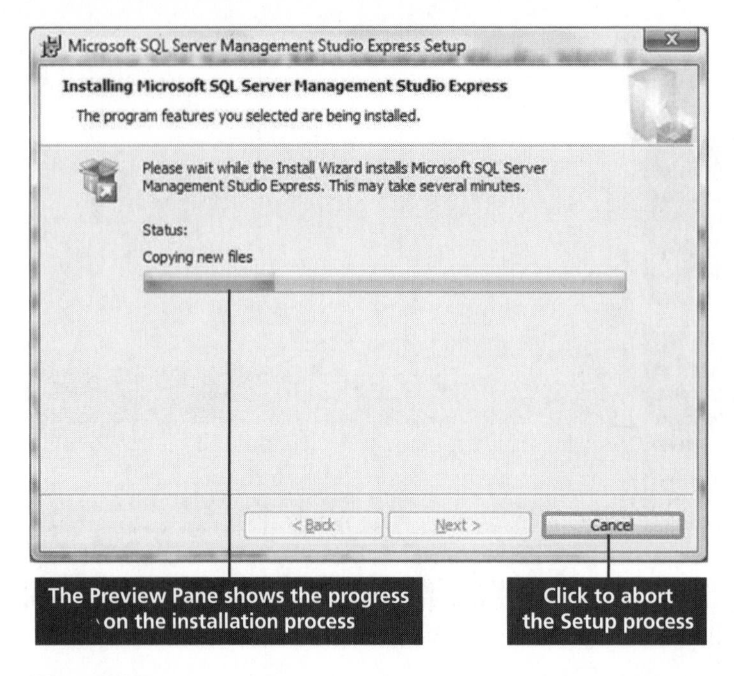

Figure 21
Installing Microsoft SQL Server Management Studio Express Page

10. On the *Installing Microsoft SQL Server Management Studio Express* page, wait until the files are copied. The **Next** button is activated only after this process. Click **Next**.

    The *Completing the Microsoft SQL Server Management Studio Express Setup* page appears.

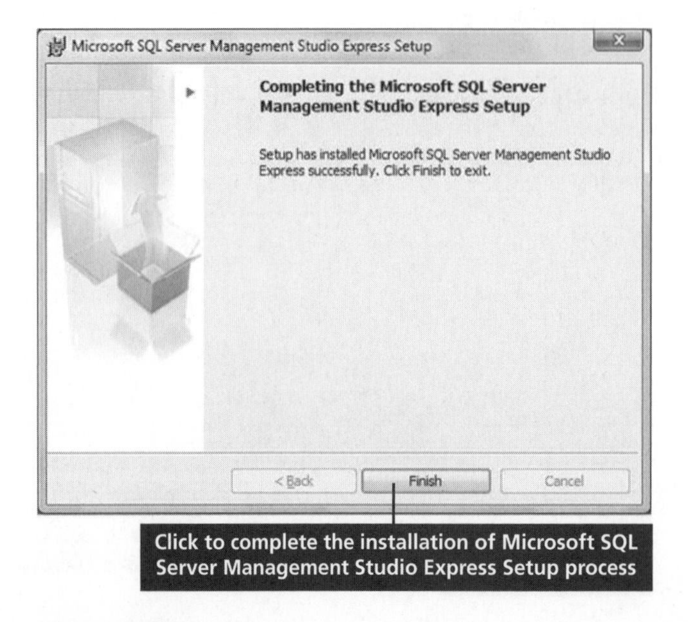

Figure 22
Completing SQL Server Management Studio Express Setup Page

The *Completing the Microsoft SQL Server Management Studio Express Setup* page confirms the successful installation of Microsoft SQL Server Management Studio Express Setup.

11. On the Completing the Microsoft SQL Server Management Studio Express Setup page, click **Finish**.

    This completes the installation of Microsoft SQL Server Management Studio Express.

INSTALLING SQL SERVER AND CONFIGURING SAMPLE DATABASES

Installing SQL Server 2005 Express	
Overview	Using the following procedure, install SQL Server and configure sample databases on a student computer.
Completion time	15 minutes

1. Open your Internet Explorer and type **http://www.microsoft.com/downloads** in the **Address** box.

2. In the **Search** text box located on top of the page, type **northwind pubs** and click **Search**.

   Search results are displayed.

3. In the search results displayed, click the **Northwind and pubs Sample Databases for SQL Server 2000** link.

   The page to download the specified database appears.

4. On the download page, download the file **SQL2000SampleDb.msi** by clicking the **Download** button and then save this file on the disk.

5. Navigate to the path where you have saved the file **SQL2000SampleDb.msi** and double click it to start running the setup program.

   The *Welcome to the Microsoft SQL Server 2000 Sample Database Scripts Setup Wizard* page appears.

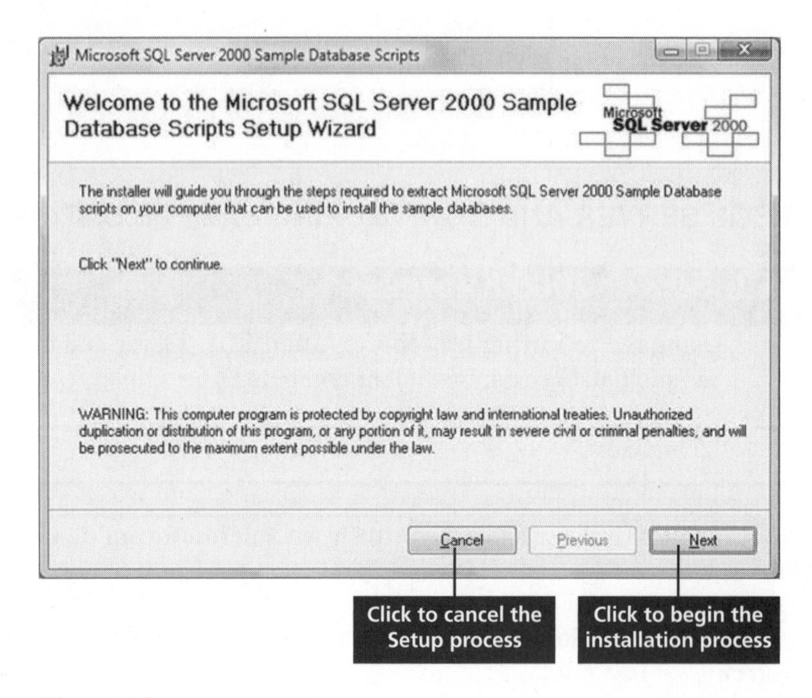

Figure 23
Welcome to the Microsoft SQL Server 2000 Sample Database Scripts Setup Wizard Page

6. On the Welcome to the Microsoft SQL Server 2000 Sample Database Scripts Setup Wizard page, click **Next**.

   A page showing the License Agreement appears.

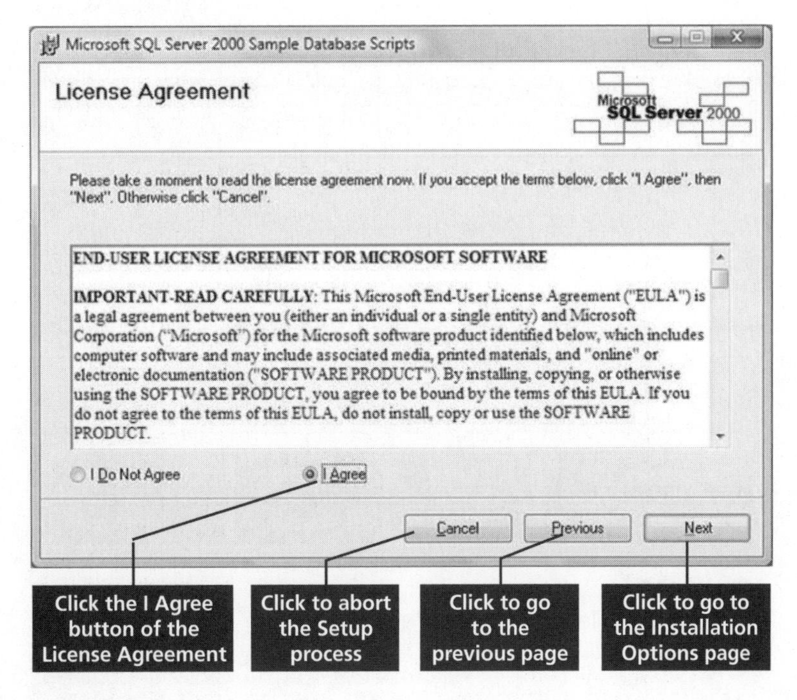

Figure 24
License Agreement Page

7. On the License Agreement page, read the license agreement, select the button beside the **I agree** option, and then click **Next**.

   The *Choose Installation Options* page appears.

> **NOTE**
>
> *You can click Cancel to abort all changes and go to the previous page.*

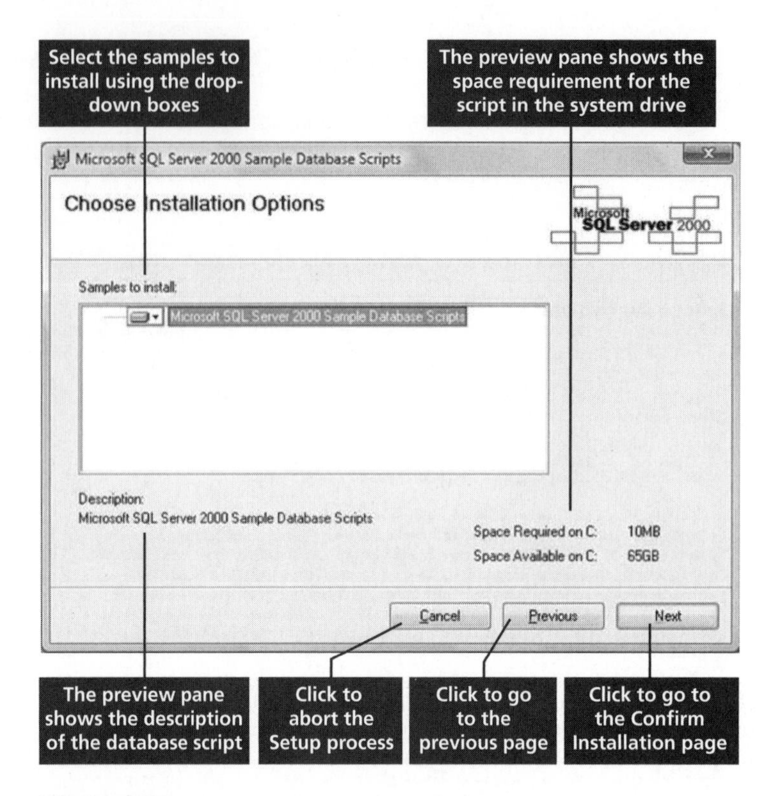

Figure 25
Choose Installation Options Page

8. On the *Choose Installation Options* page, retain the default settings, and click **Next**.

The Confirm Installation page appears.

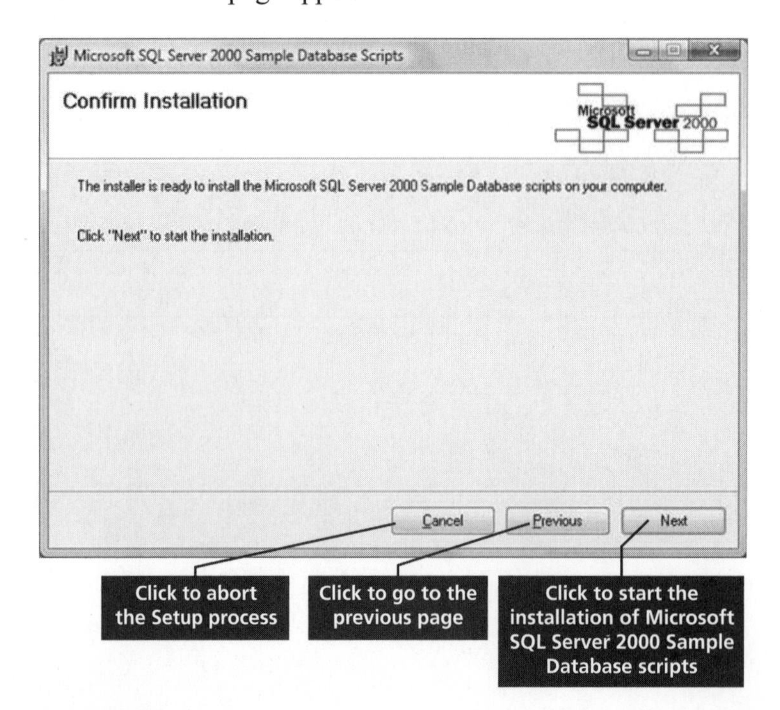

Figure 26
Confirm Installation Page

9. On the *Confirm Installation* page, click **Next** to confirm the installation process.

   A page appears, displaying the status of copying the files. After the files are copied, an *Installation Complete* page appears.

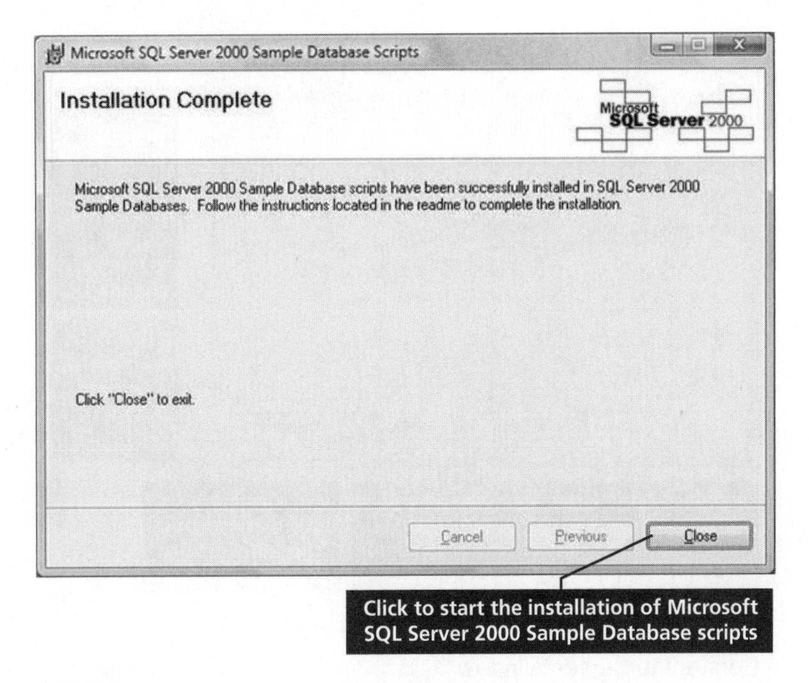

Figure 27
Installation Complete Page

10. On the *Installation Complete* page, click **Close**.

11. Navigate to C:\ SQL Server 2000 Sample Databases.

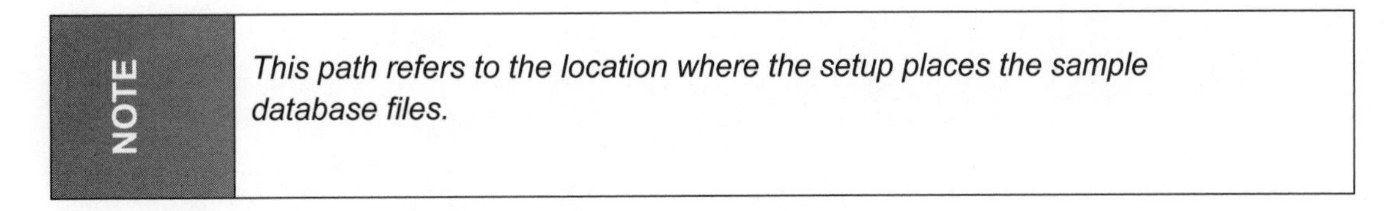
NOTE

This path refers to the location where the setup places the sample database files.

12. Copy four files (northwind.mdf, northwind.ldf, pubs.mdf, and pubs_log.ldf) and paste these at C:\Program Files\Microsoft SQL Server\MSSQL.1\MSSQL\Data.

13. Go to Start → All Programs → Microsoft SQL Server 2005, and click SQL Server Management Studio Express.

    The *Connect to Server* window appears.

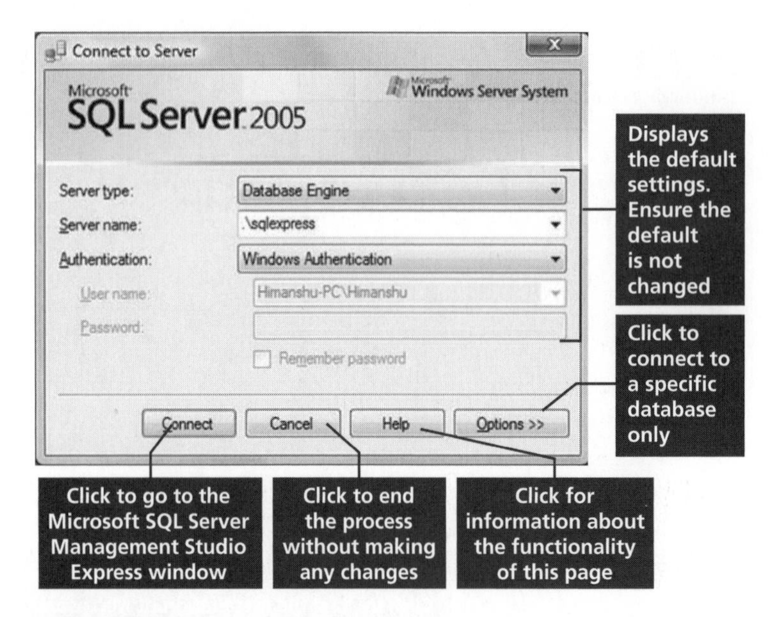

Figure 28
Connect to Server Window

14. The *Connect to Server* window displays the default settings. These settings do not need to be changed, so click **Connect**.

    The *Microsoft SQL Server Management Studio Express* window appears.

15. In the *Microsoft SQL Server Management Studio Express* window, select and right click **Databases**, and then click the **Attach** option.

    The *Attach Databases* window appears.

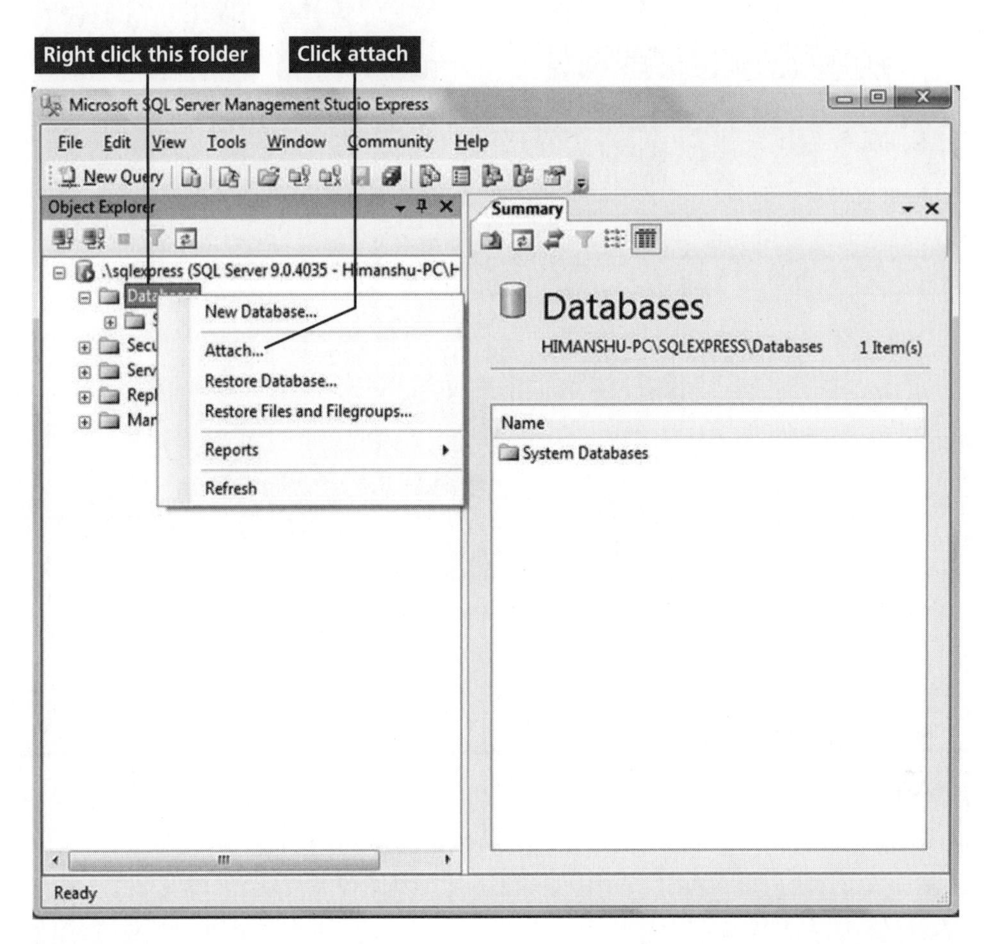

Figure 29
Attach Databases Window

16. In the *Attach Databases* window, click the **Add** button.

    Another window opens that will allow you to browse to the location of the database files (.mdf and .ldf).

17. Browse to C:\Program Files\Microsoft SQL Server\MSSQL.1\MSSQL\Data, select Northwind.mdf, and click OK.

18. Click the **Add** button, select **Pubs.mdf**, and click **OK**.

 You will see that two files are listed in the *Attach Databases* window.

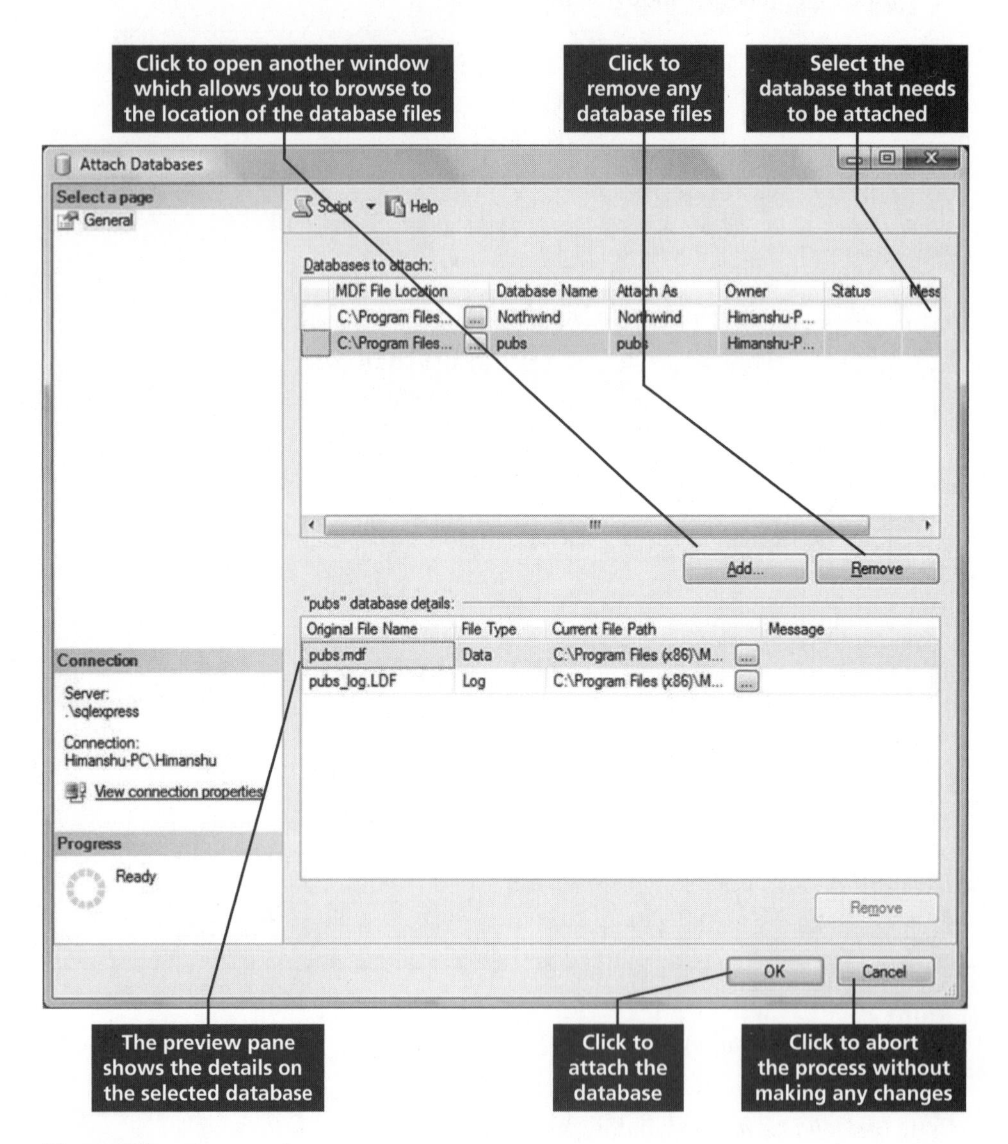

Figure 30
Attach Files Process

19. View the progress of attaching the databases.

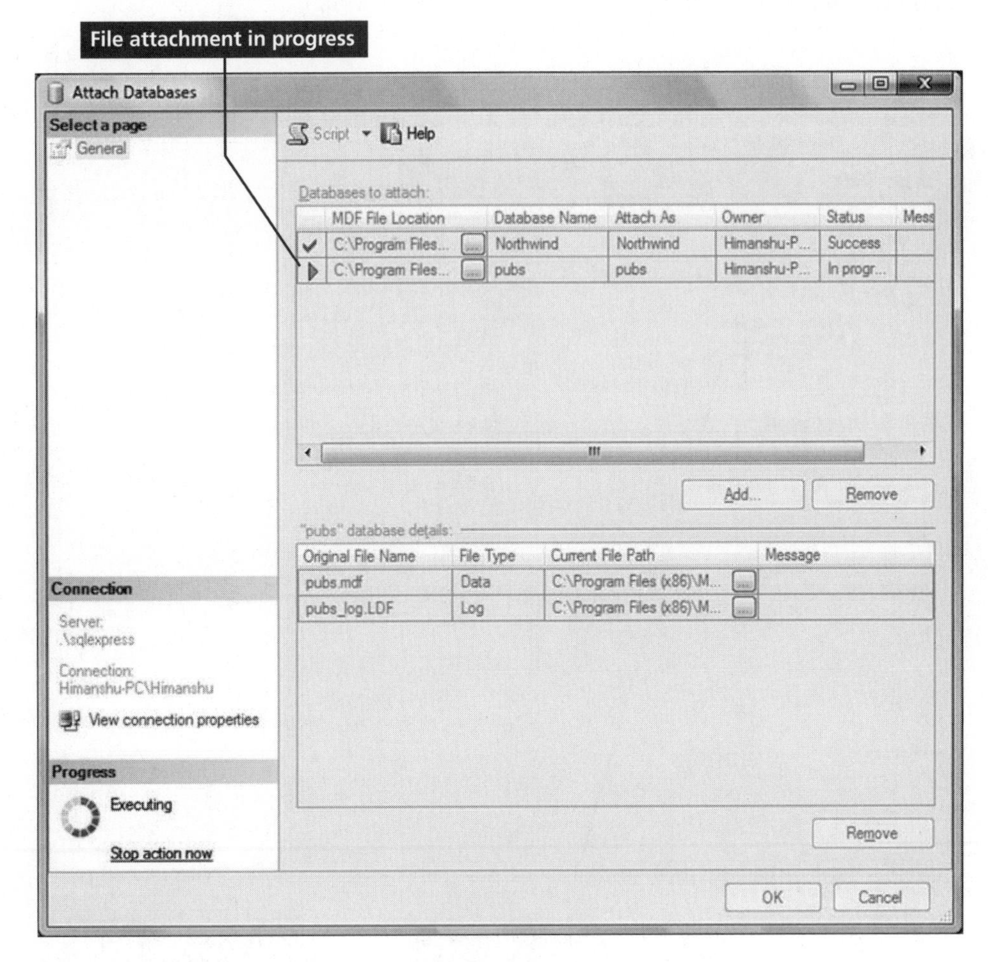

Figure 31
Progress of Attaching the Databases

20. On successful completion of attaching the databases, you will view the *Northwind* and *pubs* listed under the *Databases* node in SQL Server Management Studio Express.

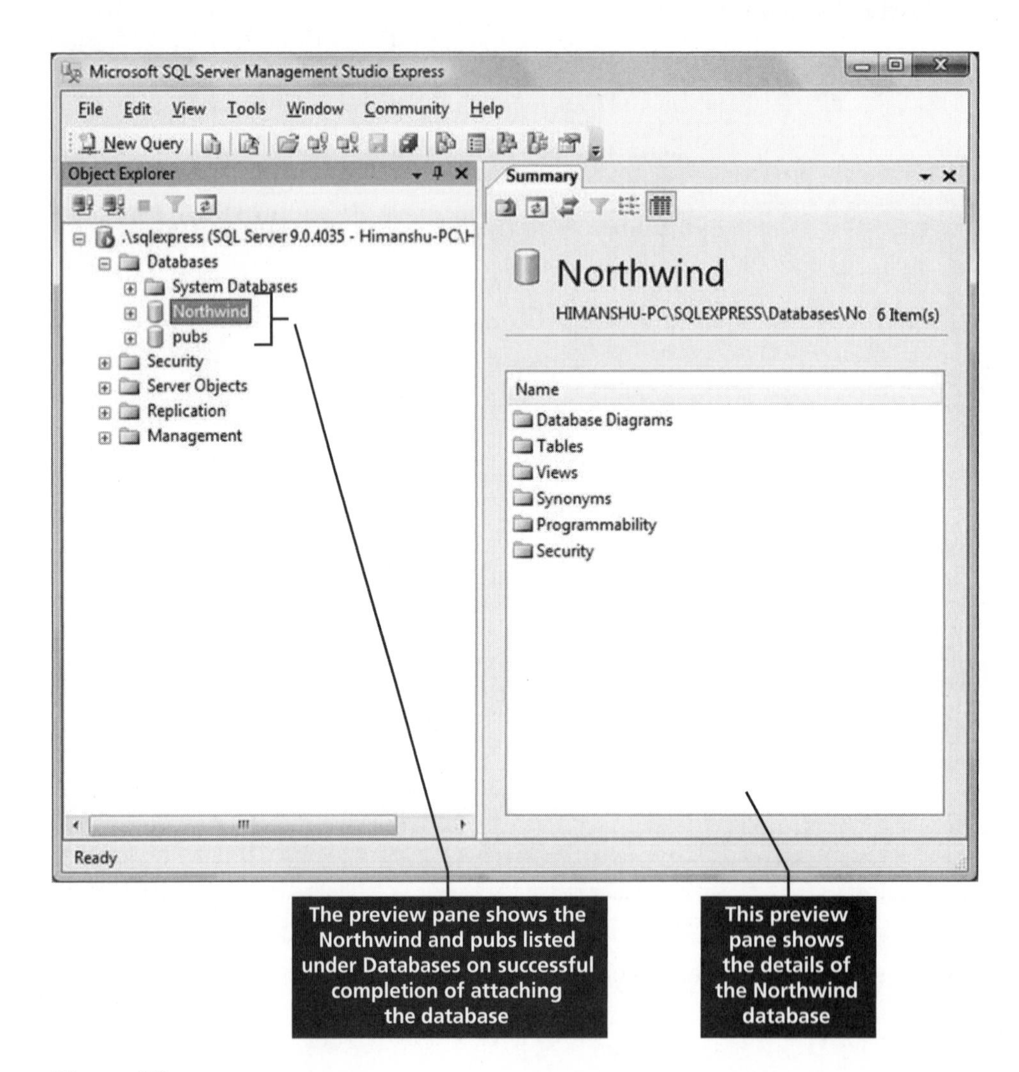

Figure 32
Listing of the New Databases